DAM PREIS FÜR ARCHITEKTUR IN DEUTSCHLAND

DAM AWARD FOR ARCHITECTURE IN GERMANY

2010|11

Treppenhalle | Staircase Hall

Treppenhalle | Staircase Hall

PETER CACHOLA SCHMAL

Mit dem Neuen Museum setzen David Chipperfield Architects einen neuen, hohen Maßstab für die Restaurierung von bedeutsamen Bauten.

With the Neues Museum, David Chipperfield Architects set a new, high standard for the restoration of important buildings.

FRIEDERIKE MEYER

Hier bleibt Geschichte in Wänden, Böden und Decken erkennbar. Die zeitgenössischen Ergänzungen und der Mut zur Wunde geben der Denkmalpflegediskussion wichtige Denkanstöße.

History remains visible here in the walls, the floors and the ceilings. The contemporary additions and the courage to show scars provide important food for thought in today's debate on historical preservation.

Detail Bacchussaal | Detail of Bacchus Room

Detail | Detail

Bacchussaal | Bacchus Room

FRANK BARKOW

Hier entsteht eine kraftvolle architektonische Dialektik zwischen dem beschädigten historischen Baubestand und einem zukunftsweisenden Eingriff.

This is a powerful architectural dialectic between a damaged historical fabric and a forward-looking intervention.

Galerie Ägyptischer Hof, Ebene 1 | Gallery Egyptian Courtyard, Level 1

Wandbilder Ägyptischer Hof, Ebene 1 | Wall Paintings, Egyptian Courtyard, Level 1

Ägyptischer Hof, Plattform Ebene 2
Egyptian Courtyard, Platform Level 2

Griechischer Saal | Greek Room

Griechischer Saal | Greek Room

KARIN LEYDECKER

Die Schönheit dieser schöpferischen Rekonstruktion liegt im Respekt vor dem, was die Geschichte in das Bauwerk eingeschrieben hat. Es ist ein Konstrukt der feinen Narbengewebe, der kunstvollen Nähte über den vielfältigen Verletzungen der Vergangenheit und der kühnen Schnitte, die neu definieren und klären.

The beauty of this creative reconstruction lies in respect for what history has inscribed onto the building.
It is a construct of fine scar tissue, of skilful seams across the manifold injuries of the past and of bold steps that clarify and define anew.

Laterne, Südkuppelsaal
Lantern, South Dome Room

Nordkuppelsaal | North Dome Room

Treppenhalle, Blick in den Modernen Saal | Staircase Hall, view into the Modern Room

AXEL SIMON

Räume, die ihre Geschichte erzählen. Allerdings jenseits von ‚damals' und ‚heute', bar jeder Ideologie, von welcher Seite auch immer.

Rooms that tell their own story. But that go beyond "that was then and this is now", barring any ideology, regardless from which side.

WOLFGANG BACHMANN

David Chipperfields Miyake-Shop, hieß es, zeige japanische Tugenden: Leere, Ordnung, Tradition. Wie kaum ein anderer Architekt hat er aus dieser Beschränkung auch im großen Maßstab hinreißende Bauten geschaffen.

David Chipperfield's shop he designed for Miyake was said to display Japanese virtues: emptiness, order, tradition. From this restraint, Chipperfield has been able like no other architect to create fascinating buildings, and to do so on a large scale.

Ethnographischer Saal | Ethnographical Room

ARCHITEKT | ARCHITECT

DAVID CHIPPERFIELD ARCHITECTS

GEBÄUDE | BUILDING

WIEDERAUFBAU NEUES MUSEUM

MUSEUMSINSEL BERLIN

TEXT PETER CACHOLA SCHMAL

01

ARCHITEKTEN | ARCHITECTS

David Chipperfield Architects
Gesellschaft von Architekten mbH
Joachimstraße 11
10119 Berlin
www.davidchipperfield.com

MITARBEITER | TEAM

WETTBEWERB
COMPETITION, **PH 1**
PROJEKTLEITER
PROJECT ARCHITECT

Jamie Fobert

GUTACHTERVERFAHREN
COMPETITION, **PH 2 + 3**
PROJEKTLEITER
PROJECT ARCHITECT

Mark Randel

PROJEKTTEAM WETTBEWERB
COMPETITION,
PH 1 – GUTACHTERVERFAHREN
COMPETITION, **PH 2 + 3**

Philipp Auer, Renato Benedetti, Franz Borho, Nathalie Bredalla, Jan Coghlan, Eamon Cushanan, An Fonteyne, Robin Foster, Mario Hohmann, Martin Kley, Madeleine Lambert, Harvey Langston-Jones, Genevieve Lilley, Claudia Marx, Patrick McInerney, Ian McKnight, Guy Morgan-Harris, Rik Nys, Eva Schad, Alexander Schwarz, Jonathan Sergison, Haewon Shin, Steven Shorter, Zoka Skorup, Graham Smith, Henning Stummel, Simon Timms, Giuseppe Zampieri, Mark Zogrotzski

VORPLANUNG–
OUTLINE PROPOSALS–
AUSFÜHRUNGSPLANUNG
PRODUCTION INFO

Harald Müller, Martin Reichert, Eva Schad, Alexander Schwarz (Direktoren | directors)
Martin Reichert, Eva Schad (Projektleiter | project architect)

PROJEKTTEAM | TEAM

Christiane Abel, Arnaud Bauman, Thomas Benk, Johannes Bennke, Daniela Bruns, Katja Buchholz, Janna Bunje, Nils Dallmann, Florian Dirschedl, Maryla Duleba, Adrian Dunham, Harald Eggers, Matthias Fiegl, Annette Flohrschütz, Michael Freytag, Anke Fritzsch, Katja Gursch, Isabelle Heide, Anne Hengst, Christoph Hesse, Isabel Karig, Michael Kaune, Regine Krause, Paul Ludwig, Martina Maire, Marcus Mathias, Werner Mayer-Biela, Christiane Melzer, Virginie Mommens, Max Ott, Peter Pfeiffer, Martina Pongratz, Robert Ritzmann, Mariska Rohde, Franziska Rusch, David Saik, Elke Saleina, Sonia Sandberger, Antonia Schlegel, Gunnar Schmidt, Lukas Schwind, Doreen Souradny, Florian Steinbächer, Christian Stiller, Annika Thiel, Barbara Witt, Sebastian Wolf

BAUHERR | CLIENT

Stiftung Preußischer Kulturbesitz vertreten durch das Bundesamt für Bauwesen und Raumordnung

TRAGWERK | STRUCTURE

Ingenieurgruppe Bauen, Karlsruhe / Berlin

RESTAURIERUNGSARCHITEKT
RESTORATION ARCHITECT

Julian Harrap Architects, London

FACHPLANUNG / -BAULEITUNG (RESTAURIERUNG)
CONSULTANT / SITE SUPERVISION (RESTORATION)

Pro Denkmal GmbH, Bamberg / Berlin

LANDSCHAFTSARCHITEKT
LANDSCAPE ARCHITECT

Levin Monsigny Landschaftsarchitekten GmbH, Berlin

AUSSTELLUNGSDESIGN
EXHIBITION DESIGN

Architetto Michele de Lucchi S.r.L., Mailand | Milan

GEBÄUDETECHNIK (HEIZUNG / LÜFTUNG / SANITÄR)
SERVICES ENGINEER (HEATING, VENTILATION, SANITARY)

JMP Ingenieurgesellschaft mbH, Stuttgart

GEBÄUDETECHNIK (ELEKTRO- UND SICHERHEITSTECHNIK)
SERVICES ENGINEER (ELECTRICAL AND SECURITY)

KMS Beratungs- und Planungsgesellschaft mbH, Berlin

BAUPHYSIK | BUILDING PHYSICS

Ingenieurbüro Axel C. Rahn GmbH, Berlin

LICHTPLANUNG
LIGHTING CONSULTANT

Kardorff Ingenieure Lichtplanung, Berlin

BAULEITUNG | SITE MANAGEMENT

Lubic & Woehrlin GmbH, Berlin

PROJEKTSTEUERUNG
PROJECT MANAGEMENT

Ernst & Young Real Estate GmbH, Berlin

ERÖFFNUNG | OPENING

Oktober 2009 | October 2009

STANDORT | LOCATION

Bodestraße 1
10178 Berlin
www.neues-museum.de

FOTOS | PHOTOS

Hélène Binet

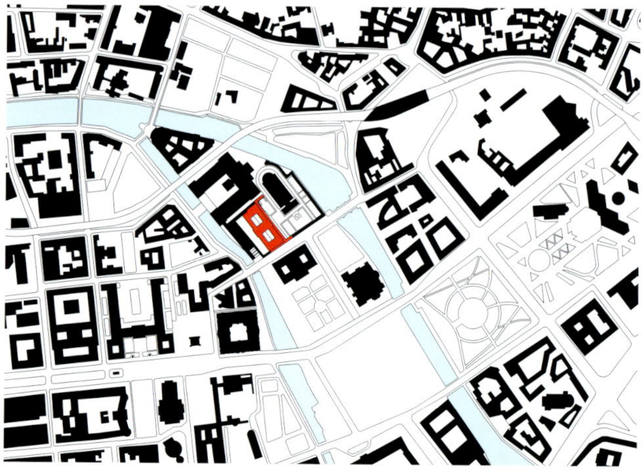

Lageplan Neues Museum, Museumsinsel Berlin
Site plan, Neues Museum, Museum Island Berlin

„Weder vom Publikum noch von denen, deren Obhut die öffentlichen Baudenkmäler anvertraut sind, wird die wahre Bedeutung des Wortes ‚Wiederherstellung' (Restaurierung) verstanden. Heute bedeutet sie die vollständigste Zerstörung: eine Zerstörung, aus der keine Bruchstücke gerettet werden können, von einer falschen Vorstellung des zerstörten Werkes begleitet. Täuschen wir uns doch nicht über diesen wichtigen Punkt: Es ist ganz ‚unmöglich', so unmöglich wie die Toten zu erwecken, irgendetwas wiederherzustellen, das jemals groß oder schön in der Baukunst gewesen ist."
John Ruskin (1849)[1]

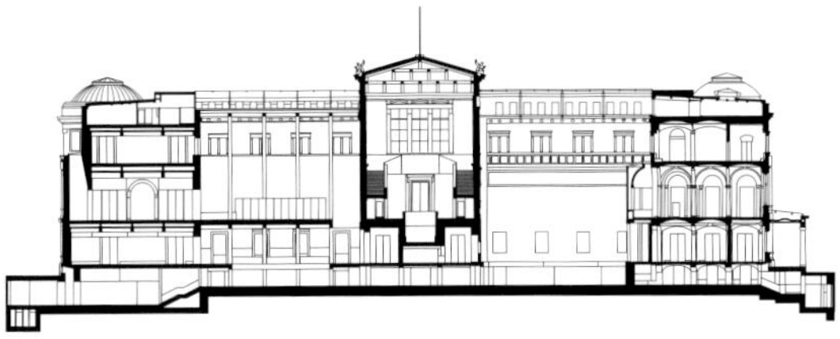

Längsschnitt durch die Höfe und die Treppenhalle
Longitudinal section of courtyards and stairway hall

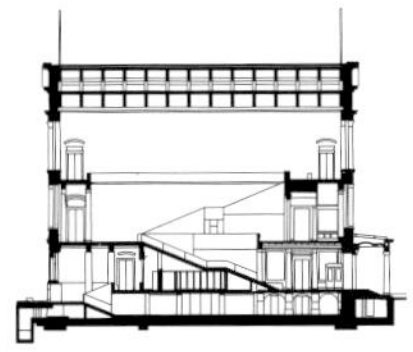

Querschnitt durch die Treppenhalle | Cross-section of stairway hall

David Chipperfield sagte bei der Eröffnung des Neuen Museums im März 2009: „Es wäre viel einfacher gewesen, eine Kopie des Gebäudes zu schaffen, statt seine Geschichte behutsam zu bewahren." Vermutlich hätte eine rekonstruierte Kopie des untergegangenen klassizistischen Meisterwerks des Schinkelschülers Friedrich August Stüler, erbaut von 1841 bis 1859, Politik und Öffentlichkeit nicht weniger begeistert als diese von Chipperfield Architects unter den denkbar höchsten eigenen Ansprüchen realisierte architektonische Verbindung von historischer Qualität und zeitgemäßer Gestaltung. Es ist diese Haltung Chipperfields, die das Neue Museum zu einem Ort des grundsätzlichen Nachdenkens über Rekonstruktion und den Umgang mit bestehender Bausubstanz macht. In einem Land, in dem die Sehnsucht nach scheinbar wiederauferstandener Baukunst Hochkonjunktur hat, ist es Chipperfield und seinem denkmalpflegerischen Berater, dem Londoner Architekten Julian Harrap, gelungen, dem Neuen Museum eine Art neues Leben im Alten zu schenken.
Lange haben wir dergleichen in Deutschland nicht mehr gesehen. Zuletzt 1957 mit Hans Döllgasts Wiederaufbau der Alten Pinakothek in München. Indem Döllgast die Kriegswunden an dem Leo-von-Klenze-Bau lediglich mit unverputzten Trümmerziegeln ausfachte, ließ er sie im fertigen Zustand sichtbar stehen. Zusätzlich strukturierte er das Gesamtgefüge des Bauwerks um und verlegte den Eingang und die Haupterschließungen. Chipperfield geht formal einen ähnlichen Weg, behandelt aber den Bau dabei weitaus behutsamer und differenzierter. Er unterscheidet zwischen drei Arten von Beständen, die er nach eigenem architektonischem Ermessen definiert.
Zum einen sind es jene Bereiche, die aufgrund schwerer Kriegsschäden in den folgenden 50 Jahren unwiederbringlich verloren gingen. Diese versucht er in ihrem Volumen und der Logik der Raumfolgen zu „re-komplettieren", allerdings in einer vollkommen zeitgenössischen Materialität.[2] Von außen ist dies besonders am Nordwestflügel sichtbar, wo eine zurückhaltende Backsteinarchitektur die Fassadenstruktur des benachbarten, noch erhaltenen Seitenflügels aufnimmt.
Die zweite Art von Beständen sind jene Bereiche, die lediglich als Rohbau erhalten werden konnten und keinerlei Oberflächengestaltung mehr aufwiesen. Sie wurden mit neuen Materialien, die sich in ihrer Farbigkeit und Textur den bestehenden unverputzten Materialien unterordnen, ergänzt und komplettiert. Am deutlichsten ist dies in der großen Treppenhalle und dem Griechischen Hof sichtbar. Auch die neu geschaffenen Tontopfkuppeln oder die Apsis im Griechischen Hof gehören zu dieser Kategorie.

"Neither by the public, nor by those who have the care of public monuments, is the true meaning of the word restoration understood. It means the most total destruction which a building can suffer: a destruction out of which no remnants can be gathered; a destruction accompanied with false description of the thing destroyed. Do not let us deceive ourselves in this important matter; it is impossible, as impossible as to raise the dead, to restore anything that has ever been great or beautiful in architecture."
John Ruskin (1849) [1]

At the opening of the Neues Museum in March 2009, David Chipperfield said: "It would have been much easier to create a copy of the building instead of carefully preserving its history." Presumably, the reconstructed replica of the destroyed Neoclassical masterpiece that Schinkel's pupil Friedrich August Stüler erected from 1841 to 1859 would have inspired no less enthusiasm on the part of politicians and the public than the architectural conjoining of historical quality and contemporary design that has now been achieved in the most demanding manner imaginable by Chipperfield Architects. It is Chipperfield's attitude that makes the Neues Museum a place for asking fundamental questions on the reconstruction and treatment of historical building fabric. In a country where there is a widespread yearning to resurrect the architecture of the past, Chipperfield and his adviser on historic preservation, London architect Julian Harrap, have succeeded instead in breathing new life into the old stones at the Neues Museum.
We have not seen anything like this in Germany in a long time. Not since Hans Döllgast's reconstruction of the Alte Pinakothek in Munich in 1957. Döllgast merely filled in the war wounds in Leo von Klenze's original building with unrendered bricks salvaged from the war, leaving them visible in the final edifice. In addition, he restructured the entire layout of the building, shifting the entrance and main access routes. Chipperfield takes a similar approach in formal terms, but treats the building with much greater care and in a more nuanced fashion. He distinguishes between three kinds of building fabric that remain, defining them at his own architectural discretion.
The first category comprises areas that were heavily damaged in the war and hence irretrievably lost during the ensuing 50 years. He attempted to, as he says, "recomplete" these in their volumes and the logic of their spatial sequences, but using completely contemporary materials. This is particularly conspicuous on the exterior of the north-west wing, where a reserved brick architecture echoes the lines of the preserved elements of the neighbouring side wing.
The second type of building fabric consists of areas where only the structural shell remains, the surface work no longer extant. These sections were augmented and completed with new materials whose colours and textures subordinate themselves to the existing

Schließlich sind es die Reste der originalen, farbenfrohen Innendekoration von Stüler, der jeden einzelnen Raum entsprechend der Inhalte der weitgefächerten humanistischen Sammlung gestaltete. Diese Reste wurden, getreu der Charta von Venedig, „im ganzen Reichtum ihrer Authentizität" erhalten und mit allen historischen Schichten und Wunden sorgfältig und mit großer Liebe restauriert. Schöne Beispiele sind der Ägyptische Hof, der Mythologische Saal oder der Nordkuppelsaal, in dem die Büste der Nofretete wieder residiert.
Chipperfield und Harrap beweisen ein hohes Maß an Stilsicherheit, indem sie die vorhandenen Wand- und Deckenausmalungen nicht einfach komplettieren.
Mithilfe von gefärbten Putzen versuchen sie in manchen Räumen den Eindruck der früheren Gesamtfarbigkeit oder des vorherrschenden Tons wiederzugeben, in anderen Räumen hingegen verwirrt eine Art Leopardenmuster von originalen Farbresten auf kontrastvollen Untergründen. Es wird eine unendliche Bandbreite an individuellen Lösungen präsentiert, die jede denkbare Möglichkeit im Umgang mit dem Bestand demonstriert, individuell unterschiedlich von Raum zu Raum. Es ist dies eine Haltung, die keinen imaginierten, reinen Zustand in der Vergangenheit anstrebt, fabrikneu glänzend und ohne Patina, sondern die Geschichte als eine Abfolge von Geschichten und Schichtungen versteht. Im Neuen Museum sind diese Zeitläufe, inklusive der Jahrzehnte als kriegsversehrte Ruine in der DDR, spürbar und für die Zukunft als wahrhaftiges Zeugnis erhalten geblieben. „Man kann nicht so tun, als sei nichts geschehen", so Chipperfield.
Es ist das große Verdienst der Planer, sich auf das Bauwerk eingelassen und eine Lösung für jede einzelne Situation gefunden zu haben. Damit setzten sie, auch international, einen neuen, sehr hohen Maßstab für die Restaurierung von bedeutsamen Bauten. Fortan kann das Neue Museum als Vorbild für den Umgang mit historischen Werken betrachtet werden.
„Der außergewöhnlich hohe Standard der handwerklichen Ausführung bei diesem Projekt erzeugte in mir die höchste Demut."[3], so David Chipperfield. Diese hohe Qualität über zwölf lange Jahre zwischen Wettbewerbsgewinn und Fertigstellung durchgestanden und realisiert zu haben, ist vor allem das Verdienst des Berliner Büros von Chipperfield Architects unter der Leitung von Christoph Felger, Harald Müller, Mark Randel, Martin Reichert, Eva Schad und Alexander Schwarz, das mit über der Hälfte der insgesamt 150 Mitarbeiter die größte der vier Chipperfield-Niederlassungen (neben London, Mailand und Shanghai) ist und beständig durch außergewöhnliche Arbeiten auffällt. In den letzten Jahren waren dies das Berliner Galeriege-

[1] John Ruskin, Die sieben Leuchter der Baukunst (1849), Zit. nach: John Ruskin, Ausgewählte Werke in vollständiger Übersetzung, Bd. 1, Eugen Diederichs Verlag Dresden, 1900, S. 363ff.
„Neither by the public, nor by those who have the care of public monuments, is the true meaning of the word restoration understood. It means the most total destruction which a building can suffer : a destruction out of which no remnants can be gathered; a destruction accompanied with false description of the thing destroyed. Do not let us deceive ourselves in this important matter; it is impossible, as impossible as to raise the dead, to restore anything that has ever been great or beautiful in architecture.", in: The Seven Lamps of Architecture, John Wiley New York, 1852.
[2] Im Original von Chipperfield: „recomplete"
[3] „The most humbling thing about this project has been the extraordinary level of craftsmanship."

unrendered materials. This is most noticeable in the great Stairway Hall and the Greek Courtyard. The newly fabricated clay pot domes and the apse in the Greek Courtyard likewise belong to this category. Finally, there were still remains of the original, colourful interior decoration designed by Stüler, which was coordinated in each room to match the exhibits it presented from the extremely diverse humanistic collection. In keeping with the Charter of Venice, these remnants were preserved "in all the richness of their authenticity", with all their historical layers and traumas, and were painstakingly and lovingly restored. Beautiful examples include the Egyptian Courtyard, the Mythological Room and the North Dome Room, where the bust of Nefertiti has once again taken up regal residence.
Chipperfield and Harrap demonstrate a high degree of self-assurance in matters of style by not simply completing the missing parts of the existing wall and ceiling paintings. With the help of coloured slurries, they try instead in some of the rooms to recreate the impression of the overall colour scheme or the predominant tonality, while in other places a kind of leopard-print pattern of original paint residues on contrast-rich backgrounds bewilders the eye. A seemingly infinite spectrum of individual solutions is presented here, demonstrating every conceivable way of handling the existing building fabric, individually tailored to the disparate circumstances from room to room. This is an approach that does not strive for any imagined, pure state of the building as it might have looked in the past, factory-fresh and without patina, but rather comprehends history as a sequence of stories and layers. In the Neues Museum, the course of time, including the decades during which the building stood as a war ruin in East Germany, becomes palpable and has been preserved for posterity as an authentic testimony to its history. "One can't simply pretend that nothing has happened," says Chipperfield.
It is to the great credit of the planners that they have immersed themselves in the intricacies of this structure and have managed to find a solution for each and every circumstance therein. They are setting a new, extremely high standard, on both the local and international levels, for the restoration of important buildings. Henceforth, the Neues Museum can be considered exemplary for the handling of historical works of architecture.
"The most humbling thing about this project has been the extraordinary level of craftsmanship," David Chipperfield noted. To have maintained this exceptionally high quality over twelve long years between the beginning of the competition and completion of the project is above all the merit of the Berlin office of Chipperfield Architects, under the direction of Christoph Felger, Harald Müller, Mark Randel, Martin Reichert, Eva Schad und Alexander Schwarz. This is the largest Chipperfield branch (alongside London, Milan and Shanghai) with over half of the total 150 staff members, and it continually attracts attention with extraordinary projects. In recent years these have included the Gallery Am Kupfergraben 10 in Berlin, the Museum of Modern Literature and interior renovation of the Schiller National Museum in Marbach, Hamburg's Empire Riverside Hotel and the Folkwang Museum in Essen.
The German Architecture Museum is proud to give the DAM Award for Architecture in Germany 2010/11 to the Neues Museum in Berlin, and to its architects, David Chipperfield and his Berlin office with all the professional planners involved in the project, as well as to his client, the State Museums of Berlin – Prussian Cultural Heritage Foundation.

[1] John Ruskin, "The Seven Lamps of Architecture", John Wiley New York, 1865, p. 161.

bäude Am Kupfergraben 10, das Literaturmuseum der Moderne und die Innensanierung des Schiller-Nationalmuseums in Marbach, das Hamburger Empire Riverside Hotel und das Essener Folkwang Museum.
Das Deutsche Architekturmuseum ist stolz, den „DAM Preis für Architektur in Deutschland 2010/11" dem Neuen Museum in Berlin verleihen zu können, und damit seinen Architekten David Chipperfield und seinem Berliner Büro mit den beteiligten Fachplanern sowie seinen Bauherrn, Die Staatlichen Museen zu Berlin – Stiftung Preußischer Kulturbesitz, zu ehren.

DAS NEUE MUSEUM AUS SICHT DES BAUHERRN

Die Wiedereröffnung des Neuen Museums war für die Stiftung Preußischer Kulturbesitz ein Höhepunkt im Jahr 2009 und ein Meilenstein bei der Realisierung des Masterplans Museumsinsel: Erstmals seit mehr als siebzig Jahren sind damit wieder alle fünf Häuser auf der Museumsinsel geöffnet. Zudem darf die Wiederherstellung des Hauses wohl als eine der komplexesten Konservierungs- und Bauaufgaben der letzten Jahrzehnte bezeichnet werden.
Das Neue Museum war das im Zweiten Weltkrieg am stärksten beschädigte, in Teilen sogar zerstörte Gebäude auf der Museumsinsel. Im Gegensatz zu den übrigen Häusern wurde es jahrzehntelang nicht saniert oder wiederaufgebaut, sondern blieb Wind und Wetter ausgesetzt, bevor 1984 mit ersten Sicherungs- und Vorbereitungsmaßnahmen zur Wiederherstellung begonnen wurde. Nach der Wiedervereinigung Deutschlands kam die Museumsinsel in die Obhut der Stiftung Preußischer Kulturbesitz, die ein umfangreiches Sanierungs- und Bauprojekt in Gang setzte, um das Gebäude zur zeitgemäßen Präsentation der Sammlungen des Ägyptischen Museums, des Museums für Vor- und Frühgeschichte mit ausgewählten Objekten der Antikensammlung herzurichten. Die Frage nach dem ‚wie' der Wiederherstellung war während der gesamten Planungs- und Bauzeit Gegenstand zahlloser kontroverser Diskussionen in Expertenkreisen und in der breiteren Öffentlichkeit. David Chipperfield hat gemeinsam mit Restauratoren, Denkmalpflegern und dem Bauherrn in einem offenen konstruktiven Dialog Lösungen erarbeitet, die mit dem Begriff „Behutsames Weiterbauen" beschrieben werden können.
Ab 2003 waren rund 300 Fachfirmen (davon etwa 150 Restauratoren) beteiligt. Das Ergebnis überzeugte – auch die ehemaligen Kritiker – und weist mit seinen neuen konservatorischen Ansätzen weit über den Einzelfall hinaus. Bei Eröffnung im Oktober 2009 war das Medienecho im In- und Ausland immens. Seitdem besuchen rund 4 000 Berliner und Gäste der Stadt täglich das Haus.

Prof. Dr. Hermann Parzinger
Präsident Stiftung Preußischer Kulturbesitz

THE CLIENT COMMENTS ON THE NEUES MUSEUM

The reopening of the Neues Museum was a highlight in the year 2009 for the Stiftung Preußischer Kulturbesitz (Prussian Cultural Heritage Foundation) and a milestone in the realisation of the masterplan for the Museum Island. For the first time in more than seventy years, all five museums on the island are now open again for visitors. What's more, the restoration of the Neues Museum was surely one of the most complex conservation and construction projects of the last few decades.
Of all the buildings on the Museum Island, the Neues Museum was the most severely damaged in the Second World War, with whole sections even destroyed completely. Unlike the other museums, it was not restored or rebuilt and remained exposed to the elements for decades, until in 1984 the first efforts were finally undertaken to secure the remaining structure and to prepare for the building's restoration. Following the reunification of Germany, the Museum Island came under the custody of the Prussian Cultural Heritage Foundation, which initiated an extensive restoration and construction project to prepare the building for a modern presentation of the collections of the Egyptian Museum, the Museum of Prehistory and Early History and selected objects from the Collection of Classical Antiquities. The question as to the "how" of this reconstruction was the subject of countless heated debates in expert circles and amongst the wider public during the entire planning and construction period. David Chipperfield, in conjunction with, and in an open and constructive dialogue with restorers, monument conservators and the client, managed to work out solutions that might be described as "gentle rebuilding". Starting in 2003, some 300 professional firms (about 150 of them restorers) participated in the undertaking. The results have convinced even former critics, in the process inaugurating new conservatorial strategies that provide valuable insights for future projects of this kind. The museum's opening in October 2009 was met by a resounding response on the part of the German and international media. Since then, the museum has welcomed around 4,000 Berliners and other visitors each day.

Prof. Dr. Hermann Parzinger
President Stiftung Preußischer Kulturbesitz

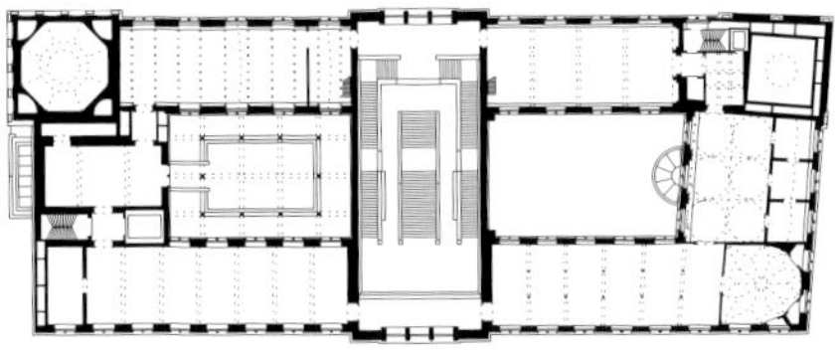

Grundriss Ebene 3
Floor plan Level 3

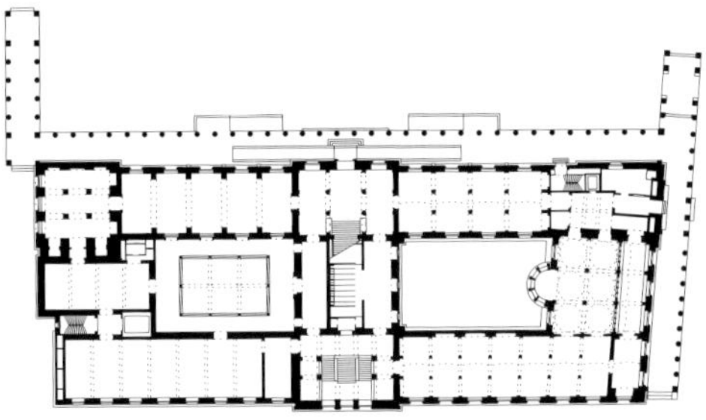

Grundriss Ebene 1
Floor plan Level 1

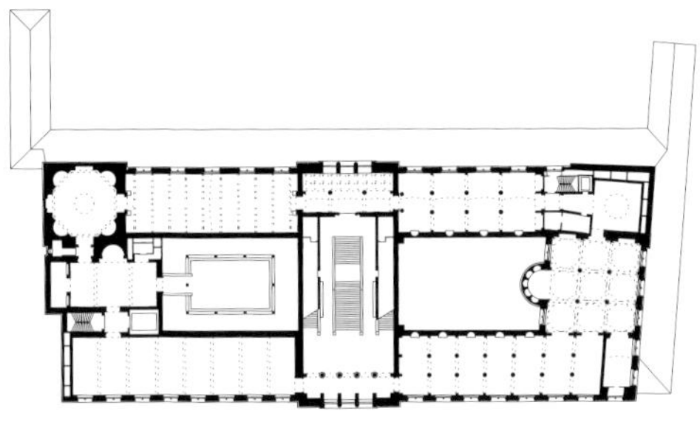

Grundriss Ebene 2
Floor plan Level 2

Griechischer Hof | Greek Courtyard

DEUTSCHES ARCHITEKTUR JAHRBUCH

GERMAN ARCHITECTURE ANNUAL

2010|11

DEUTSCHES ARCHITEKTURMUSEUM FRANKFURT AM MAIN
PRESTEL VERLAG MÜNCHEN | BERLIN | LONDON | NEW YORK

DEUTSCHES ARCHITEKTUR JAHRBUCH | GERMAN ARCHITECTURE ANNUAL

VORWORT | FOREWORD

PETER CACHOLA SCHMAL
YORCK FÖRSTER

Das Deutsche Architektur Jahrbuch, herausgegeben vom Deutschen Architekturmuseum (DAM), hat sich ohne Zweifel etabliert, ebenso der „DAM Preis für Architektur in Deutschland" und die begleitende Ausstellung im DAM. Wir sind dabei, das Konzept zu einer Wanderausstellung für Goethe-Institute weltweit weiterzuentwickeln, das Institut in Sofia soll den Anfang machen. Das entspricht unserer Intention herausragende zeitgenössische Architektur in und aus Deutschland zu einer möglichst breiten Bekanntheit zu verhelfen.

Die diesjährigen Träger des DAM Preis für Architektur, David Chipperfield Architects, sind alles andere als unbekannte Akteure im Architekturgeschehen. Das ausgezeichnete Projekt, das Neue Museum in Berlin, hat ein ungeteiltes Echo sowohl in Fach- wie Publikumszeitschriften hervorgerufen. Das Deutsche Architektur Jahrbuch hat immer wieder von Bauten des Büros berichtet, sei es das Literaturmuseum der Moderne in Marbach (2006) oder das Galeriegebäude am Kupfergraben (2008/09). Und schon jetzt gilt unsere besondere Neugier einem ihrer aktuellen Projekte in nächster Nachbarschaft. Das historische Gesellschaftshaus im Frankfurter Palmengarten erfährt eine Neugestaltung, ein erster Umbau des Gebäudes fand 1929 nach Plänen von Martin Elsaesser und Ernst May statt. Das Thema der historischen Zeitschichten dürfte auch hier eine große Rolle spielen.

Wir freuen uns sehr, dass sich die Jahrbuch-Jury für das Neue Museum als Preisträger entschieden hat und sind stolz, zusammen mit David Chipperfield Architects eine kleine Ausstellung im Ungerschen Haus-im-Haus im 3. OG, dem Herzstück des DAM, pünktlich zur Eröffnung der Ausstellung „DAM Preis 2010. Die 23 besten Bauten in/aus Deutschland" am 28. Januar 2011 präsentieren zu können.

ESSAYS

Haben die Rekonstruktionsdebatten der letzten Jahre eine neue Tendenz ausgelöst? Kommt nach ‚Reko' jetzt ‚Retro'? Grob überschlagen gut ein Drittel der Projekte im Jahrbuch zitiert historische Haltungen, teils mit etwas Augenzwinkern, teils mit

The German Architecture Annual, published by the German Architecture Museum (DAM), has without doubt become a fixed feature on the architecture scene, as can also be said for the DAM Award for Architecture in Germany and the accompanying exhibition at DAM. We are currently in the process of developing a concept for a touring exhibition for Goethe Institutes all over the world, starting in Sofia. This undertaking reflects our ambition to bring outstanding contemporary architecture to the attention of as many people as possible, both in Germany and beyond.

This year's DAM Award winners, David Chipperfield Architects, are anything but unknowns in the architectural field. Both the trade and popular press have greeted their award-winning project, the Neues Museum in Berlin, with unreserved praise. The German Architecture Annual has reported frequently in past years on buildings produced by this firm, including the Museum of Modern Literature in Marbach (2006) and the Gallery Am Kupfergraben 10 (2008/09). And we are already curious about how a current project right in our own neighbourhood will develop. The historic Gesellschaftshaus (Society House) in Frankfurt's Palmengarten, renovated in 1929 according to the plans of Martin Elsaesser and Ernst May, is now being redesigned by David Chipperfield and his firm. The theme of layers of history, a key to the approach taken to the Neues Museum, can be expected to play a major role here as well.

We are delighted that the jury for our German Architecture Annual chose the Neues Museum as winner, and are proud to present in conjunction with David Chipperfield Architects a small exhibition on this project in Ungers' "house within a house" on the third floor, the heart of the DAM, to coincide with the opening of the show "DAM Award 2010. The 23 Best Buildings in/from Germany" on 28 January 2011.

ESSAYS

Have all the debates on reconstruction during recent years set off a new trend? Is "recon" now being replaced by "retro"? Roughly a third of the projects in this year's Annual quote historical stances, sometimes a bit tongue-in-cheek and in other cases simply as a matter of course. This was reason enough for us to ask the polemical Arno

größter Selbstverständlichkeit. Für uns war das ein Grund, den streitbaren Arno Lederer um einen Essay zu bitten. Vielleicht haben, so argumentiert er, eine technikbegeisterte exaltierte Moderne und die heimelige Vergangenheitsverklärung mancher Rekonstruktionen mehr gemeinsam, als es zunächst scheinen mag. Denn die eigentliche Herausforderung ist eine Architektur, die sich ihrer Vergangenheit bewusst ist und aus der Gegenwart die Zukunft denken kann. Denn letztlich geht es immer darum, die Architektur nicht isoliert zu verstehen, sondern sie in einem Zusammenhang mit dem Ort und der Gemeinschaft, der sie dienen soll, zu denken. So verstanden haben wir es nicht mit einer ‚Retro'-Tendenz zu tun, sondern mit dem Bemühen der Architekten, Kontinuität herzustellen. Sein Essay ist ein Plädoyer für die Verantwortung der Architektur gegenüber der Stadt.

Ganz direkt um die Stadt geht es auch in dem zweiten Essay, hier um die neue Hafenstadt Lingang New City bei Shanghai. Das Büro von Gerkan, Marg und Partner hat den Wettbewerb für die neue Großstadt 2002 für sich entschieden. Statt eines baulich verdichteten Zentrums bildet ein kreisrunder See von 2,5 Kilometern Durchmesser das Herz der neuen Stadt, mit einem kontinuierlichen Strand für die Bewohner, eine Art große Binnenalster. Eine Alternative zu den wuchernden Stadtwüsten des chinesischen Ostens? Dirk Meyhöfer zieht nach acht Jahren ein erstes Resümee des Projekts, das sehr positiv ausfällt.

DIE JURY DES JAHRBUCHS

Die Vorauswahl und Nominierung von Projekten zu der Jurysitzung für das Jahrbuch erfolgte in bewährter Weise durch die Kuratoren und wissenschaftlichen Mitarbeitern des DAM sowie den externen Jurymitgliedern. In diesem Jahr konnten wir als solche gewinnen: den Chefredakteur der Zeitschrift „Baumeister", Wolfgang Bachmann; die freie Architekturkritikerin Karin Leydecker; Friederike Meyer, Redakteurin der „Bauwelt", und Axel Simon, Redaktor Architektur der Schweizer Zeitschrift „Hochparterre". Frank Barkow, Träger des „DAM

Lederer to write an essay for us on the theme. It might be, he argues, that the Modernist exaltation of technology and the nostalgic glorification of the past found in many a reconstruction have more in common than first meets the eye. The real challenge is after all to create an architecture that remains aware of its past while being able to envision a future based on its present state. It's always important that we try to understand architecture not in isolation, but rather in the context of its setting and the community it is meant to serve. Viewed from this standpoint, what we are witnessing today is not a "retro" wave, but instead the efforts of many architects to establish continuity. Lederer's essay makes a plea for the responsibility of architecture to the city.

And the city is also the subject of the second essay, specifically the new harbour town of Lingang New City near Shanghai. The architecture office of von Gerkan, Marg and Partner won the competition to design this new mega-city in 2002. Instead of a cluster of tall buildings, a round lake measuring 2.5 kilometres in diameter forms the heart of the new city, with a continuous beach for the enjoyment of the residents – a bit like Hamburg's Binnenalster, but bigger. Could this be a viable alternative to the proliferating urban jungles of eastern China? After eight years, Dirk Meyhöfer takes stock of the project and draws some very positive conclusions.

THE JURY OF THE GERMAN ARCHITECTURE ANNUAL

Putting together a shortlist and nominating projects for the jury session was entrusted this year as always to the capable hands of the curators and research assistants at the DAM as well as external jury members. Joining us this year in that capacity were: Wolfgang Bachmann, editor-in-chief of "Baumeister" magazine; freelance architecture critic Karin Leydecker; Friederike Meyer, editor of "Bauwelt"; and Axel Simon, architecture editor for the Swiss magazine "Hochparterre". Frank Barkow, winner of the DAM Award for Architecture in Germany in 2009, likewise sat on the jury. The team from DAM was made up of director Peter Cachola Schmal, curators Annette Becker and Oliver Elser, archive director Inge Wolf, freelance staff member Michaela Busenkell and co-editor Yorck Förster. The jury session

Preises für Architektur in Deutschland" 2009 war ebenfalls bereit mitzuwirken. Von Seiten des DAM waren, neben seinem Direktor Peter Cachola Schmal und den Kuratoren Annette Becker und Oliver Elser, die Archivleiterin Inge Wolf sowie die freien Mitarbeiter Michaela Busenkell und Mitherausgeber Yorck Förster Jurymitglieder. Am 25. und 26. Januar 2010 fand die Jurysitzung im Archiv des DAM statt. In mehreren Durchgängen mit intensiven Diskussionen sichtete die Jury die rund 90 nominierten Projekte aus dem In- und Ausland und wählte die 23 Bauwerke aus, die hier vorgestellt werden. In seltener Einstimmigkeit fiel die Wahl des neuen Preisträgers auf David Chipperfield Architects für die Wiederherstellung des Neuen Museums in Berlin. Daneben gab es aber noch ein Projekt, das eine besondere Aufmerksamkeit der Jury hervorrief – Max Dudlers Jacob-und-Wilhelm-Grimm-Zentrum in Berlin. Wir haben dem Gebäude deshalb in diesem Buch eine etwas längere Darstellung als üblich eingeräumt.
Für die Bilddokumentation des Neuen Museums freuen wir uns, wieder einmal die britische Fotografin Hélène Binet gewonnen zu haben, die Anfang Juni eine Reise nach Berlin unternahm, um dieses außerordentliche Projekt zu fotografieren.

ARCHITEKTUR IN DEUTSCHLAND

Wie wohnen? Die Beispiele dafür reichen in diesem Jahrbuch vom Haus in Niederbayern bis zum Wohnen in Metropolen. Beginnen wir beim Maßstab XS: den Maisonettbungalows für Studenten im ehemaligen Olympischen Dorf in München. Nach Plänen einer Arbeitsgemeinschaft von Werner Wirsing und bogevischs buero sind dort zwölf Bestandshäuser saniert worden und 1052 Bungalows neu entstanden. In Hamburg haben sich SPRINGER ARCHITEKTEN der Sanierung von 1950er-Jahre Wohnzeilen am Altenhagener Weg angenommen und die Substanz für eine qualitätvolle neue Interpretation genutzt. In der Nähe von Passau haben Florian Fischer und Katharina Leuschner ein Haus geplant, das Schlichtheit mit einem Spiel architektonischer Codes verbindet und dabei den Bewohnern wunderbar lichte Räume bietet. Ein Haus für

took place at the DAM archive on 25 and 26 January 2010. In several run-throughs, accompanied by intensive discussions, the jury selected from some 90 nominated projects in Germany and abroad the 23 buildings that are now presented here. In a rare unanimous decision, the award went to David Chipperfield Architects' reconstruction of the Neues Museum in Berlin. But there was also another project that commanded special attention from the jury – Max Dudler's Jacob and Wilhelm Grimm Centre in Berlin. We have therefore devoted somewhat more space in this book to this second building as well.
For the pictorial documentation of the Neues Museum, we are pleased to have been able to retain the services once again of British photographer Hélène Binet, who made a special trip to Berlin in early June to photograph this extraordinary project.

ARCHITECTURE IN GERMANY

How do we want to live today? Examples in this Annual range from a house in Lower Bavaria to life in the big city. Let's start with size XS: the maisonette bungalows for students in the former Olympic Village in Munich. To plans by a consortium of Werner Wirsing and bogevischs buero, twelve existing houses have been refurbished there and 1,052 new bungalows erected. In Hamburg, SPRINGER ARCHITEKTEN took on the renovation of a group of 1950s apartment blocks on Altenhagener Weg and were able to make use of the existing building stock for a high-quality reinterpretation. Near the town of Passau, Florian Fischer and Katharina Leuschner conceived a home whose pared-down style subtly alludes to common codes in domestic architecture, resulting in wonderfully light and airy rooms for its residents. A home for a family of bookworms was designed in Berlin-Pankow by brandt + simon as a sculptural structure enveloped in 8,350 beaver-tail tiles in graduated shades of green. Genteel elegance is embodied in the urban villas set in Herderpark in Bad Tölz, built according to plans by Goetz Hootz Castorph.
Can a newly built hotel seem both matter-of-course and personally appealing? It certainly can when it's the Hotel Louis in Munich designed by Hild + K, which feels just as if it had always been there.

eine Familie und viele Bücher wurde von brandt + simon in Berlin-Pankow als ein skulpturaler Bauköper, der von 8350 Bieberschwanzziegeln in unterschiedlichen Grüntönen umhüllt ist, entworfen. Distinguierte Noblesse verkörpern die Stadtvillen im Herderpark in Bad Tölz, die nach Plänen von Goetz Hootz Castorph entstanden.
Kann ein neu errichtetes Hotel selbstverständlich und persönlich wirken? Sehr wohl, beinahe sogar als sei es schon immer dagewesen, wie das Beispiel des Louis Hotels in München, entworfen von Hild und K, zeigt.
Die Breite möglicher architektonischer Haltungen spiegelt sich in den beiden Verwaltungsbauten in diesem Jahrbuch wider. Der von Christoph Mäckler entworfene OpernTurm in Frankfurt am Main setzt im Hochhauscluster der Stadt als steinerner Turm einen neuen Akzent und schließt zudem mit seiner Sockelbebauung die verlorene Platzkante am Opernplatz. Fast schon einem unter vollen Segeln fahrenden Schiff dagegen gleicht die ETFE-Fassadenhülle der Unilever Hauptverwaltung für den deutschsprachigen Raum, die Behnisch Architekten in der Hamburger HafenCity errichtet haben.
Zwei Bildungseinrichtungen dokumentiert das Jahrbuchs: In einer kaum zu überbietenden Lage mit Blick auf den Bodensee haben Lederer Ragnarsdottír Oei den Schulbau des Klosters Hegne um einen neuen Flügel ergänzt. In der Mitte Berlins ist als größte deutsche Präsenzbibliothek das bereits erwähnte Jacob-und-Wilhelm-Grimm-Zentrum mit einem beeindruckenden zentralen Lesesaal nach einem Entwurf von Max Dudler errichtet worden.
Empfangsbauwerke sind in Dachau und Dresden entstanden. Für die KZ-Gedenkstätte Dachau hat Florian Nagler ein Besucherzentrum entlang des Zugangsweges entworfen, das eine unaufdringliche Präsenz entfaltet. Dem Residenzschloss Dresden wiederum fehlte ein Empfangsbereich für den enormen Besucherzustrom. Peter Kulka hat zusammen mit Philipp Stamborski zu diesem Zweck den Kleinen Schlosshof mit einer flach über die Renaissancegiebel gespannten Kuppel überwölbt. Ein kleinteiliges Ensemble moderner und regionaler Elemente hat Gregor Sunder-Plassmann für das Museum Kunst der

The breadth of possible attitudes to architecture becomes evident in the two office buildings featured in this Annual. Christoph Mäckler's OpernTurm in Frankfurt am Main is a stone-clad tower that adds a new feature to the cluster of high-rises that dominate the city centre, while also with its well-conceived base forming a congenial border to the Opernplatz square. By contrast, the EFTE membrane enclosing Unilever's German headquarters building in Hamburg's HafenCity, conceived by Behnisch Architekten, makes it look almost like a ship gliding by with wind-filled sails.
Two educational facilities are documented in this year's Annual. Lederer Ragnarsdottír Oei have added a new wing to the school at Hegne Monastery, located in an unrivalled scenic setting with a view of Lake Constance. And in the centre of Berlin, Max Dudler has given Germany's biggest open-stack library, the above-mentioned Jacob and Wilhelm Grimm Centre, an imposing central reading room.
New visitors' buildings were constructed this year in Dachau and Dresden. For the Dachau Concentration Camp Memorial Site, Florian Nagler designed a visitor centre that asserts a low-key presence along the access path. The Dresden Royal Palace also needed a reception area for its crowds of visitors. To create a suitable space, Peter Kulka and Philipp Stamborski roofed over the Small Courtyard with a shallow transparent dome stretched between the Renaissance gables of the surrounding structures.
An intricate ensemble of both modern and traditional regional buildings was strung together by Gregor Sunder-Plassmann for the Museum Kunst der Westküste in Alkersum on the island of Föhr. In Herzog & de Meuron's VitraHaus in Weil am Rhein, by contrast, twelve elements in the shape of elongated gable houses are stacked one on top of the other, interpenetrating to form a complex geometry. What is certainly the most provocative new building Berlin has seen in recent years comes from the drawing board of Brandlhuber+ ERA, Emde, Schneider. The gallery on Brunnenstrasse uncompromisingly assimilates all the references found in its setting and cultivates a raw aesthetic of the changeable and unfinished.
Berlin is likewise home to a new building for the Frische Paradies Lindenberg catering suppliers, designed by ROBERTNEUN™ as a symbolic gigantic wooden delivery pallet. Another iconic form, a dark, heavy monolith resting on a waterway, was used by

Dem Prestel Verlag sei an dieser Stelle für sein großes Engagement gedankt. Ebenso dem gesamten Team des Deutschen Architekturmuseums und allen Architekten und Fotografen für die große Unterstützung bei Nominierung und Auswahl, Publikation und Ausstellung.

We would like to take this opportunity to thank Prestel Verlag for its hard work and dedication in putting together this German Architecture Annual. Many thanks as well to the team at the Deutsches Architekturmuseum and all architects and photographers involved for their generous support with the nomination and selection process, publication and exhibition.

Westküste in Alkersum auf Föhr geplant. Dagegen bildet ein Stapel aus zwölf übereinander geschichteten und sich durchdringenden Giebelhäusern das VitraHaus in Weil am Rhein, entworfen von Herzog & de Meuron. Der sicherlich provokativste Neubau der letzten Jahre in Berlin stammt von Brandlhuber+ ERA, Emde, Schneider. Kompromisslos nimmt das Galeriehaus in der Brunnenstraße alle vorgefundenen Bezüge auf und kultiviert eine raue Ästhetik des Veränderbaren und Unfertigen. Ebenfalls in Berlin befindet sich ein Neubau für das Frische Paradies Lindenberg, den ROBERTNEUN™ als eine signethafte Riesenpalette entworfen haben.
Als puren, schweren Monolithen, der auf einer Wasserader lagert, haben SYRA – SCHOYERER ARCHITEKTEN ein Hochwasserpumpwerk in Mainz gestaltet.
Stadtentwicklung durch einen „situativen Urbanismus" zu induzieren, war die Absicht von KARO* beim Lesezeichen in Magdeburg-Salbke, das sowohl Treffpunkt, Ortsmitte und Konzertbühne ist.

EXPORT

Unter den Auslandsprojekten findet sich in diesem Jahr ein Beispiel eines umfassenden Kulturexports. In einer Zusammenarbeit des Kommunikationsnetzwerks PLATOON mit Graft Beijing und Baik, Jiwon ist in Seoul aus 28 Containern die „PLATOON Kunsthalle" entstanden – als Veranstaltungsort und die beste Möglichkeit, in Korea Kässpätzle zu essen.
Für eine möglichst breite Nutzung offen sein sollte auch die 193 x 31 Meter große „Platine" genannte Halle, die LIN Finn Geipel + Giulia Andi für die Cité du design in Saint-Étienne, Frankreich, konzipiert haben. Einen dezidierten Ort erhalten hat die Auenlandschaft der Mur bei Gosdorf in Österreich durch den Turm, der von terrain: loenhart&mayr entworfen wurde. Schließlich richten wir den Blick noch nach Hangzhou in China. Dort entstand die Culture Wave City und der City Balcony nach Plänen von OBERMEYER.

SYRA – SCHOYERER ARCHITEKTEN for a floodwater pumping station in Mainz. Inducing urban development through "situational urbanism" was KARO*'s declared intention in their design for the Lesezeichen open-air library in Magdeburg-Salbke, which functions at once as meeting point, town centre and concert stage.

EXPORT

Amongst the foreign projects featured this year, one is a fine example of a comprehensive cultural export. In a cooperative project of the PLATOON communication network with Graft Beijing and Baik, Jiwon, the PLATOON Kunsthalle was built in Seoul out of 28 shipping containers – as an event location and the best place to dine on cheesy spaetzle noodles in Korea. Also open to a wide variety of uses is a 193 x 31 metre hall, "Platine", conceived by LIN Finn Geipel + Giulia Andi for the Cité du design in Saint-Étienne, France. The floodplains of the Mur River near Gosdorf in Austria have been given a new focal point in the form of an observation tower by the architects terrain: loenhart&mayr. Finally, we turn our gaze to China and the city of Hangzhou, where Culture Wave City and the City Balcony have been built according to plans by OBERMEYER.

Im Bild die Installation von Barkow Leibinger als Sieger des Preises 2009 mit ihrem Betriebsrestaurant in Ditzingen.
Seen here is the installation by Barkow Leibinger, winner of the DAM Award in 2009 for their company restaurant in Ditzingen.

Das DAM zeigt seit 2008 alle Projekte des Deutschen Architektur Jahrbuchs in einer Ausstellung. Der Preisträger des DAM Preis für Architektur in Deutschland 2010, das Neue Museum in Berlin, wird wieder im „Haus im Haus“ präsentiert werden.

Since 2008 the DAM has shown all projects featured in the German Architecture Annual in an exhibition. The winner of the DAM Award for Architecture in Germany 2010, the Neues Museum in Berlin, will be presented, like previous winners, in the “House within a House”.

EIN PLÄDOYER FÜR DIE VERANTWORTUNG DER ARCHITEKTUR GEGENÜBER DER STADT
A PLEA FOR SOCIALLY RESPONSIBLE URBAN ARCHITECTURE

DIE ZUKUNFT AUS DER VERGANGENHEIT DENKEN
ENVISIONING THE FUTURE FROM THE PAST

ARNO LEDERER

E1

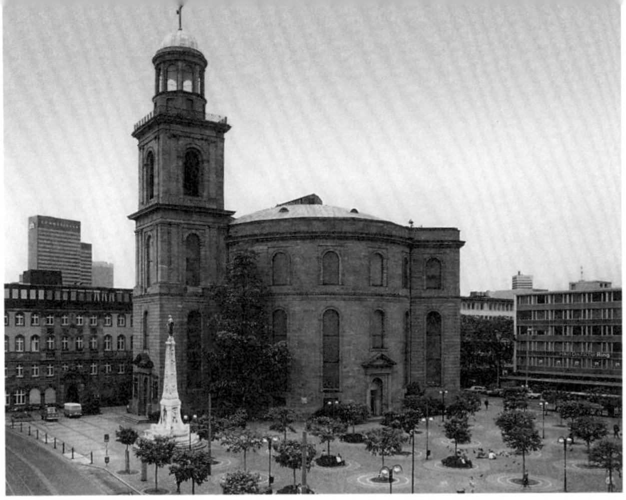

Wiederaufbau der Paulskirche, Frankfurt am Main (1946–1948), Architekten: Eugen Blanck, Gottlob Schaupp, Rudolf Schwarz, Johannes Krahn; Außenansicht, 1983 | Reconstruction of St Paul's Church, Frankfurt/Main (1946–1948), architects: Eugen Blanck, Gottlob Schaupp, Rudolf Schwarz, Johannes Krahn; exterior view, 1983

Wiederaufbau der Paulskirche, Frankfurt am Main (1946–1948), Architekten: Eugen Blanck, Gottlob Schaupp, Rudolf Schwarz, Johannes Krahn, Saal, 1967. Im Innenraum sollte die durch die Bomben freigelegte schlichte Raumdimension erhalten bleiben.
Reconstruction of St Paul's Church, Frankfurt/Main (1946–1948), architects: Eugen Blanck, Gottlob Schaupp, Rudolf Schwarz, Johannes Krahn; assembly hall, 1967. The aim was to preserve the simple spatial dimensions exposed by the wartime bombings.

Als die Sektkorken zu Silvester des neuen Jahrhunderts knallten, dachte jeder, es würde anders. Besser auf jeden Fall. Denn das 20. Jahrhundert, das sich so sehr als ein Fortschrittliches betrachtete und nur nach vorne schaute, erfuhr nun, an seinem Ende, eine zwiespältige Beurteilung. Die Architektur selbst ist es, die wie ein Bilderbogen Hoffnung, Zweifel und Verzweiflung dieser Epoche widerspiegelt. Jetzt, zehn Jahre später, kann man besser Resümee ziehen als direkt an der Schwelle, die man empfand, als das Jahr 2000 eingeläutet wurde.
Nirgendwo wird die zunehmende Spaltung der Gesellschaft greifbarer als in der Architektur und im Städtebau, man kann hier von einer Verfestigung der unterschiedlichen Strömungen sprechen. Das hat sich auch durch die vehemente Art, mit der das Internet seinen Siegeszug fortsetzte, nicht geändert. Nach wie vor fordert der analoge Raum, die materialisierte Umwelt, den Menschen mehr zu einem Urteil heraus als jede virtuelle Darstellung. Denn Architektur ist der Bummelzug der Kultur. Erdacht zu einem Zeitpunkt, dessen Fenster schon lange wieder geschlossen sind, wenn die langwierige Planungs- und Bauphase überwunden ist.

ARCHITEKTUR, ORT UND GEMEINSCHAFT

Jahrhundertelang gehörte das Bauen für die Kirche zu den vornehmsten Aufgaben der Architektur. Kein Ort, keine Stadt in der Bundesrepublik, und sei sie noch so arm an baukünstlerisch wertvollen Häusern, hat nicht wenigstens einen Kirchenbau, der, unabhängig seines Baujahres, mit Sorgfalt entworfen wurde. Dass die Kirche schön zu sein hat, ist eine Sache, die unmittelbar mit dem Glauben verbunden ist. Die gewünschte Schönheit, oder besser gesagt der ästhetische Reichtum, kann ja auch als eine Ehrerweisung gegenüber dem Himmel beschrieben werden. Sie ist damit Teil der Verherrlichung durch

When the champagne corks popped on New Year's Eve to usher in the new century, everyone thought things would be different. Surely better. The 20th century, which had viewed itself as so progressive and forward-looking, was now coming to an end with mixed reviews. Like a picture album, architecture reflects the hopes, misgivings and despair of this era. Now, ten years later, the picture is clearer than at the threshold of New Year 2000.
Nowhere is the growing division of society as apparent as in architecture and city planning, where we can speak of a consolidation of different trends. Even the vehemence with which the internet has continued its triumphal march has not changed anything. Analogue space and the material environment still demand human judgements more than any virtual world. Architecture is a cultural slow-train, conceived in a time window that has long since closed again by the time the drawn-out planning and construction phase has been completed.

ARCHITECTURE, LOCATION AND COMMUNITY

Building for the Church has been one of the most distinguished architectural tasks for centuries. There is not one town or city in Germany, even those otherwise utterly bereft of any edifice of architectural merit, which does not have at least one church designed with care, regardless of the year of its construction. The fact that churches must be beautiful is directly linked with religious faith. The desired beauty or, more precisely, aesthetic richness, may also be described as a tribute of honour to heaven. It is hence part of glorification through faith. In this respect it is perfectly understandable that churches are always built in the most distinguished locations. This is accepted as a matter of course. Wherever a church stands, the adjacent city districts and the layout of the city itself are planned around this one special building. The spatial structure of our cities is therefore not only based on commerce and traffic, but also on faith. This, too, is a truism. But no one questions whether the interdependence of worldly and religious

Sächsischer Landtag, Dresden (1991–1997), Architekt: Peter Kulka; Elbflügel des Neubaus mit dem Bürgerportal. Für Heinrich Klotz ein Beispiel der „neuen Einfachheit" | Saxon State Parliament, Dresden (1991–1997), architect: Peter Kulka; Elbe wing of the new building with the "citizens' portal". For Heinrich Klotz, an example of the "new simplicity".

Ansicht von Westen auf den Neubau der Europäischen Zentralbank neben der ehemaligen Großmarkthalle in Frankfurt am Main (Rendering); Architekten: Coop Himmelb(l)au
Views from the west of the new European Central Bank building, next to the former market hall in Frankfurt/Main (rendering); architects: Coop Himmelb(l)au

den Glauben. Insofern ist nur allzu verständlich, dass Kirchen immer auf einem der vornehmsten Plätze der Stadt platziert sind. Eine Selbstverständlichkeit, über die nicht weiter nachgedacht wird. Denn dort, wo Kirchen stehen, sind die benachbarten Quartiere und somit der Plan der Stadt auf den besonderen Bau ausgerichtet. Die räumliche Ordnung unserer Städte hat also nicht nur etwas mit Handel und Verkehr zu tun, sondern auch mit dem Glauben. Auch das ist eine Binsenweisheit. Niemand stellt sich jedoch die Frage, ob diese beidseitige Abhängigkeit zwischen weltlicher und religiöser Macht, die die Ordnung der Stadt prägt, nicht eine Sache ist, die nicht die Kirche allein betrifft, sondern auch umgekehrt die Stadt und den Staat.

Es ist also eine weitergehende Frage, eine des Städtebaus und der Architektur, die sich mit dem Abriss oder der Umnutzung von Kirchen verbindet. Dazu gehört umgekehrt auch die Frage der Qualität von Gotteshäusern anderer Religionen, bezogen auf ihre städtebauliche Stellung und ihre baukünstlerische Ausprägung. Die peripheren Lagen, vornehmlich in Gewerbegebieten, zementieren bildlich im Grundriss der Städte den Umgang mit Andersgläubigen. Aber auch die Frage der Architektur des Gebäudes selbst. Bauten der Kirche hatten immer Vorbildfunktion und damit einen enorm positiven Einfluss auf die Baukultur des Profanen.

Sichtbar hat in der Stadt die Bedeutung der Religion abgenommen und damit verschwindet auch peu à peu der Bedarf an Räumen, die nicht dem Primat der Ökonomie untergeordnet sind, gleichwohl Bauten der Religion für sich genommen einen Wert im Sinne der Immobilienwirtschaft darstellen. Uns kommen dadurch aber auch ‚zweckfreie Räume' in der Stadt abhanden, Räume, die das sichtbare Gegengewicht zum Zweckhaften, zu Konsum und Verwaltung darstellen. Könnte es sein, dass dieses Thema eines der großen zukünftigen Felder ist, dem sich Architektur und Städtebau annehmen müssen?

power prevalent in cities might in fact be a matter that concerns not the Church alone, but rather also the city and the state.

A more far-reaching question, concerning both urban planning and architecture, must therefore be posed with regard to the demolition or conversion of churches. This issue conversely involves determining the quality of places of worship of other religions with regard to their position in the urban fabric and its architectural characteristics. Their peripheral locations, primarily in industrial areas, figuratively cement in a city's layout how it deals with people of different religions. As do the architectural aspects of the building itself. Church buildings always set an example and hence have had a very positive influence on secular building practices.

Today, the significance of religion has declined visibly in our cities. Little by little, the demand for spaces that are not subject to the primacy of economic dictates is diminishing, although religious buildings in themselves still represent a value for the real estate industry. What we lose, however, are "purpose-free spaces" in the city, spaces that form a tangible counterweight to those dedicated to a specific purpose, to consumption or administrative use. Could this be one of the major issues that must be addressed in future by architects and city planners?

INCENTIVE ARCHITECTURE

This type of architecture would seem to be necessary in view of the functional buildings erected by banks, insurance companies and corporations. Here the trends have if anything gained momentum. Those who said they were surprised by the financial crisis at the end of the decade could have seen it coming had they opened their eyes while walking through the city. The huge trend towards incentive architecture during the last ten years would have been proof enough. The arrogance with which capital has left signs of its power everywhere in the purlieus of our cities is astounding. In the early 1990s architects were still making efforts to recover from the excesses of Postmodernism and return to a more reduced and in the best sense

Max-Planck-Institut für Bildungsforschung, Berlin (1965–1974), Architekten: Hermann Fehling + Daniel Gogel | Max Planck Institute for Human Development, Berlin (1965–1974), architects: Hermann Fehling + Daniel Gogel

Max-Planck-Institut für Bildungsforschung, Berlin (1965–1974), Architekten: Hermann Fehling + Daniel Gogel | Max Planck Institute for Human Development, Berlin (1965–1974), architects: Hermann Fehling + Daniel Gogel

BONI-ARCHITEKTUR

Mit Blick auf die Zweckbauten, wie man jene von Banken, Versicherungen und Unternehmen nennen kann, scheint dies geboten. Denn hier hat die Entwicklung eher noch an Fahrt zugenommen. Wer von der Finanzkrise am Ende des Jahrzehnts sagt, man sei davon überrascht worden, hätte es sehen können, wenn er offenen Auges durch die Stadt spaziert wäre. Denn die Massivität, in der sich die Boni-Architektur in der letzten Dekade breit gemacht hat, wäre allein schon Zeichen genug gewesen. Die Arroganz, mit der das Kapital Zeichen seiner Macht im Weichbild der Stadt hinterlassen hat, ist erstaunlich. Noch Anfang der 1990er-Jahre gebaren Architekten den Begriff der ‚neuen Einfachheit' und gaben sich Mühe, nach der Postmoderne zu einer reduzierten und im besten Sinne bescheidenen Sprache zurückzukehren. Das Zeichen, das das Bauvorhaben der Europäischen Zentralbank mit dem Entwurf von Coop-Himmelb(l)au setzt, spricht gleich in mehrfacher Hinsicht Bände. Einmal natürlich die Überheblichkeit, mit der das Gebäude allen anderen, voran der Markthalle von Elsaesser, bedeutet, Landpomeranzen zu sein. Zum anderen wird wohl kaum jemand die Auffassung vertreten können, dass trotz allen technischen Schnickschnacks das Haus dem Gebot eines sorgfältigen Umgangs mit Ressourcen gerecht wird. (Wobei Kultur und Geschichte auch als Ressourcen anzuführen wären.) Das Gebäude zeigt dagegen sehr gut, was Architektur heute kann und ganz sicher kann man ihm auch nicht ein hohes Maß an baukünstlerischem Raffinement wie auch architektonisches Können absprechen.

DIE VERGESSENE BESCHEIDENHEIT

Es scheint so, dass in der Architektur dieser und ähnlicher Gebäude sichtbar wird, dass die Tugend der Bescheidenheit, die wirklich reiche und vom Wohlstand gesegnete Unternehmen auszeichnete, in Vergessenheit geraten ist. Dazu gehört auch

modest architectural idiom, inventing the term "new simplicity". The fact that the European Central Bank then chose a building designed by Coop Himmelb(l)au speaks volumes. First, there is the presumption with which the edifice implies that all others before it, such as the Market Hall by Elsaesser, are mere country bumpkins. Secondly, no one can possibly defend the view that, despite all its technical gadgets, the building thoroughly fulfils the obligation to use resources with care. (Whereby culture and history must also be cited as resources). What the bank building does show very successfully is the power of architecture today, and one cannot deny the high level of architectural refinement and skill it represents.

FORGOTTEN MODESTY

The architecture in this and similar buildings seems to demonstrate that the virtue of modesty, which once characterised truly wealthy and successful companies, has been forgotten. This includes a sense of social responsibility. What do these over-styled façades say? What they definitely do not convey is a willingness to form a community with the rest of the city's architectural landscape. Or should these buildings be considered one last defiant uprising of Modernism, a brand of Modernism that is (still) based on the love of technology, but which has taken leave of its roots? One forgets all too easily that the first quarter of the last century was borne by a great social ideal. It seems that the heirs of supposedly contemporary architecture have little to do with this ideal.

Those who are not content with this assumption should look at publications of exemplary projects online or in the media. Floor plans or sectional drawings, which are equivalent to the musical scores of architecture, have been replaced by gorgeous pictures of buildings that will never look the way they are depicted. The electronic image is so beautiful and precise that no company or craftsman could ever convert it into reality. The design process has now been reversed.

In the 1980s, one read in a book how the architects Fehling and Gogel, who had already drawn the floor plans and sectional drawings,

Berliner Schloss/Humboldtforum, Architekt: Francesco Stella; Blick von der Liebknecht-Brücke auf das Schloss
Berlin City Palace/Humboldt Forum, architect: Francesco Stella; view of the palace from Liebknecht Bridge

Bauhaus Europa, Aachen (2006), Architekt: Wolfgang Tschapeller. Das Projekt sollte zwischen Pfalzkapelle und Rathaus anstelle eines Verwaltungsgebäudes aus den 1950er-Jahren entstehen. In einem Bürgerentscheid votierten die Aachener gegen die Realisierung. | Bauhaus Europa, Aachen (2006), architect: Wolfgang Tschapeller. The project was meant to replace a 1950s administrative building between the Palatine Chapel and the Town Hall. In a referendum Aachen's citizenry voted against its realisation.

ein Gespür für soziales Verhalten. Was sagen aber in diesem Sinne die super gestylten Fassaden? Auf jeden Fall nicht, mit den anderen Häusern der Stadt eine Gemeinschaft eingehen zu wollen. Oder kann man diese Gebäude als ein letztes Aufbäumen der Moderne verstehen, einer Moderne, die (immer noch) ihre Gestalt aus der Begeisterung für die Technik bezieht, aber ihre eigenen Wurzeln verlassen hat? Man vergisst allzu leicht, dass das erste Viertel des letzten Jahrhunderts von einer großen sozialen Idee getragen wurde. Damit haben die Nachfahren scheinbar zeitgenössischer Architektur wenig zu tun.

Wem diese These nicht behagt, der möge sich in den Medien oder im Netz die Veröffentlichungen vorbildlicher Projekte ansehen. Grundrisse oder Schnitte, die die eigentliche Partitur der Architektur bedeuten, weichen den tollen Bildern von Gebäuden, die man so nie sehen wird. Denn das elektronische Bild ist so schön und präzise, dass kaum ein Unternehmen, kaum ein Handwerker in dieser Art das Bild umzusetzen vermag. Der Entwurfsprozess hat sich umgekehrt. In den 1980er-Jahren las man in einem Buch über das Büro Fehling und Gogel, wie die Architekten Grundrisse und Schnitte bereits angefertigt hatten, sich aber plötzlich dem Problem gegenübersahen, die Fassade noch nicht gezeichnet zu haben. Heute versucht man, vereinfacht gesagt, den umgekehrten Weg: Aus dem Bild von außen entstehen die Grundrisse und Schnitte. So ist die Hülle, besser gesagt, deren Design, zunehmend zum wichtigsten Thema der letzten zehn Jahre geworden.

Man kann nun freilich das alles beklagen und zum wiederholten Male den Untergang der abendländischen Architektur beschwören. Die geschilderte Entwicklung führte aber in den letzten Jahren, und das ist nun durchaus ein neues Phänomen, zu einer radikalen Gegenbewegung. Diese beschränkt sich jedoch nicht nur auf professionelle Verteidigungsminister der europäischen Stadt, die im Sinne der Rekonstruktion die urbanen Räume des 19. Jahrhunderts wiederherzustellen

suddenly realised that they still had to design the façade. Today, simply put, architects are trying out the reverse method: floor plans and sectional drawings emerge from the outer image. The "wrapping", or its design, has become the most important element in the last ten years.

We can certainly lament all of this and once again attest the downfall of occidental architecture. The developments presented have, however, led to a radical counter-movement during the past few years, and this is by all means a new phenomenon. This movement is not limited to the professional defence ministers of the European city, who are attempting to restore the city spaces of the 19th century in the spirit of reconstruction. No, it is the citizens themselves who are increasingly speaking out strongly against contemporary architecture. This causes problems for the business on various levels, especially when the scene goes radical and blindly calls for a past that never existed, not in terms of craftsmanship and certainly not with respect to social structure. Behind the homely atmosphere of old buildings was a specific user group, whose social function and significance were directly linked to those edifices. Now, a clientele who have nothing in common with the previous occupants are taking possession of the new old buildings. One might well wonder whether both types of architecture, that of the so-called Modernists and that produced by the adherents of reconstruction, are not in fact one and the same. It is beyond dispute that each type has its highs and lows, and whether an architect belongs to one side or the other is irrelevant in terms of design reputation, because there are buildings of remarkable quality in both camps.

The impression that architecture has relegated itself to a right and left corner of a symmetrical room is apparent in large-scale building projects. Exasperating discussions about the reconstruction of palaces, whether in Brunswick, Potsdam or especially with respect to Stella's project for Berlin, are just as tedious as the debate about the "Bauhaus Europa" in Aachen, for which the Austrian architect Tschapeller received first prize in the 2006 competition. Tschapeller's project, as we all know, landed in the rubbish bin – a fate not yet shared

Bauhaus Europa, Aachen (2006), Architekt: Wolfgang Tschapeller. Der Ausstellungsbereich war als fließende ‚Geschichtslandschaft' gedacht. Darüber sollte sich eine fahrbare Brücke – als Reminiszenz an einen historische Verbindungsgang zwischen Königshalle und Pfalzkapelle – rotierend bewegen. | Bauhaus Europa, Aachen (2006), architect: Wolfgang Tschapeller. The exhibition area was conceived as a flowing "landscape of history". Overhead a mobile bridge would rotate – to recall the historical passageway between the Kings' Hall und Palatine Chapel.

Wiederaufbau Gürzenich, Köln (1951–1955), Architekten: Rudolf Schwarz und Karl Band. Die Außenmauern der Kirchenruine St. Alban bilden den Raumabschluss der Wandelhalle. Reconstruction of the Gürzenich, Cologne (1951–1955), architects: Rudolf Schwarz and Karl Band. The exterior walls of the ruins of St Alban's Church enclose the foyer.

versuchen. Nein, zunehmend ergreifen auch Bürger das Wort, die sich massiv gegen zeitgenössische Architektur wehren. Das macht das Geschäft an der einen oder anderen Stelle mühsam, besonders dann, wenn sich die Szene radikalisiert und mit Blindheit eine Vergangenheit eingefordert wird, die es so nie gab: weder in der handwerklichen Ausführung und schon gar nicht in der sozialen Konstellation. Denn hinter der heimeligen Atmosphäre alter Bauten stand eine bestimmte Nutzerschicht, deren gesellschaftliche Funktion und Bedeutung unmittelbar mit den Baulichkeiten in Verbindung stand. Nun werden die neuen alten Gebäude von einer Klientel in Besitz genommen, die mit den Vorgängern, die diese Häuser nutzten, nichts mehr zu tun hat. Man kann deshalb der Überlegung nachgehen, ob beide Arten von Architektur, die der sogenannten Modernen und jene der rekonstruktiven Haltung, nicht ein und dasselbe sind. Auf beiden Seiten, das ist unbestritten, gibt es Höhen und Tiefen, und ob einer da oder dort steht, sagt zunächst über seine gestalterische Reputation wenig aus, da sowohl auf der einen wie anderen Seite bemerkenswert hochwertige Gebäude zu finden sind.

Der Eindruck, die Architektur habe sich in eine rechte und linke Ecke eines symmetrischen Raums verrannt, wird bei großen Bauvorhaben deutlich. Die leidige Diskussion um den Wiederaufbau von Schlössern, ob in Braunschweig, Potsdam oder ganz besonders bei Stellas Projekt für Berlin, kann einem ebenso zum Hals heraushängen wie der Streit um das „Bauhaus Europa", für das der österreichische Architekt Tschapeller 2006 den ersten Preis erhielt. Tschapellers Aachener Projekt ist bekanntlich im Papierkorb gelandet, was beim Humboldtforum noch nicht erfolgt ist. Manchmal ist die Ökonomie doch ein guter Ratgeber oder gar ein Gottesgeschenk. Vielleicht ist es ein Zeichen des Himmels, dass es etwas anderes, etwas Drittes geben müsse.

by the Humboldt Forum in Berlin. Sometimes economy is actually a good counsellor and even a godsend. Perhaps it is a sign from up above that something else, a third option, is needed.

THE CHALLENGE OF CONTINUITY

There is, in fact, a growing discussion concerning continuity and the concept of building on what went before. It is about architecture that, on the one hand, is conscious of history and its own past and, on the other, does not seek to evade current challenges. This model is related to the idea that only those who live in the present are able to envision the future and the past. This is the self-image of the relay runner who takes the baton and, after contributing his own efforts, passes it on. The Modernists rightly thought that they were faster without the baton. But when they arrived at the finish line, a crucial element of victory was missing.

But this is nothing new. Döllgast, Tessenow, Plečnik, Schwarz, Bienefeld: the 20th century produced a whole series of great architects who thought in this way. What is new is that opinions on certain architects have changed, and their real value is only now being rediscovered. The Schmitthenner exhibition curated by Wolfgang Voigt at the German Architecture Museum, and his forthcoming venture to exhibit the works of Paul Bonatz, have provided, and will provide, a better picture of the quality of this architecture. We should also recall in this context the pioneering work of Vittorio Magnago Lampugnani, whose writings on the "other modernists" opened up the narrow viewpoint taken in the uptight contemplation of the theme to date. This already occurred back in 1992. But as I said earlier: architecture is a cultural slow-train.

There is an undisputedly new and promising development in architecture. Building on the past is a topic that has arrived in Germany in the most various forms. Architects have recognised the creative potential inherent in the existing building stock. Not in the familiar spirit of "Noli me tangere" from the St John's Gospel, as was still academic duty in the 20th century: with visible and often inferior glass joints

Wiederaufbau Alte Pinakothek, München (1952–1957), Architekt: Hans Döllgast | Reconstruction of the Alte Pinakothek, Munich (1952–1957), architect: Hans Döllgast

Ljubljana – Die „Drei Brücken", Architekt: Jože Plečnik. Die Franziskanerbrücke von 1842 ergänzte er um zwei fächerförmig angeordnete Fußgängerstege (1929–1932). Ljubljana – "Triple Bridge", architect: Jože Plečnik. He added two footbridges with fan-like staircases to the 1842 Franciscan Bridge (1929–1932).

KONTINUITÄT ALS HERAUSFORDERUNG

In der Tat entwickelt sich eine Diskussion, die sich mit der Frage der Kontinuität oder dem Begriff des Weiterbauens beschäftigt. Es geht um eine Architektur, die sich auf der einen Seite der Geschichte und ihrer eigenen Vergangenheit bewusst ist und sich auf der anderen Seite aber ebenso den Herausforderungen der Gegenwart nicht entzieht. Dieses Modell beruht auf dem Gedanken, dass nur der in die Zukunft und Vergangenheit denken kann, der in der Gegenwart steht. Man begreift sich als einen Läufer, der den Staffelstab aufnimmt und ihn nach eigener Anstrengung auch weitergeben kann. War es nicht so, dass die Moderne dachte, ohne Staffelstab sei man schneller, was ja auch stimmt. Aber am Ziel angekommen, fehlte dann doch etwas Entscheidendes zum Sieg.

Nun ist das keine neue Erfindung. Döllgast, Tessenow, Plečnik, Schwarz, Bienefeld: Das 20. Jahrhundert hat eine ganze Reihe von großartigen Architekten hervorgebracht, die in diese Richtung dachten. Neu ist aber, dass sich die Sichtweise auf bestimmte Architekten ändert und deren Wertschätzung erst heute richtig wiederentdeckt wird. Die von Wolfgang Voigt kuratierte Ausstellung über Schmitthenner im DAM ebenso wie sein kommendes Vorhaben, Paul Bonatz eine Ausstellung zu widmen, haben und werden dazu beitragen, das Bild über die Qualität dieser Architektur zurechtzurücken. Man erinnere sich auch an die dazu bereits geleistete Pionierarbeit von Vittorio Magnago Lampugnani, der mit seinen Arbeiten zur ‚anderen Moderne' den eingeengten Blick einer bislang verklemmten Betrachtung aufbrechen konnte. Das war bereits im Jahr 1992. Aber wie hatte ich eingangs bemerkt: Architektur ist der Bummelzug der Kultur.

Unstreitig zeichnet sich eine neue und vielversprechende Entwicklung in der Architektur ab. Weiterbauen ist als Thema in der Bundesrepublik in ganz unterschiedlichen Facetten angekommen. Man hat die gestaltende Kraft des Bestands

separating the old from the new with supposed scientific precision. Whether in Zumthor's Kolumba or Chipperfield's Neues Museum, the carefree intertwining and juxtaposition of old and new is suddenly as possible as it was in centuries past, when it was unabashedly common practice. The Neues Museum, despite its great popularity, still raises the question however of whether the original character of the building has lost something in all the enthusiasm for the treatment of its chequered history. We can recognise in much current architecture, in particular in the work of smaller and still-young offices, that history for them is not an unpleasant, compulsory exercise, and that it indeed forms an inspiration for the architecture of the future. Architecture is being created today that integrates the past in both a tongue-in-cheek and fondly pedantic manner – and that is certainly cause for excitement.

Hauptbahnhof, Stuttgart (1911–1927), Architekt: Paul Bonatz; Ansicht von Nordwesten
Main Station, Stuttgart (1911–1927), architect: Paul Bonatz; view from north-west

Kolumba, Kunstmuseum des Erzbistums Köln (1997–2007), Architekt: Peter Zumthor; Hof mit Fragment von St. Kolumba
Kolumba, Art Museum of the Archdiocese of Cologne (1997–2007), architect: Peter Zumthor; courtyard with fragment of St Kolumba

erkannt. Nicht in der Art des bekannten „Noli me tangere" des Johannes Evangeliums, wie es im 20. Jahrhundert noch akademische Pflicht war: mit den sichtbaren und meist weniger gut geglückten Glasfugen, mit denen vermeintlich wissenschaftlich korrekt das Alte vom Neuen getrennt wurde. Ob bei Zumthors Kolumba oder bei Chipperfields Neuem Museum: Das unbekümmerte In- und Aneinander ist plötzlich wieder so möglich, wie es in weiter zurückliegenden Jahrhunderten ungeniert gang und gäbe war. Wobei sich beim Neuen Museum, das sich so großer Popularität erfreut, die Frage stellt, ob bei aller Begeisterung für den Umgang mit der Geschichte das gelitten hat, was das Wesen des Baues ursprünglich ausmachte. Grundsätzlich erkennt man in vielen Arbeiten, vor allem den kleineren und noch jungen Büros, dass für sie Geschichte nicht eine unerfreuliche Pflichtübung darstellt und dass die Architektur auch mit ihr in die Zukunft blicken kann. Dass es darunter Arbeiten gibt, die sowohl mit einem Augenzwinkern als auch liebevoll pedantisch mit der Vergangenheit umgehen, macht die Sache spannend.

Kolumba, Kunstmuseum des Erzbistums Köln (1997–2007), Architekt: Peter Zumthor; Fragment von St. Kolumba und Sakramentskapelle von Gottfried Böhm (1956/57) | Kolumba, Art Museum of the Archdiocese of Cologne (1997–2007), architect: Peter Zumthor; fragment of St Kolumba and Blessed Sacrament Chapel by Gottfried Böhm (1956/57)

ARCHITEKTUR IN DEUTSCHLAND
ARCHITECTURE IN GERMANY

02–19

DEUTSCHLAND
GERMANY

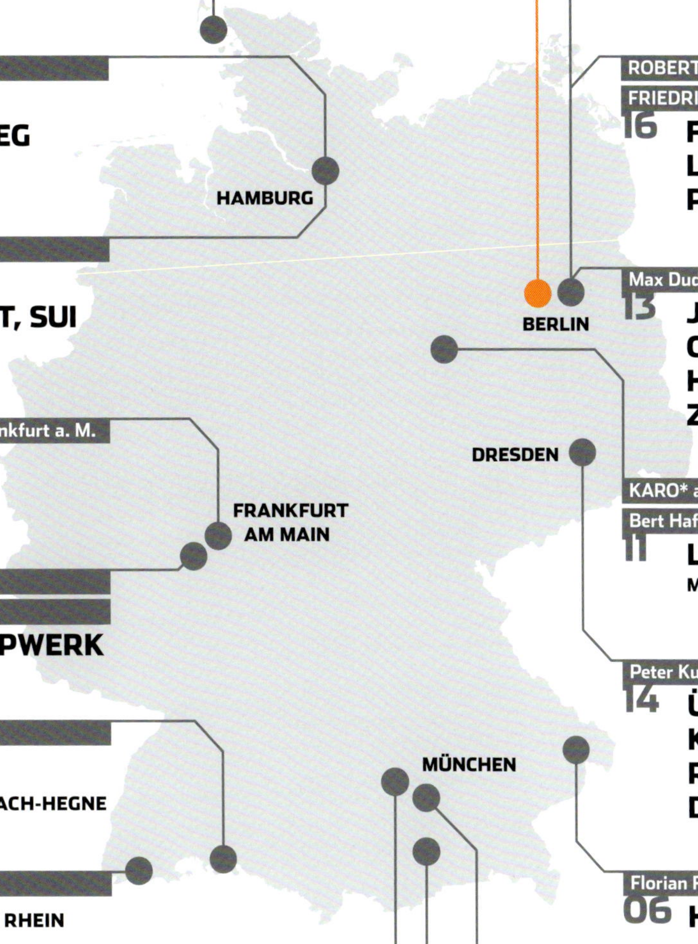

Sunder-Plassmann Architekten, Kappeln
18 **MUSEUM KUNST DER WESTKÜSTE** ALKERSUM / FÖHR

SPRINGER ARCHITEKTEN, Berlin
17 **WOHNQUARTIER ALTENHAGENER WEG**
HAMBURG

Behnisch Architekten, Stuttgart
03 **FIRMENZENTRALE UNILEVER, GER, AUT, SUI**
HAMBURG

Prof. Christoph Mäckler Architekten, Frankfurt a. M.
15 **OPERNTURM**
FRANKFURT AM MAIN

SYRA – SCHOYERER ARCHITEKTEN, Mainz / Frankfurt am Main
19 **HOCHWASSERPUMPWERK**
MAINZ

Lederer + Ragnarsdóttir + Oei, Stuttgart
12 **KLOSTER HEGNE MARIANUM** ALLENSBACH-HEGNE

Herzog & de Meuron, Basel
09 **VITRAHAUS** WEIL AM RHEIN

Florian Nagler Architekten, München
07 **BESUCHERGEBÄUDE DER KZ-GEDENKSTÄTTE DACHAU**

Goetz Hootz Castorph Architekten und Stadtplaner, München
08 **STADTVILLEN IM HERDERPARK** BAD TÖLZ

David Chipperfield Architects, Berlin
01 **WIEDERAUFBAU NEUES MUSEUM MUSEUMSINSEL BERLIN**

Brandlhuber+ ERA, Emde, Schneider, Berlin
04 **GALERIE- UND ATELIERGEBÄUDE BRUNNENSTRASSE 9**
BERLIN

brandt + simon architekten, Berlin
05 **EINFAMILIENHAUS MAXIMILIANSTRASSE**
BERLIN

ROBERTNEUN™ BAECKER BUSCHMANN FRIEDRICH, Berlin
16 **FRISCHE PARADIES LINDENBERG – PRENZLAUER BERG** BERLIN

Max Dudler, Berlin
13 **JACOB-UND-WILHELM-GRIMM-ZENTRUM HUMBOLDT-UNIVERSITÄT ZU BERLIN**

KARO* architekten, Antje Heuer, Stefan Rettich, Bert Hafermalz, Leipzig
11 **LESEZEICHEN SALBKE**
MAGDEBURG

Peter Kulka Architektur, Dresden
14 **ÜBERDACHUNG KLEINER SCHLOSSHOF, RESIDENZSCHLOSS DRESDEN**

Florian Fischer und Katharina Leuschner, München
06 **HAUS POLZ** NEUKIRCHEN AM INN

arge werner wirsing bogevischs buero hofmann ritzer architekten, München
02 **STUDENTENWOHNANLAGE IM OLYMPISCHEN DORF**
MÜNCHEN

Hild und K Architekten, München
10 **LOUIS HOTEL** MÜNCHEN

ARCHITEKT | ARCHITECT

ARGE WERNER WIRSING BOGEVISCHS BUERO HOFMANN RITZER ARCHITEKTEN

GEBÄUDE | BUILDING

STUDENTENWOHNANLAGE
IM OLYMPISCHEN DORF MÜNCHEN

TEXT YORCK FÖRSTER

02

ARCHITEKTEN | ARCHITECTS

arge werner wirsing bogevischs buero hofmann ritzer architekten
Dreimühlenstraße 19
80469 München | Munich
www.bogevisch.de

MITARBEITER | TEAM

Prof. Werner Wirsing, Rainer Hofmann, Ritz Ritzer, Sven Gosmann, Michael Drenhaus, Kerstin Engelhardt, Viktor Filimonov, Sebastian Helbig, Katrin Zauner, Sebastian Seyboth, Christina Patz, Nicole Ploschnik, Thomas Hirsch

BAUHERR | CLIENT

Studentenwerk München, Anstalt des öffentlichen Rechts vertreten durch Frau Dr. Wurzer-Fassnacht

AUSFÜHRUNGSPLANUNG
EXECUTION PLANNING

arge werner wirsing bogevischs buero hofmann ritzer architekten

BAULEITUNG
PROJEKTSTEUERUNG
SITE MANAGEMENT
PROJECT MANAGEMENT

arge werner wirsing bogevischs buero hofmann ritzer architekten
Studentenwerk München | Munich

TRAGWERK | STRUCTURE

Sailer Stepan und Partner GmbH
Beratende Ingenieure für Bauwesen VBI,
München | Munich

HAUSTECHNIK | M & E ENGINEERS

HLS-Planung
HVAC & plumbing design
Konrad Huber GmbH
Ingenieurbüro für Technische Gebäudeausrüstung,
München | Munich
Elektro-Planung | electrical planning
Rücker+Schindele Beratende Ingenieure GbR,
München | Munich

ENERGIEKONZEPT
ENERGY CONCEPT

Konrad Huber GmbH
Ingenieurbüro für Technische Gebäudeausrüstung,
München | Munich

LANDSCHAFTSARCHITEKTEN
LANDSCAPE ARCHITECTS

Keller & Damm Landschaftsarchitekten Stadtplaner Partnerschaft,
München | Munich

FERTIGSTELLUNG | COMPLETION

Mai 2010 | May 2010

STANDORT | LOCATION

Connollystraße 3
80809 München | Munich

FOTOS | PHOTOS

Jens Masmann,
München | Munich

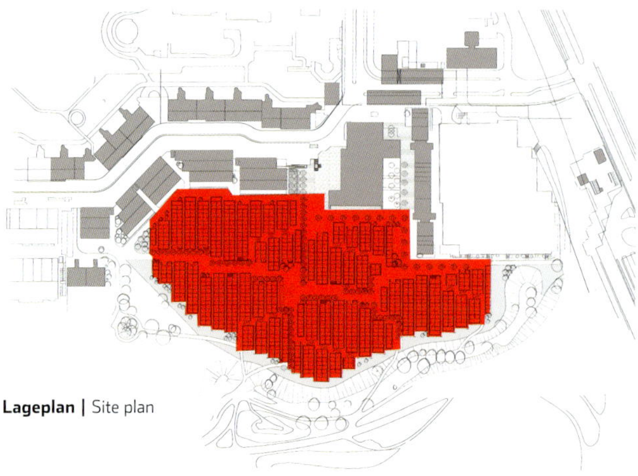

Lageplan | Site plan

In der Studentenwohnanlage im Olympischen Dorf hat jeder Bewohner sein eigenes Haus mit eigener Haustür. Die Gassen mit ihren Aufweitungen bilden den informellen Kommunikationsraum. | In the student housing at the Olympic Village, each resident has his own house and door. The alleyways widen to form informal communication spaces.

Es ist das eigentümlichste und – mit entsprechenden Wartezeiten – eines der beliebtesten Wohnangebote des Studentenwerks München: das ehemalige olympische Frauendorf. Ein Feld von 800 Bungalows bildete eine Art Endmoräne des überwiegend aus markanten Terrassenhäusern bestehenden Sportlerdorfs der Olympiade 1972. Von Werner Wirsing wurden die Maisonette-Bungalows mit 24 Quadratmetern Wohnfläche als Studentenwohnanlage konzipiert, später wurden sie in die Olympiaplanungen einbezogen. Nach den Spielen belegten wieder die Studenten das Dorf.
Jeder Studentin, jedem Studenten ein eigenes Haus, eine eigene Tür, ein eigener Briefkasten, lautete das Konzept Wirsings. Das scheint etwas paradox, denn während die Studentenbewegung das Kollektiv der Kommune betonte, entstanden hier Bungalows als individuelle Miniatur-Reihenhäuser. Zu der hohen Beliebtheit dürfte aber geführt haben, dass andere Studentenwohnanlagen Zufallsgemeinschaften waren. Das „Olydorf", wie es von den Studenten genannt wird, bot dagegen immer die Rückzugsmöglichkeit in die ‚eigene Bude'. Gleichzeitig bilden die nur 2,30 Meter breiten Gassen zwischen den Wohnzeilen einen informellen Kommunikationsraum. Der Ausgleich von Privatheit und Gemeinschaft hat in Werner Wirsings Studentendorf eine

It is the most idiosyncratic and – for those willing to put up with long waiting times – one of the most popular residential areas for students in Munich: the former Olympic women's village. A field dotted with 800 bungalows forms a kind of terminal moraine at one end of the athletes' village for the 1972 Summer Olympics, which consists primarily of distinctive terraced houses. The maisonette bungalows with 24 square metres of living space were originally conceived by Werner Wirsing as student apartments and were only later incorporated into the plans for Olympic housing. After the games, the students re-occupied the village.
Every student would have his own house, own door, own mailbox – that was Wirsing's idea. It might appear paradoxical that bungalows were being built here as miniature row houses in the days when the student movement was emphasising the collective nature of the commune. But their great popularity can probably be attributed to the way that other student accommodations force their residents to become part of randomly constituted

Das Olympische Dorf mit den Studentenbungalows im Vordergrund. Links noch die ursprünglichen Bauten, rechts die ersten der Neuplanung.
The Olympic Village with student bungalows in the foreground. On the left the original buildings can still be seen and on the right the first new structures.

Mock-up eines neuen Bungalows im ehemaligen Bestand
Mock-up of a new bungalow made from the former building stock

konsequent moderne Form gefunden. Und noch etwas war besonders im Olympiadorf: Jeder Bewohner hatte das Recht, die Hausfassade nach eigenen Wünschen zu gestalten. Konsequenter wurde die Forderung nach Individualisierung des seriell gefertigten Wohnungsbaus aus Hundertwassers Verschimmelungsmanifest wohl kaum umgesetzt.
Jetzt ist das Studentendorf nach Plänen der arge werner wirsing bogevischs buero neu entstanden. Der energetische Standard und Feuchtigkeitsprobleme waren Gründe dafür, vor allem aber erwies sich die komplett erdverlegte Installation als ein Hindernis für eine wirtschaftlich vertretbare Sanierung. In Abstimmung mit dem Denkmalschutz wurden lediglich zwölf der Bestandshäuser saniert, die übrigen aber neu errichtet. Bestehen blieb der Grundriss des Ensembles aus Nord-Süd orientierten Gassen mit Aufweitungen und Platzsituationen. Ebenso beibehalten blieb das Prinzip der Maisonettewohnungen, jedoch wurde – auch um Fördermöglichkeiten ausnutzen zu können – eine Nachverdichtung vollzogen. Das Achsmaß der Häuser ist um ein Viertel von 4,20 Meter auf 3,15 Meter geschrumpft, dadurch konnten nun 1052 Einheiten entstehen.
In den alten Bungalows waren zur Gasse hin der Sanitärbereich (als vorgefertigte geschlossene Kunststoffzelle ausgeführt) und ein begehbarer Schrank platziert. Im hinteren Teil des Baukörpers befand sich die Wohnzone, im Obergeschoss der Studienbereich. Ein rund ein Viertel der Grundfläche einnehmender Luftraum schuf eine räumliche Differenzierung und war wesentlich für die Belichtung und Belüftung des Erdgeschosses. Der hohe Raum war für die Bewohner auch eine Gelegenheit,

communities. By contrast, the "Olydorf", as the students like to call it, always offered the option of retiring to one's own "digs". At the same time, the narrow, 2.3-metre-wide alleyways between the rows of flats create a kind of informal communication forum. The balance between privacy and togetherness hence took on a thoroughly modern form in Werner Wirsing's student village. And there was somethingelse that was special in the Olympic Village: each resident had the right to design the façade of his house as he saw fit. A more logical implementationof the demand for individualisation of serially fabricated apartments made by Hundertwasser in his "Mouldiness Manifesto" can hardly be conceived.
Now the student village has been recreated according to the plans of the architects arge werner wirsing bogevischs buero. New energy standards and dampness problems were among the reasons for the rebuilding, but the completely underground plumbing posed an even greater obstacle to economical refurbishment. In consultation with the historic preservation office, only 12 of the existing houses were renovated and the rest rebuilt from the ground up. The layout of the whole ensemble, with the north-south orientation of the alleys and their widenings and squares, was maintained. Also preserved was the principle of the maisonette apartment; however, the space has now been compressed – in part to take advantage of funding opportunities. The dimension between the axes of the houses has been reduced by a quarter, from 4.20 to 3.15 metres, making it possible to now build 1,052 units.
In the old bungalows the bathrooms (self-contained prefabricated plastic cells) and a walk-in closet were placed on the street side. At the rear was a living zone, and on the upper level a study area. The air space, which made up about one quarter of the floor area, created a spatial differentiation and was essential for the lighting and ventilation of the lower floor. The high ceiling also tempted residents to try their hand at building a loft bed, which then however plunged the living space below into darkness.
With the reduction in the floor area, the layout of the floor plan was also adjusted; the new plan was then tested at the site based on a 1:1 mock-up. The living area now abuts the alleyway and the bathroom is set at the back. This makes the house more open to visitors, while a small kitchen area underscores the studio character and a built-

Im Vordergrund einer der sanierten ursprünglichen Bungalows, im Hintergrund der neue Typ. | In the foreground is one of the refurbished original bungalows and in the background the new model.

Gasse im Studentendorf | Alleyway in student village

sich im Bau von Hochbetten zu versuchen; entsprechend dunkel wurde dann der Wohnbereich.
Das Grundrisslayout erfuhr mit der Verkleinerung der Grundfläche eine Neujustierung, die an einem 1:1 Mock-up auf dem Gelände überprüft wurde. Der Wohnbereich ist jetzt zur Gasse hin angeordnet, die Sanitärzelle hingegen im rückwärtigen Teil. Damit ist das Haus offen für Besucher, eine kleine Kochgelegenheit unterstreicht den Charakter eines Studios, ein Einbauschrank unter der Treppe bietet den Stauraum. Für die Belichtung im Entree des Hauses sorgt nun auch ein Bandfenster in der Fassade. Die Treppe wurde extrem kompakt gehalten. Im Obergeschoss bildet ein Regal zum Treppenschacht hin die Absturzsicherung der variabel nutzbaren Arbeits- und Schlafzone mit Dachterrasse. In einer Variation des Grundtyps sind an den Enden der Gebäudezeilen Doppelhäuser für studierende Paare entstanden. Pro Baufeld wurde für die technischen Installationen und einen Fahrradraum eine Gebäudezeile komplett unterkellert.
Ähnlich, aber nicht gleich sollte das neue Studentendorf werden. Am zentralen Platz (‚Marienplatz') befand sich eine überdachte Zone mit öffentlichen Fernsprechapparaten. Nun wurde daraus ein beschirmender Stahlbetonpilz, daneben, hinter einem leuchtend gelben Stahltor, findet sich die nötige Ausstattung für Grillfeste – im Studentenjargon heißt der Ort inzwischen ‚Tankstelle'.
Nach gut einem halben Jahr Nutzung sind die Sichtbetonelemente immer noch makellos, nicht einmal die Spur eines Graffito ist in dem Dorf zu sehen, auch wenn jeder Bewohner weiterhin seine Fassade bemalen darf. Der Wunsch nach

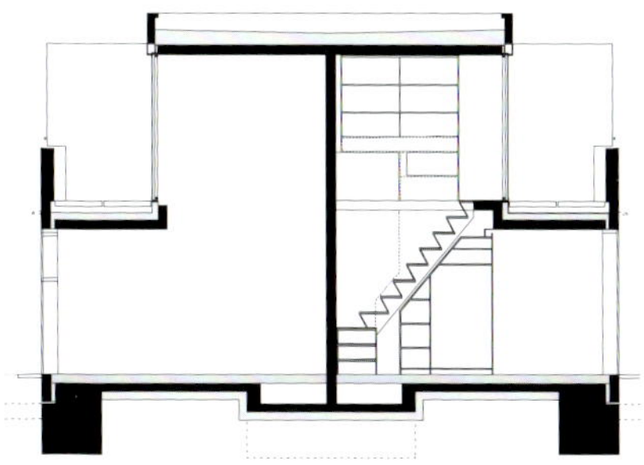

Schnitt | Section

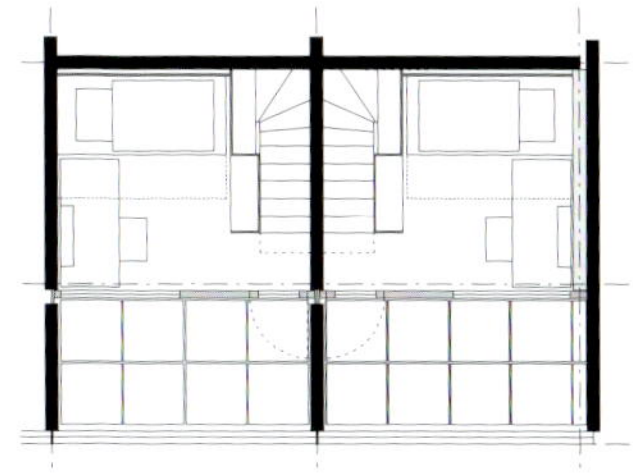

Obergeschoss | Upper level

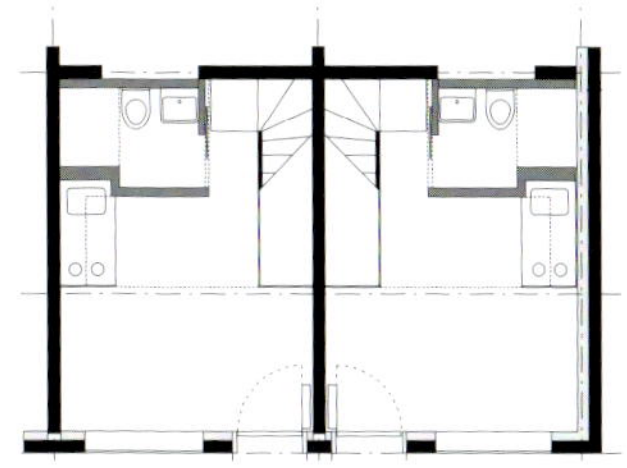

Erdgeschoss | Ground floor

Eingangssituation | Entrance situation

Kochecke, im Hintergrund die Treppe zum Obergeschoss
Cooking niche with stairs to the upper level in the background

Schlaf- und Studierbereich mit Terrasse im Obergeschoss | Sleep and study area with balcony on upper level

Individualisierung hat einen anderen Weg gefunden. Auf die Wandinnenseite der Gassenfenster können als Blickschutz transluzente Plexiglastafeln gehängt werden. Schnell haben die Studenten erkannt, dass sich diese Fenstervitrinen bestens als Ausstellungsraum für alles, was im eigenen Leben wichtig ist, eignen. Auch das ist eine Form der Transformation im Sinne eines kritischen Denkmalschutzes.

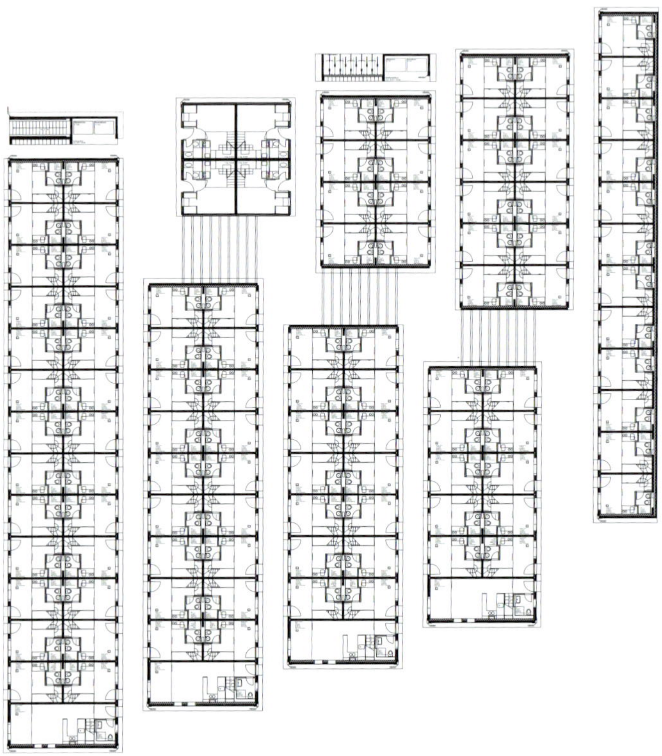

Zeilengrundriss mit Gassen und Aufweitungen
Plan of bungalow blocks with alleyways and widenings

in closet underneath the stairs offers storage space. The entrance is now lit by a band of windows in the façade. The stairs were kept extremely compact. On the upper floor a bookshelf bordering the stairwell provides a safety barrier for the variably utilisable work and sleep zone, complete with rooftop terrace. In a variation on the basic model, semi-detached houses have been built at the ends of the rows for student couples. One row of houses per building field has been equipped with cellars for technical installations and a bicycle room.
The new student village was meant to be similar to the old one, but not identical. At the central square (Marienplatz) there was once a roofed area with public telephones. Now this has become a sheltering mushroom of steel-reinforced concrete; next to it, behind a bright yellow steel gate, is all the equipment needed for a BBQ – the students have in the meantime dubbed this area the "Tankstelle" (petrol station).
After a good six months of use, the exposed concrete elements here are still immaculate; not a trace of graffiti is to be found in the village, even though each resident is still permitted to paint his own façade. The desire for individuality has taken a different path. On the inner side of the windows onto the alleyway, translucent plexiglass panels can be put up for privacy. The students quickly realised that these provide ideal display cases to exhibit all that is important to them. This, too, is a form of transformation in the spirit of critical monument protection.

Blick in das Erdgeschoss eines Doppelhauses für studierende Paare | View of the lower level of a double bungalow for student couples

„Marienplatz" im Studentendorf | "Marienplatz" in the student village

ARCHITEKT | ARCHITECT

BEHNISCH ARCHITEKTEN

GEBÄUDE | BUILDING

FIRMENZENTRALE UNILEVER
DEUTSCHLAND, ÖSTERREICH UND SCHWEIZ

TEXT ULRICH HÖHNS

03

ARCHITEKTEN | ARCHITECTS

Behnisch Architekten
Stefan Behnisch, David Cook, Martin Haas
Rotebühlstraße 163A
70197 Stuttgart
www.behnisch.com

MITARBEITER | TEAM

Projektleiter | project manager **Peter Schlaier,**
Projektarchitekt | project architect **Stephan Zemmrich,**
Projektteam | project team **Mandana Alimardani, Jens Berghaus, Andreas Leupold, Irina Martaler, Andreas Peyker, Eckart Schwerdtfeger, Dennis Wirth**

BAUHERR | CLIENT

Strandkai 1 Projekt GmbH c/o HOCHTIEF Projektentwicklung

TRAGWERK | STRUCTURE

Weber Poll Ingenieurbüro für Bauwesen , Hamburg (Entwurf Tragwerk für Weber Poll structural design for Weber Poll) **Pfefferkorn Ingenieure, Beratende Bauingenieure VBI, Stuttgart**

ENERGIEKONZEPT ENERGY CONCEPT

Transsolar Energietechnik GmbH, Stuttgart (in der Wettbewerbsphase | in the competition phase)

HAUSTECHNIK | M & E ENGINEERS

HKP Ingenieure GmbH, Hamburg

OBJEKTÜBERWACHUNG SITE SUPERVISION

360grad+ Architekten GmbH, Hamburg

TAGESLICHTTECHNIK DAYLIGHT TECHNOLOGY

Licht 01 Lighting Design – Diplom-Ingenieure Winkelmann / von Sichart GbR, Hamburg

FASSADENBERATUNG FAÇADE CONSULTING

Prof. Michael Lange Ing. GmbH, Hamburg

FASSADENBERATUNG FOLIENFASSADE FAÇADE COSULTING FOR EXTERIOR MEMBRANE

form TL ingenieure für tragwerk- und leichtbau gmbh, Radolfzell

ORGANISATORISCHE GEBÄUDEPLANUNG BUILDING ORGANISATION

QUICKBORNER TEAM Gesellschaft für Planung und Organisation mbH, Hamburg

LANDSCHAFTSPLANUNG LANDSCAPE PLANNING

Entwurfsphase | design phase **EMBT Enric Miralles – Benedetta Tagliabue, Barcelona, Spanien** | Spain
Ausführungsplanung execution planning **Behnisch Architekten, Stuttgart**

FERTIGSTELLUNG | COMPLETION

September 2009

STANDORT | LOCATION

HafenCity Hamburg
Strandkai 1
20457 Hamburg

FOTOS | PHOTOS

Adam Mørk, Kopenhagen | Copenhagen

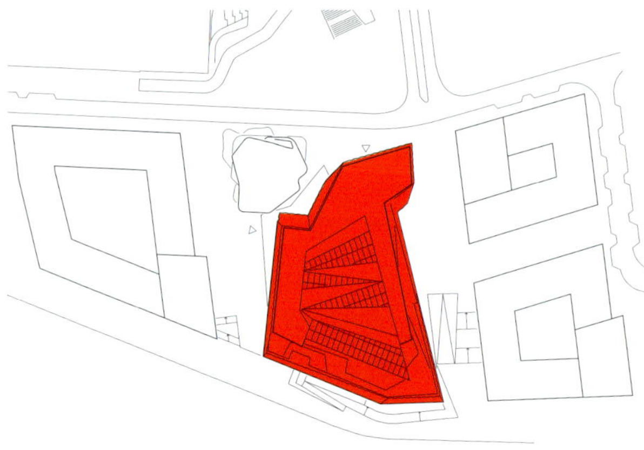

Lageplan | Site plan

Ansicht vom Strandkai von Südwest | View from Strandkai from sout-west

Das Gespür für die Kraft der Marke ist für einen Konzern wie Unilever, dessen Produkte von „Rama" bis „Omo" manchmal schon seit Jahrzehnten die neutrale Warenbezeichnung ersetzt haben, einer der Pfeiler des wirtschaftlichen Erfolgs. Als William Hesketh Lever 1888 die pittoreske Gartenstadt Port Sunlight bei Liverpool für die Arbeiter seiner Seifenfabrik gründete, nahm die Herausbildung einer auch sozial

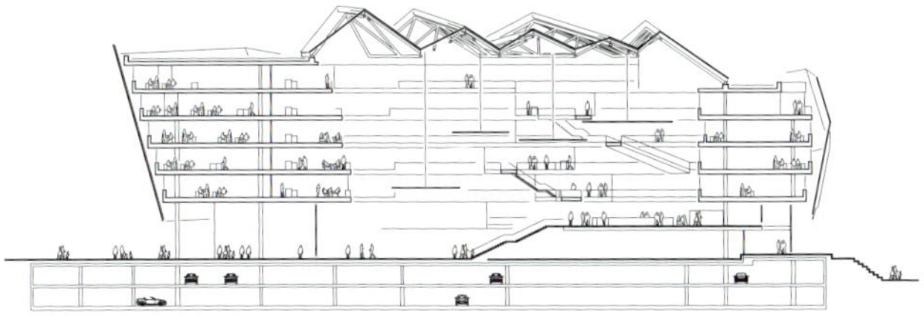

Schnitt | Section

A feeling for the power of branding is essential to the business success of a corporation like Unilever, some of whose trademarks, from Vaseline to Domestos, have long since become synonymous with the product category. When William Hesketh Lever built the picturesque garden city of Port Sunlight near Liverpool for workers in his soap factory in 1888, he inaugurated the idea of inculcating a "corporate identity" in the social as well as the business sphere, an element that no global enterprise today can do without. In Hamburg, the company's German headquarters, it took on a national and in particular a local identity for

Fassade Westseite, Weg zur Elbe
West façade, path to Elbe

Ansicht von West | View from west

verstandenen ‚corporate identity' ihren Anfang, ohne die heute ein weltweit agierendes Unternehmen kaum bestehen könnte. In Hamburg, dem Sitz der deutschen Zentrale, gewann es mit dem 1964 fertiggestellten Unilever-Hochhaus am Dammtorwall von Helmut Hentrich und Hubert Petschnigg erstmals eine nationale und in besonderem Maße auch eine lokale Identität. 2009 verließ das Unternehmen mit seinen 1200 Hamburger Mitarbeitern diese zwar etablierte, wegen der vertikalen Erschließung aber nicht mehr brauchbare Landmarke und bezog stattdessen ein für die gewachsenen kommunikativen Bedürfnisse maßgeschneidertes Seezeichen an der Elbe. Die neue Firmenzentrale für Deutschland, Österreich und die Schweiz liegt direkt am großen Strom, am südlichsten Kai der HafenCity.

Das Erkennungsmerkmal des Hauses, das trotz seiner sechs Geschosse eher niedrig erscheint, ist die transparente Kunststoff-Folie, die es vom ersten Obergeschoss bis über die Traufen umhüllt. Ein größerer Kontrast zum steinernen Ernst der meisten Neubauten in der HafenCity ist nicht denkbar.

Die Folie könnte ein Segel vor der Fassade sein, gehalten von einem weißen Tragwerk und dann rahmenweise durch eine filigrane Seilkonstruktion schlagfrei abgespannt, sodass Reihen von Prismen entstehen. Dieses Kleid aus Ethylen-Tetrafluorethylen ist zwar weit geschnitten, aber es sitzt straff und faltenfrei. Blickwinkel und Lichteinfall entscheiden darüber, ob es für das Haus gestaltbestimmend und dank Schrägstellungen und Scharfkantigkeit dessen Dynamik überzeichnend wirkt, oder ob diese Haut an den Schattenseiten bzw. bei Dämmerung und Dunkelheit entmaterialisiert zurücktritt und ein diszipliniert gegliedertes und gebändertes Bürohaus freilegt. Die Folie schützt die Fassaden und den außen liegenden Sonnenschutz an diesem exponierten Ort vor Wind und die Büroräume mit frei zu öffnenden Fenstern vor den Abgasen der Kreuzfahrtschiffe, die direkt nebenan festmachen und ihre Motoren auch während der Liegezeiten nicht abstellen.

Unregelmäßig geformte und zueinander gestellte schmale Riegel und tiefere Bauteile erzeugen gemeinsam eine komplexe Gesamtgeometrie des Gebäudes. Eine öffentlich zugängliche

the first time with the completion in 1964 of the Unilever high-rise on Dammtorwall, designed by Helmut Hentrich and Hubert Petschnigg.

By 2009, however, the company with its 1,200 Hamburg staff members was forced to abandon this established landmark due to its strict and limiting verticality and has now moved into waterfront premises on the Elbe River, custom-built for the requirements of increased communication. The new company headquarters for Germany, Austria and Switzerland commands a prominent location on HafenCity's southernmost quay.

The distinguishing feature of the building, which despite its six storeys appears to be quite low-slung, is the transparent plastic membrane that encases it from the first floor up to the eaves. A greater contrast to the stony earnestness of most new buildings in HafenCity is hard to imagine.

This skin might be a sail billowing out from the façade, held in place by a white framework to which it is anchored at regular intervals by a filigree configuration of cables, creating a series of prisms. This ethylene-tetrafluoroethylene mantle is roomy, but is nonetheless stretched taut. The viewer's vantage point and the fall of light determine whether it dictates the shape of the building, exaggerating its dynamism with its angles and sharp edges, or whether – where the building is cast in shadow, or at twilight and in the dark – the skin recedes into the background to the point of dematerialisation, revealing behind it an office building articulated by disciplined bands. In its exposed setting, the membrane protects the façade and the outside sun shades from wind, and the people in the offices, who can open their windows individually, from the diesel fumes of the cruise ships at the adjacent terminal, which leave their engines running even when moored.

Eine Fassade aus ETFE-Folien als zweite Hülle schützt die Bürobereiche vor Zug und den Sonnenschutz vor den an diesem Ort erheblichen Windbelastungen. | An EFTE membrane as second skin protects the offices and sunshades from the considerable wind in this exposed location.

Passage mit Läden und einem Café durchläuft den Baukörper vom nördlichen Eingang bis zum Elbufer. Im Zentrum ist sie aufgeweitet zu einem zentralen, lichtdurchfluteten Platz, der als Atrium von einem Stahl-Glas-Faltwerk überdeckt ist.
Die Innenwelt des Hauses entfaltet ein intensives Farbenspiel für die Brüstungen, die Möbel und die vielen Zeichen an den Wänden und auf den Besprechungsboxen, die alle in einem gestalterischen Zusammenhang mit den Markenprodukten stehen und sich nun Gelb, Grün, Orange oder Lila vor weißem Grund zu Bändern, Inseln und Räumen zusammenschließen. Brücken, Stege und Treppen durchziehen und flankieren die große Halle, die Innenfassaden öffnen sich an Knoten und Gelenken zu viel frequentierten Treffpunkten. Transparenz und eine Fülle direkter Kommunikationsmöglichkeiten waren gefordert und wurden in einem selten gesehenen Maße auch erreicht. Der Arbeitsplatz kann hier überall sein. Und es könnten auch andere als die heutigen entstehen, denn die

The interplay of irregularly shaped and cantered narrow bars and more deep-set building components generates a complex overall geometry. A public arcade with shops and a café runs through the building from the northern entrance to the banks of the Elbe. In the centre of the building this space widens to form a light-flooded atrium topped by a folded steel-and-glass roof.
In the interior, a variety of intense colours plays across the railings, furniture and the many designs patterning the walls and the meeting boxes, all of which echo the product brands, coming together in yellow, green, orange or purple on a white background to form bands, islands and rooms. Bridges, ramps and steps run through and flank the big hall, and the interior façades open up at nodes and joints to become highly frequented meeting points.

Meeting Point Hafencity | Meeting point in Hafencity

Atrium von Osten, abends | Atrium from the east, evening

maßgeschneiderte Architektur ist flexibel genug angelegt, um betriebliche Umstrukturierungen bis hin zu unterteilbaren Fremdnutzungen zu ermöglichen.
Noch verläuft die breite Nord-Süd-Achse des Grasbrooks, in deren südliches Ende sich das Unilever-Haus fast unmerklich, aber stadträumlich wirksam hineindreht, ins Leere. Seine Alleinstellung wird beendet sein, wenn eines Tages westlich und östlich weitere Bauten errichtet werden. Schon jetzt spürbar ist dagegen der auf die Erzeugung einer skulpturalen Dauerspannung angelegte Dialog mit dem direkt benachbarten, ebenfalls von Behnisch Architekten entworfenen Marco Polo Tower. Der kühn modellierte, sich nach oben verbreiternde Wohnturm ist zwar nicht mehr, wie im Wettbewerb vorgesehen, in der Außengestalt zackig wie das Bürogebäude, aber trotz seiner weichen, gefälligeren Form mit unregelmäßig geschichteten Ebenen und organisch gerundeten Fassaden bleibt er als ein aus der Taille herausgerücktes vertikales Passstück zum Unilever-Haus erkennbar.

Transparency and an abundance of opportunities for direct communication were what Unilever wanted – and this goal has been achieved here to a degree rarely witnessed. A workplace can be anywhere in the building. And new ones can be created besides those that exist today, because the customised, open-floor architecture has been designed to be flexible enough to enable operational restructurings that might even go as far as separating off areas for third-party utilisation.
Grasbrook, the north-south axis into whose southern end the Unilever headquarters turns almost imperceptibly and yet with a significant impact on the urban space, still ends in a void. But this isolation will end some day when additional buildings are erected on the western and eastern sides. By contrast, a deliberate, ongoing sculptural tension can already be felt in the dialogue between the Unilever building and the directly adjacent Marco Polo Tower, likewise designed by Behnisch Architekten. The daringly modelled residential tower, which splays out toward the top, no longer shares the office building's zigzagging exterior as originally planned in the competition entry, but despite the softer, more accommodating curves of its irregularly layered levels and organically rounded façades it nonetheless remains recognisable as a vertical counterpart of the Unilever building, seemingly shifted out from its middle.

Ansicht Elbseite von Süden, nachts | View of Elbe side from the south, night

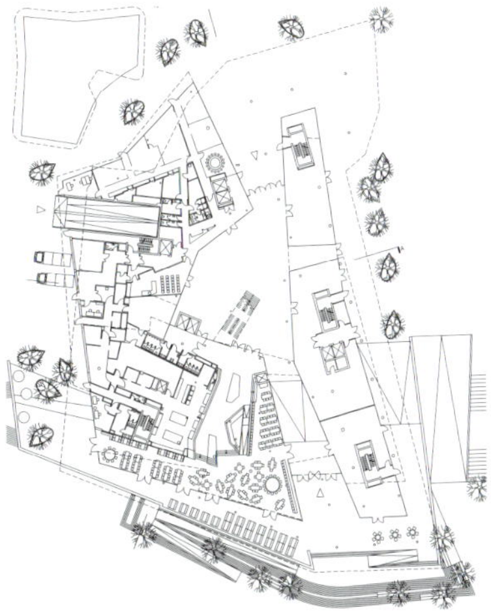

Ebene 0 | Level 0

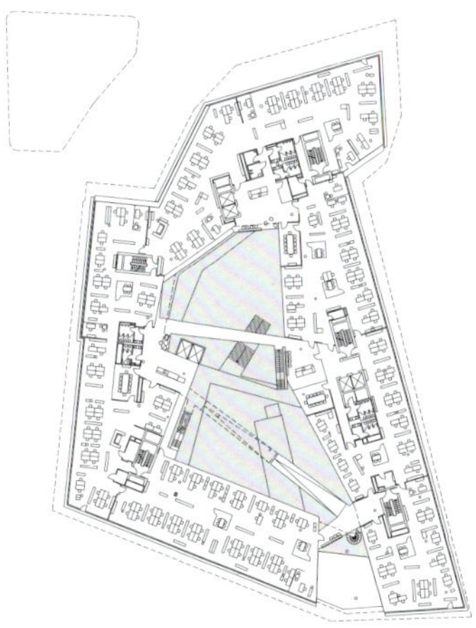

Ebene 3 | Level 3

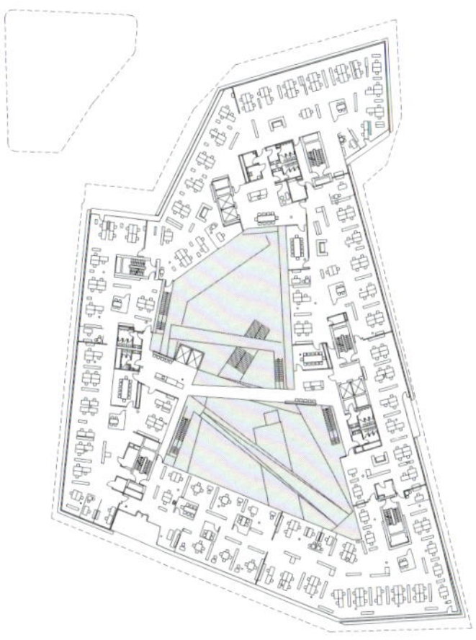

Ebene 5 | Level 5

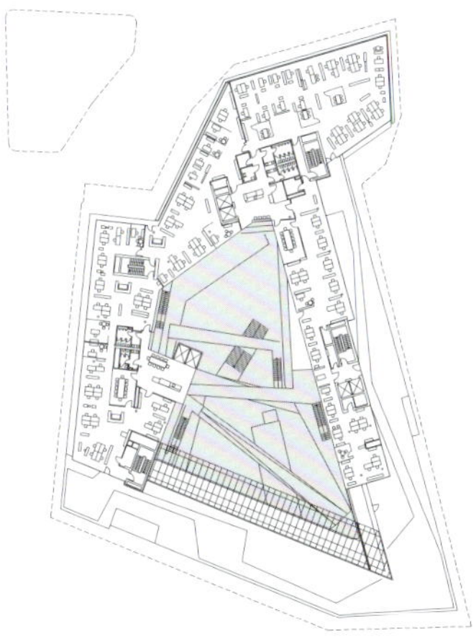

Ebene 6 | Level 6

ARCHITEKT | ARCHITECT

BRANDLHUBER+ ERA, EMDE, SCHNEIDER

GEBÄUDE | BUILDING

GALERIE- UND ATELIERGEBÄUDE BRUNNENSTRASSE 9

TEXT FRANK BARKOW

04

ARCHITEKTEN | ARCHITECTS

Brandlhuber+ ERA, Emde, Schneider
Brunnenstraße 9
10119 Berlin
www.brandlhuber.com

MITARBEITER | TEAM

Thomas Banek, Arno Brandlhuber, Bruno Ebersbach, Markus Emde, Silvia Farris, Christian Geisser, Tobias Hönig, Andriana Ivanda, Katharina Jankowski, Philipp Reinfeld, Thomas Schneider, Florian Steinbeck, Jan Winterstein

BAUHERR | CLIENT

Arno Brandlhuber

AUSFÜHRUNGSPLANUNG | EXECUTION PLANNING

Brandlhuber+ Emde, Schneider

BAULEITUNG | SITE MANAGEMENT

Markus Emde, Thomas Schneider

LANDSCHAFTSPLANUNG | LANDSCAPE PLANNING

terraform (Sandra Bartoli, Andreas Ziegeler)

KUNST AM BAU | ART

Mark Bain, Amsterdam

FERTIGSTELLUNG | COMPLETION

Dezember 2009 | December 2009

STANDORT | LOCATION

Brunnenstraße 9
10119 Berlin

FOTOS | PHOTOS

Michael Reisch, Köln | Cologne
Nathan Willock, London

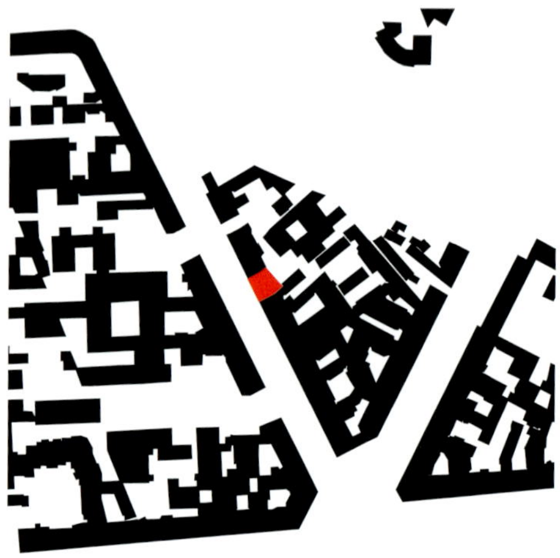

Lageplan | Site plan

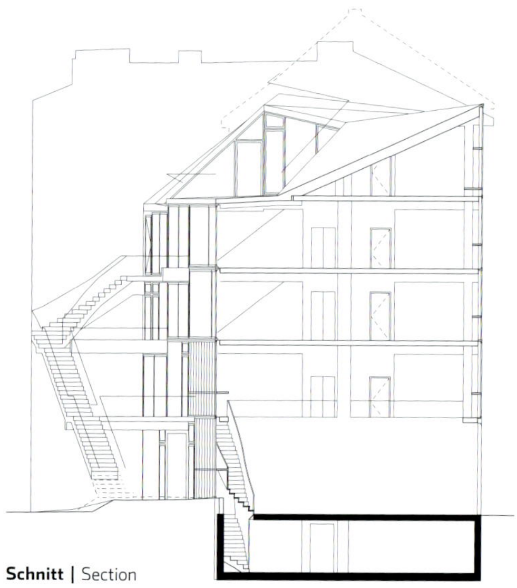

Schnitt | Section

Das Galeriehaus nimmt die unterschiedliche Höhe der Traufkanten der Nachbarbauten auf. Die Fassade besteht teils aus Glas, teils aus Polycarbonattafeln. | The gallery building takes up the varying heights of the eaves of the neighbouring buildings. The façade is part glass, part polycarbonate panels.

Die Brunnenstraße 9, ein von Arno Brandlhuber zur Mischnutzung konzipiertes Gebäude in Berlin, wirkt wie der geradezu zwangsläufige architektonische Inbegriff des kulturellen Milieus in Berlin-Mitte nach dem Mauerfall. Überraschend ist dabei, dass in Berlin nicht mehr Projekte wie dieses existieren, Projekte, die mehr der im Ausland verbreiteten Vorstellung von der kulturell-künstlerischen Identität der Stadt entsprechen, als der Realität vor Ort. Denn die Stadt ist nicht unbedingt bekannt für bahnbrechende konzeptuelle Arbeiten. Von der eigenen ikonografischen Kontinuität besessen, wird kontextuelles Bauen in der Stadt und ihren Behörden eher als ein historisches/stilistisches Problem interpretiert und weniger als ein abstrakt konzeptuelles.
Brandlhubers Ansatz gegenüber dem Ort ist sowohl ausnutzend (in einem architektonischen Sinn) als auch pragmatisch (einem Verfahren folgend). Das Gebäude verweigert sich sowohl einer technizistischen Könnerschaft (zugunsten von Einfachheit) als

Arno Brandlhuber's Brunnenstrasse 9, a mixed-use building located in Berlin, strikes one as the inevitable architectural embodiment of the post-wall cultural milieu of Mitte. What is surprising is that Berlin is not populated by more projects like this one that seem to be more in line with its cultural/artistic identity as projected abroad than with the reality on the ground. This is, after all, a city whose bar for groundbreaking conceptual work has been consistently low. Obsessed with its own iconographic continuity, Berlin and its agencies have favoured contextualism as a historical/stylistic problem rather than a conceptual one.
Brandlhuber's approach to the site is an exploitative one, architecturally speaking, and process-based. Defiant to both technical proficiency (in favour of simplicity) and historicism (in favour of abstraction)

Blick von der Straße in die Galerieräume
View from the street into the galleries

Ansicht der Hofseite mit außen liegender Erschließungstreppe. Die Dachform entstand, um die Besonnung eines rückwärtigen Gebäudes zu erlauben. | View of courtyard side with outdoor access stairs. The shape of the roof allows sun to reach a building behind it.

auch dem Historizismus (zugunsten von Abstraktion). Eine regelorientierte Interpretation des Bestandes und der Bauvorschriften bestimmen die Organisation. Dieser ‚Taschenspielertrick', ein Projekt so zu konzipieren als wäre es selbstgenerierend, ist nicht nur sehr überzeugend, sondern auch eine kluge Taktik, den selbstreferenziellen Formalismus oder den öden Historizismus, der die Berliner Diskussion seit Langem beherrscht, zu vermeiden. Auf diese Weise positioniert sich der Architekt weniger als Entwerfer denn als ‚constructeur' der organisatorische Rahmenbedingungen festlegt, die ihrerseits ein zu Beginn nicht völlig vorhersehbares Resultat bestimmen. Diese Anti-Haltung ist auch im Kontext einer übertechnologischen Baukultur, die in der Regel technische Kompetenz konzeptuellem Einfallsreichtum vorzieht, von nicht geringer Bedeutung. In diesem Fall heißt das Einfachheit, geringe Kosten und hohe Sensibilität für Standardware. Eine Galerie, die Redaktion einer Zeitschrift, ein oder zwei Ateliers und eine Wohnung werden programmatisch lässig und offen in- und aneinandergefügt, ohne diesen Ansatz dabei zu überlasten. Zwei Strategien sind hier im Spiel. Die erste, nämlich Aneignung, beginnt mit der Umnutzung der hinterlassenen Investorenruine im Untergeschoss. Der Neubau erweitert den existierenden

the building is organised by a series of rule-based readings of both the existing site and building regulations. This conceptual "sleight of hand" of conceiving a project that seems self-generating is a powerful one and one of the best exit strategies for avoiding self-referential formalism or, say, the tedious historicism that has dominated the Berlin discussion for so long. In this way the architect positions himself less as a designer than a constructeur who establishes organisational parameters that determine an outcome that cannot from the outset be entirely predictable. This defiance is also significant in the context of a hyper-technical building culture that generally privileges technical competency over conceptual inventiveness. Here much of that gives way to simplicity, low-cost, or an off-the-shelf sensibility. Programmatically nonchalant, a gallery, a magazine, a studio or two and an apartment are open-ended and do not overburden this approach. Two strategies are at work here. The first, appropriation, begins with the reuse, as found, of the abandoned developers' ruins

Aufzugsschacht und nutzt die Umfassungswände und die teilweise vorhandene Bodenplatte des Erdgeschosses um daraus im neuen Plan einen im Untergeschoss beginnenden doppelgeschossigen Raum zu entwickeln. Die zweite Strategie basiert auf Anpassung, um Gebäudevolumen und Geschosshöhen zu bestimmen. Eines der am offensichtlichsten ‚übernommenen' Elemente ist das Dachprofil. Es entstand, indem eine Diagonale vom Dachfirst des benachbarten Gebäudes auf der gegenüberliegenden Seite der Brunnenstraße bis hin zur Fensterbretthöhe der Hinterhofwohnung im ersten Stock gezogen wurde. Die Dachlinie des Neubaus passt genau unter diese Linie, sodass Tageslicht nach wie vor in den Hinterhof fallen kann. In einer eher rhetorischen Geste wurden die Geschossdecken der Nachbarbebauung auf den Neubau projiziert.

Am Übergang der dadurch gebildeten Ebenen entsteht jeweils ein kleiner Höhenversatz (der an der vorderen Fassade sichtbar ist), der gleichzeitig auf geniale Weise die schlanken Balkenprofile aufnimmt, die aus der rückwärtigen Fassade herausragen und die außen liegende Treppe tragen. Diese Anpassungen bewirken eine Transformation in dem Gebäude: von einer rechtwinkligen/versetzten Anordnung in den unteren Geschossen zu einer vieleckigen facettierten Geometrie in der Dachwohnung und der den Hof überblickenden Dachterrasse. Zwei geometrische Strategien werden hier zur Lösung zweier unterschiedlicher Probleme eingesetzt.

Die öffentliche, der Straße zugewandte Fassade des Gebäudes ist didaktisch und explizit enthüllend (erklärend) in Bezug auf die Logik des Gebäudeschnitts, sie ist eher ein de facto Ergebnis des Baues als dass sie eine unabhängig entworfene Fassade wäre. Gebildet wird die Fassade sowohl aus preisgünstigen transluzenten Polycarbonattafeln als auch klaren Iso-Glasumfassungen, die theoretisch von zukünftigen Mietern beliebig modifiziert werden können.

Die Innenräume sind durch die alternierenden Deckenhöhen belebt, bis hin zu doppelgeschossigen Räumen, die von zukünftigen Nutzern je nach Bedarf modifiziert oder geschlossen werden können.

in the basement level. The new construction extends the existing elevator shaft, utilises the perimeter retaining walls, and partially covered ground-floor decking, which the new scheme exploits to generate a double-height space beginning at the lower level. The other strategy uses alignment to determine the building volume and floor heights. Instrumentalised most evidently, the roof profile is determined by drawing a diagonal line from the roof ridge of the neighbouring building across Brunnenstrasse to the sill height of the first-floor apartment in the back courtyard. The roofline of the new construction fits exactly under this limit, allowing light into the rear courtyard. More rhetorically, the side neighbouring floor plate heights are projected into the site of the new building, planes whose intersections create small split-levels internally (visible in the front façade) that, at the same time, ingeniously create small beam depths that project to the rear façade and support the out-board circulation/stairs. Through these alignments the building transforms from an orthogonal/offset organisation at the lower levels to the polygonal faceted geometry of the roof apartment and terrace facing the courtyard. Two geometric strategies are assigned to two different problem-solving roles.

The public façade of the building to the street is didactic and explicit, revealing (explaining) the logic of the building section as the de facto conclusion of the building rather than being composed independently. This façade is enclosed by either low-cost polycarbonate panels or by clear iso-glass enclosures, which can theoretically be modified as wished by future tenants.

The interior sections are animated by the up-and-down hydraulics of the double-height spaces, which also could be modified or closed at a future date as needed. This alleged flexibility, congruent with

Galeriefläche im Untergeschoss | Gallery space in basement

Treppe aus dem Untergeschoss zum Hof
Stairs leading from basement to courtyard

Studio im 4. Obergeschoss | Studio on 4th floor

Diese vermeintliche Flexibilität, die dem modernen Ziel der Umwandlungsfähigkeit entspricht, scheint gleichwohl mit der zeitgenössischen, Lesbarkeit und Stimmigkeit in einem Widerspruch zu stehen, wie auch die Verwandelbarkeit der Fassaden.

Zwangsläufig ästhetisiert, durchdringt das Gebäude eine Logik der Materialarmut, bei der Sichtbeton vom Bauherrn ad hoc eingesetzt wird, was sowohl Zeit als auch Geld spart. Industrielle Beleuchtung und Heizungselemente, beide von der Stange, schlichte Rohrgeländer, ganz gewöhnliche Fensterrahmen und Polycarbonattafeln runden die Palette ab.

Eigentlich sollten Projekte dieser Art in Berlin fast unvermeidlich sein. Da dies dennoch nicht immer der Fall ist, sticht die Brunnenstraße 9 umso mehr als provokativ und zeitgemäß ins Auge. Dieses Gebäude ist eine Herausforderung an unser Verständnis, wie wir in einer Stadt, die sich ständig weiterentwickelt und ändert, den Raum bewohnen, benutzen und uns zu eigen machen. Es vermittelt zwischen einer Banalität und einem Radikalchic, der die wirtschaftlichen Herausforderungen der Zeit – und die Marginalisierung der Architektur – widerspiegelt: Ein Hinweis darauf, dass wohldurchdachte und provokative Gebäude immer noch entstehen und inspirieren können.

the Modernist aim for transformability, seems nonetheless at odds with the building's current legibility and coherence, as is the transformability of the façades.

Inevitably aestheticised, a material-povera logic permeates the building where fair-faced concrete is formed ad hoc at the will of the builders, saving time and money. Off-the-shelf industrial lighting and heating elements, pipe-railings, standard window frames and the polycarbonate panels complete the palette.

While this kind of project should be inevitable in Berlin, that has not always been the case, making Brunnenstrasse 9 all the more provocative and timely. It is a building that challenges the notion of how we occupy, colonise and use space in a city that continues to evolve and change. It mediates between a banality and radical chic that reflects the economically difficult times we are experiencing, where architecture has been marginalised – a reminder that thoughtful and provocative buildings can still emerge and inspire.

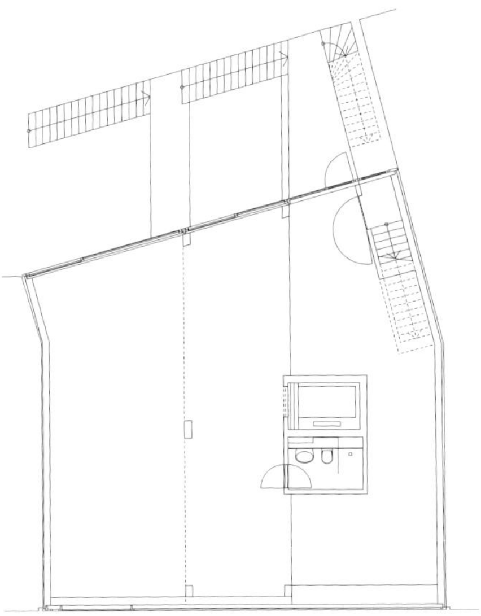

Grundriss 2. Obergeschoss | Floor plan of 2nd floor

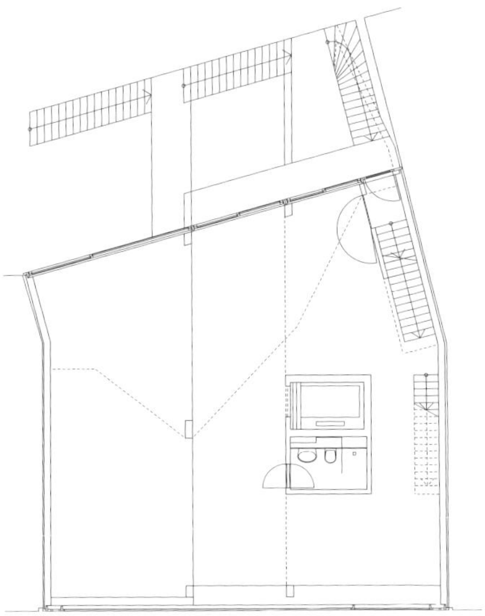

Grundriss 3. Obergeschoss | Floor plan of 3rd floor

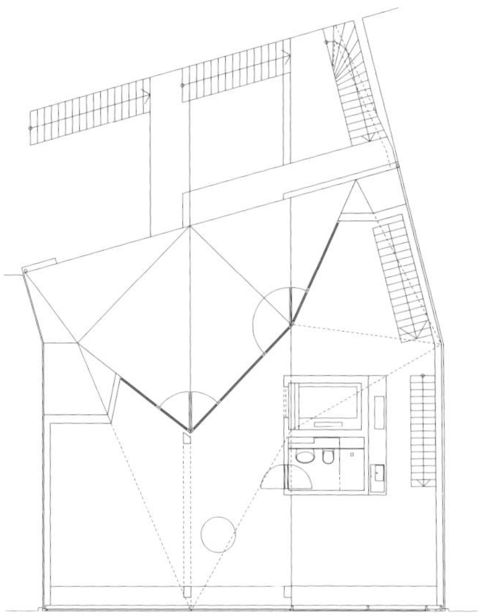

Grundriss 4. Obergeschoss | Floor plan of 4th floor

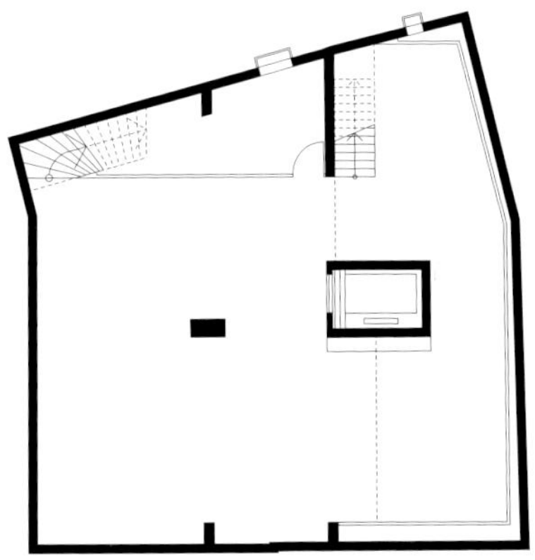

Grundriss Untergeschoss | Floor plan of basement

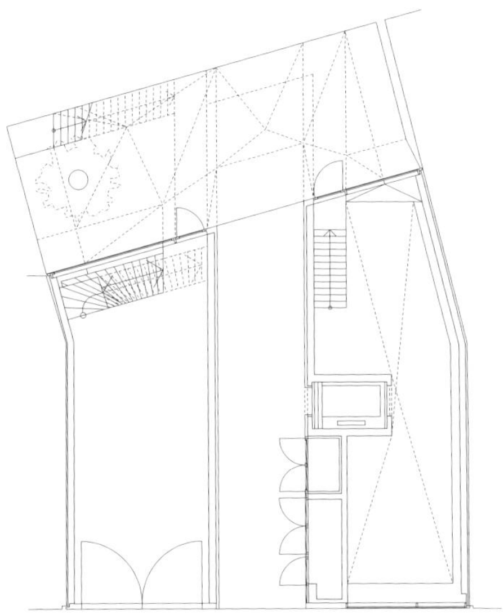

Grundriss Erdgeschoss | Floor plan of ground floor

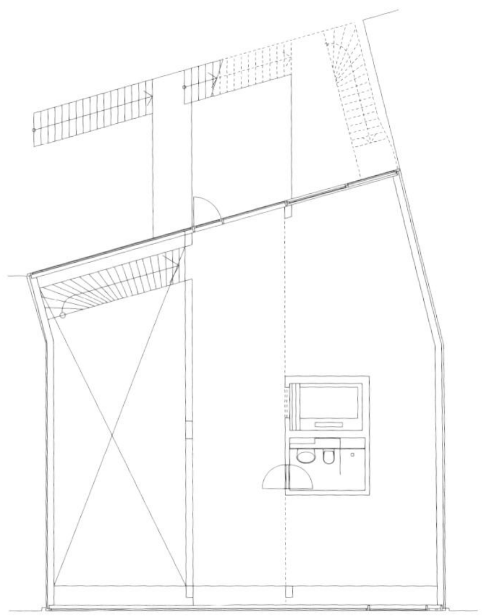

Grundriss 1. Obergeschoss | Floor plan of 1st floor

ARCHITEKT | ARCHITECT

BRANDT + SIMON ARCHITEKTEN

GEBÄUDE | BUILDING

EINFAMILIENHAUS
MAXIMILIANSTRASSE

TEXT CHRISTIAN BRENSING

05

ARCHITEKTEN | ARCHITECTS

brandt + simon architekten
Auerstraße 14
10249 Berlin
www.brandtundsimon.de

MITARBEITER | TEAM

Ralph Brandt, Martin Simon, Nina Christe

BAUHERR | CLIENT

Anke Pätsch und | and **José María Durán Medraño**

BAULEITUNG | SITE MANAGEMENT

brandt + simon architekten

TRAGWERK | STRUCTURE

Ingenieurbüro für Tragwerksplanung Dr.-Ing. Christian Müller GmbH, Berlin

FERTIGSTELLUNG | COMPLETION

Juni 2009 | June 2009

STANDORT | LOCATION

Maximilianstraße 10
13187 Berlin

FOTOS | PHOTOS

Michael Nast, Güstrow

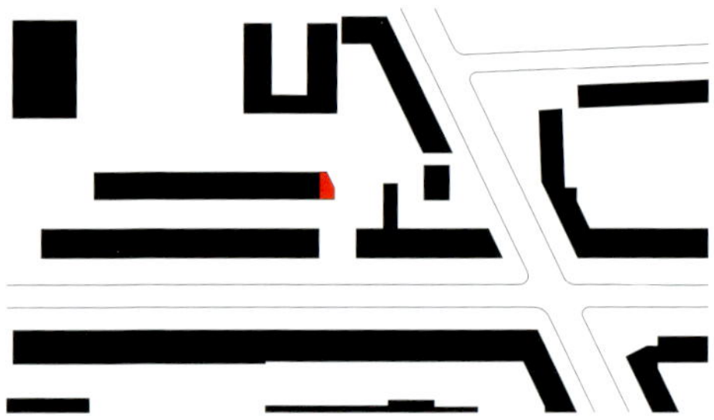

Lageplan | Site plan

Die Fenster durchstoßen die schuppenartige Hülle des Hauses aus 8350 Biberschwanzziegeln.
The windows pierce the fish-scale-like skin of the house, made up of 8,350 beavertail tiles.

Das Gebäude entstand auf einer ungewöhnlich großen Baulücke inmitten einer gründerzeiltichen Bebauung. | The house was erected in an unusually large gap between turn-of-the-century buildings.

Grüne Wiese, Gemüsebeete, ein Baum und ein grünes Haus – dies offenbart der Blick in eine Baulücke zwischen der viergeschossigen Blockrandbebauung in der Maximilianstraße, Berlin-Pankow. Größer könnte die räumliche wie bauliche Überraschung hier an der Peripherie des Stadtbezirks Prenzlauer Berg kaum sein. Inmitten gründerzeitlicher Wohngebäude wurde auf einem 850 Quadratmeter großen Grundstück, in 30 Metern Entfernung zur Straße, an die Brandwand der Hofbebauung ein 160 Quadratmeter großes Einfamilienhaus gesetzt.

Die Bauherren waren auf ihrer Suche nach einer Bleibe für die Familie auf dieses verwahrloste und mit Garagen zugestellte Grundstück gestoßen und hatten sofort dessen Potenzial erkannt. In enger Zusammenarbeit mit den Architekten wurde ein Konzept entwickelt, das den Anforderungen der Familie auf den Leib geschneidert ist. Schon aus Kostengründen musste das Heim für die Akademikerfamilie, mit entsprechend vielen Büchern, eine Maßanfertigung sein, die den individuellen Anforderungen der einzelnen Familienmitglieder genau entspricht. Die Synthese dieser vielfältigen Ansprüche und Zugeständnisse ist die durch eine Abkantung definierte Geometrie des Grundrisses sowie die des gesamten Bauvolumens an Dach und Fassade.

A green meadow, vegetable beds, a tree and a green house – a look through a gap in the four-storey perimeter block development on Maximilianstrasse in Berlin-Pankow reveals all of this. The surprise in terms of space and architecture here on the periphery of the city district of Prenzlauer Berg could hardly be greater. In the midst of Wilhelminian apartment buildings, a single-family home with 160 square metres of living space has been set down on an 850-square-metre plot, 30 metres away from the street and pushed up against the firewall of the courtyard buildings.

The clients were looking for a new home for their family, and when they happened upon this neglected site cluttered with garages they immediately recognised its potential. In close cooperation with the architects, a concept was tailor-made to fit the needs of the family. For cost reasons alone, a home for a family of academics, with shelves full of books, would have to be customised to the personal requirements of each family member. The synthesis of these diverse demands and the necessary

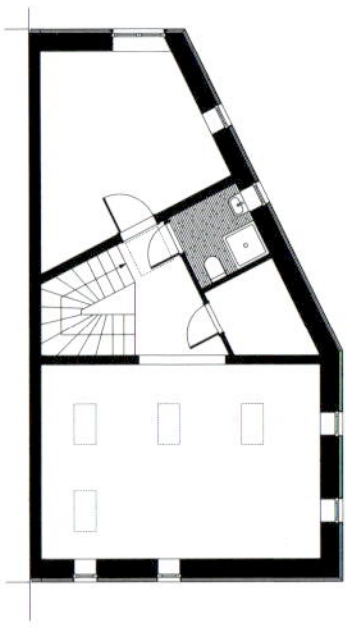

Grundriss 2. Obergeschoss
Floor plan of 2nd floor

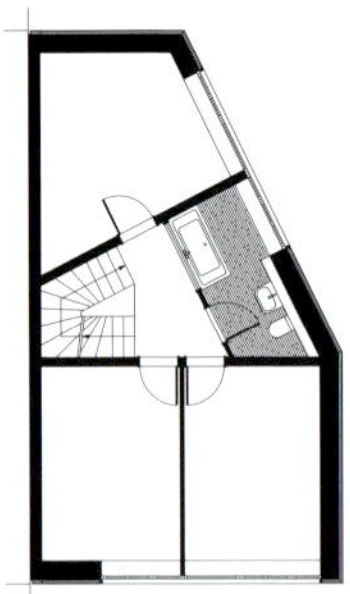

Grundriss 1. Obergeschoss
Floor plan of 1st floor

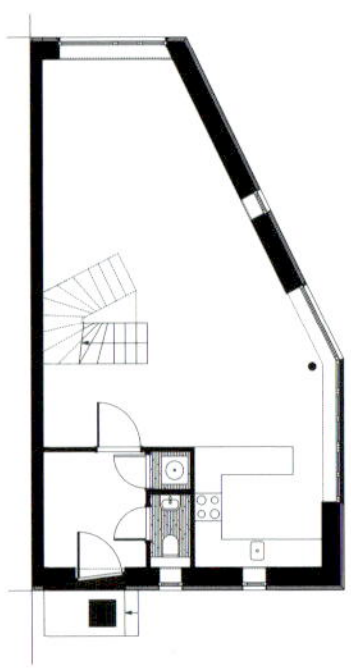

Grundriss Erdgeschoss
Floor plan of ground floor

Eigentlich deutet alles an diesem Bauwerk auf Individualität hin. Aus der Definition der eigenen Wünsche, der Begrenztheit der finanziellen Mittel und dem Anspruch an die durchgängige Nachhaltigkeit der Baumaterialien bildete sich während des Entwurfs-, aber auch des Bauprozesses ein höchst individuelles Haus heraus. Dabei wurde in allen Phasen auf konventionelle Lösungen gesetzt, die dann aber jeweils von den Architekten leicht modifiziert wurden.

Das Entwurfsprinzip von brandt + simon architekten beruht auf einer in der heutigen Architektursprache nicht unüblichen Objekthaftigkeit. Der Baukörper wird als homogenes Objekt – quasi wie ein Kunstobjekt – betrachtet, dessen Form dominant die Attribute jeglicher Funktionalität unterordnet oder gar vermeidet. So wird die äußerliche typologische Zeichenhaftigkeit eines Wohnhauses, z.B. die symmetrische Anordnung von Fenstern, Türen, Schrägdach und Schornstein, bewusst hinterfragt, wenn nicht gar negiert. Keines dieser Bauelemente entspricht hier der Norm. Die bereits erwähnte asymmetrische kubische Gebäudeform lässt vom Garten her nur in Ansätzen eine Dachform erkennen. Die homogene Dach- und Fassadeneindeckung mit 8350 Biberschwanzdachziegeln in unterschiedlichen Grünschattierungen scheint diese Aufgabe wie eine Metapher für das gesamte Haus zu übernehmen. Auch Fensterbänder und kleine Fensteröffnungen, alle mit markantem Zinkblechrahmen, entsprechen wenig dem Bild eines konventionellen Einfamilienhauses. In unterschiedlichen Größen und Ausrichtungen durchstoßen sie nach dem Prinzip, je Raum ein großes Fenster, die schuppenartige Haut des Hauses.

Trotz dieser hohen Form der Abstraktion ist der Bau nicht formal entrückt. Das dreigeschossige Einfamilienhaus stellt am Ende der um zwei Geschosse höheren Häuserzeile in seinen bescheidenen Dimensionen einen quasi natürlichen Endpunkt dar – unaufgeregt und in sich fokussiert. Die Lebendigkeit des Äußeren lässt sich ohne weiteres auch auf die in neutralem Weiß gehaltenen Innenräume und deren Einbauten übertragen. Eine jede Ebene generiert ihr eigenes unverwechselbares Raumgefühl. Das „Durchwohnen" in dem lichtdurchfluteten

Das Gebäude schließt an die Brandwand des benachbarten Hinterhauses an. | The house is aligned with the firewall of the building behind it.

concessions have resulted in a floor plan defined by a chamfered geometry, and is likewise reflected in the overall volumes of the roof and façade.

Everything in this edifice speaks of individuality. Out of the definition of the clients' wishes, along with restricted financial means and the desire for sustainability in all building materials, a highly idiosyncratic house emerged during the design as well as the construction process. All the same, conventional solutions were relied on in every phase of the project, admittedly after being slightly modified by the architects.

The design principle applied by brandt + simon architekten is based on an understanding of the building as an object that is not unusual in today's architectural idiom. The body of the building is regarded here as a homogeneous object – quasi as an art object – whose formal dominance subordinates or even avoids any functional attributes. The external iconic typology of a home, e.g. the symmetrical arrangement of windows, doors, a peaked roof and chimney, is hence deliberately called into question, if not negated outright. None of these building elements here corresponds to the norm. Topping the above-described asymmetrical cuboid building shape, a roof can be only vaguely discerned from the garden side. The homogeneous covering of the roof and façade with 8,350 beavertail tiles in various shades of green seems to take on this task as if representing a metaphor for the entire house. Nor do the ribbon windows and small window openings, all with distinctive sheet-zinc frames, correspond very closely to our picture of what a conventional single-family home looks like. In various sizes and orientations they pierce the fish-scale-like skin of the house, obeying only the principle: one big window per room.

Despite this high degree of abstraction, however, the building is not formally inaccessible. With its modest dimensions, the three-storey single-family home forms a seemingly natural end point, calm and self-contained, for the row of houses that exceed it by two storeys. The liveliness of the exterior continues into the interior spaces, all in neutral white with their built-in furnishings. Each level generates its own unmistakable spatial ambience. The living space on the open-plan, light-flooded ground floor with its three-metre ceilings, the small, intimate bedrooms on the first floor and the rooms up to 4.10 metres high on the second floor, with a north-facing office opposite the library – none of these can necessarily be discerned from the façade.

1. Obergeschoss | 1st floor

2. Obergeschoss. Jede Ebene bietet ein eigenes Raumgefühl.
2nd floor. Each floor offers a different spatial ambience.

Erdgeschoss mit 3 Metern Deckenhöhe | Ground floor with 3-metre ceilings

Erdgeschoss mit seinen 3 Metern Deckenhöhe, die kleinen intimen Schlafräume im 1. Obergeschoss und die bis zu 4,10 Meter hohen Räume im 2. Obergeschoss, mit dem nach Norden ausgerichteten Arbeitzimmer nebst gegenüber liegender Bibliothek, lassen sich von außen nicht unbedingt erahnen.
Keinesfalls von außen ist zu erkennen, dass es sich um einen vollständigen Holzbau handelt. Wegen der Kosten, der geringen Bauzeit bei relativer Wetterunabhängigkeit, der Ökologie, aber auch aus konstruktiven Gründen, wählte man diesen Baustoff. So wurden alle Bauteile vor Ort gefertigt und der komplette Rohbau von dem Bauunternehmer Wildenhayn an einem einzigen Tag aus den vorgefertigten Wandscheiben zusammengesetzt. Hier und da stößt man im Inneren auf Reminiszenzen von Holz. Zum Beispiel, die im engen Winkel aufsteigende Holztreppe und die Holzstütze im Fenster, das zur Terrasse hinausgeht, sind in Weiß gehaltene Aide mémoire der konstruktiven Genealogie. Ansonsten liegt die Holzkonstruktion verborgen hinter Gipsfaserplatten und einer Gesamtwandstärke von 50 Zentimetern mit 36 Zentimeter Dämmstärke. So erfüllt das Gebäude, inklusive der Solarpanele auf dem Dach für Warmwasser und Heizung, mühelos die Kriterien eines Niedrigenergiehauses. Mit anderen Worten, der ‚grüne' optische Eindruck des Hauses setzt sich bis in die kleinste Faser der Konstruktion und Funktion fort.

And it is by no means possible to guess by looking at the outside of the building that it is made completely of wood. This material was chosen due to its low cost, short construction time relatively independent of weather conditions, and also for structural reasons. All components could thus be made on site and the complete building shell put together in a single day by the contractor, Wildenhayn, out of prefabricated wall panels. Here and there one meets reminiscences of wood in the interior. The wooden stairway that curves up at a tight angle, for example, and the wooden support in the window onto the terrace are white-painted "aides-mémoires" of the house's structural genealogy. Otherwise, the timber framework lies hidden behind gypsum fibreboard panels and a total wall thickness of 50 centimetres, including 36 centimetres of insulation. Equipped in addition with solar panels on the roof for hot water and heating, the building hence effortlessly fulfils the criteria for a low-energy house. In other words, the "green" visual impression it makes is carried on into the smallest fibre of its construction and function.

ARCHITEKT | ARCHITECT

FLORIAN FISCHER UND KATHARINA LEUSCHNER

GEBÄUDE | BUILDING

HAUS POLZ

TEXT YORCK FÖRSTER

06

ARCHITEKTEN | ARCHITECTS

FLORIAN FISCHER
Altersheimerstr. 6
81546 München | Munich
www.florianfischer.net

KATHARINA LEUSCHNER
Esebeckstraße 20
80637 München | Munich
www.leuschner-architekten.de

MITARBEITER | TEAM

Florian Fischer, Katharina Leuschner

BAUHERR | CLIENT

Karin und Valentin Polz

TRAGWERK | STRUCTURE

Haidl Holzbau GmbH, Röhrnbach

FERTIGSTELLUNG | COMPLETION

Mai 2009 | May 2009

STANDORT | LOCATION

Rosenweg 11
94127 Neukirchen am Inn

FOTOS | PHOTOS

Michael Heinrich, München | Munich

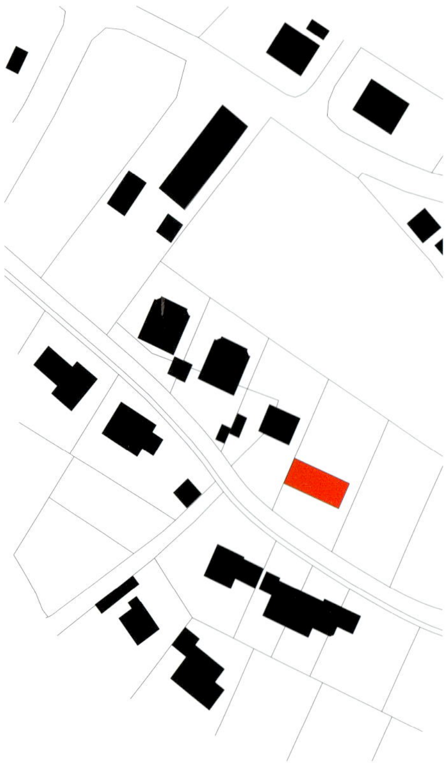

Lageplan | Site plan

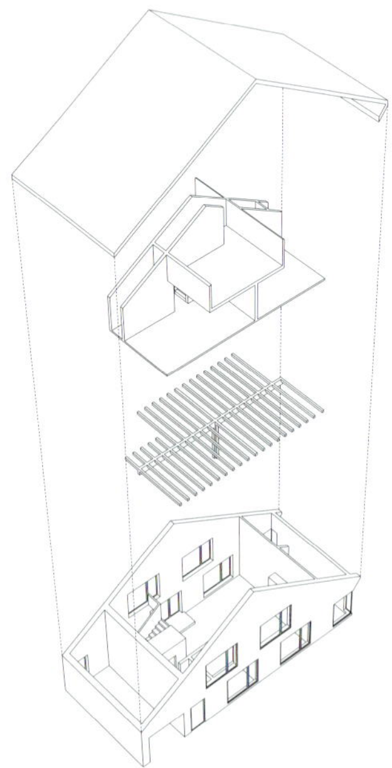

Isometrie Konstruktion | Isometric drawing structure

Das Gebäude ist als einfaches breites Satteldachhaus konzipiert. Der Giebel über der Längsseite steigert die Präsenz des eigentlich kleinen Hauses. | The building is conceived as a simple wide gabled-roof house. The gable across the longer side enhances the presence of what is actually a small house.

In einer Stichstraße am Rand des kleinen Ortes Neukirchen am Inn nahe Passau steht das Haus Polz. Florian Fischer und Katharina Leuschner haben das kleine Wohnhaus mit einer gewissen Lust am Widersprüchlichen entworfen. Formal korrekt ausgedrückt handelt es sich um ein weiß verputztes Giebeldachhaus. Es ist ein unaufgeregtes Haus, das ein Spiel mit typologischen Codes betreibt, vor allem aber eine heitere Ausdifferenzierung und Erlebbarkeit unterschiedlicher Raum- und Blickkonstellationen entfaltet.
Das Grundstück geht nach Norden hin in eine Wiesensenke mit einem Baumbestand an einem Bachlauf über. Erst jenseits der Senke befindet sich die Bebauung der angrenzenden Parzellen. Der unverbaubare Blick sollte so weit wie möglich in dem Haus erfahrbar sein.
Wegen der Erschließung des Grundstücks von Süden galt es, die Verschattung des Hauses auf den rückwärtigen Wiesengarten möglichst gering zu halten, gleichzeitig war aber auch ein zur Morgensonne exponierter Bereich gewünscht. So entstand das Konzept, den Baukörper längs zur Straße anzuordnen und relativ weit in das Grundstück einzuschieben. Zu dieser hin orientiert ist der (südliche) Vordergarten, der mehr als nur eine Vorzone des Hauses, sondern auch ein Lebensraum mit Frühstücksterrasse nebst der Küche ist.

In a cul-de-sac on the outskirts of the small town of Neukirchen am Inn near Passau stands Haus Polz. Florian Fischer and Katharina Leuschner designed the modest-sized residence with a certain relish for contradictions. In purely formal terms it can be described as a white stucco house with a gable roof. It is a tranquil structure that plays a bit with typological codes but above all opens up delightful experiences of nuanced spatial and visual constellations.
The plot verges to the north on a tree-dotted meadow that slopes down to a stream. Only on the other side of this hollow are there further buildings on the adjacent plots. The idea was thus to take advantage to the greatest extent possible of this unobstructed view.
Because access to the plot is on the south, the shadow cast by the house on the garden meadow behind was to be minimised, but the residents also wished to have an outdoor spot where they could enjoy the morning sun. These considerations gave rise to the idea of arranging the body of the building longitudinally along the street, pushing it relatively far into the plot. The (southern) front garden is now

Grundriss und Schnitt
Floor plan and section

Dominiert wird die Straßenansicht von dem Giebel über der Längsfront. Der Baukörper erhält dadurch eine kräftige horizontale Betonung, zumal auch noch die Garage ohne Absatz unter dem Dach Schutz gefunden hat. Nun könnte man sagen, das dies der Typus des alpenländischen Hauses mit seitlicher Scheune sei, wäre nicht die flächige Putzfassade, die auf jede Folklore-Applikation verzichtet. Und auch eine bergende Fülle dicker Wände sucht man vergebens. Nach den Entwürfen der Architekten wurde das Haus von einem Fertighaus-Hersteller als Holzbau realisiert, der Wandaufbau bleibt dadurch auch bei KFW-40-Standard geradezu kartondünn.

Der untersetzte, durchaus disproportionierte Charakter des Hauses wird noch unterstrichen durch die zueinander verschobenen Reihen von Panoramafenstern, die ebenfalls die Breite betonen. Geradezu athletisch straff dagegen, mit nur geringem Überstand, schließt das Dach mit dem Baukörper ab. Dieses dann keineswegs in der inzwischen üblichen Weise mit Ortziegeln an der Giebelkante, sondern ganz traditionell ausgeführt mit einer Zahnleiste unter den dann messerdünn erscheinenden Ziegeln.

Betritt man das Haus, führt eine kleine Diele in einen nahezu mittig entlang der Längsachse angeordneten kurzen Korridor. Damit wird eine Blickachse definiert, die die zentrale kreuzförmige Stütze im Erdgeschoss des Hauses streift und die abschließende Raumwand und den Durchgang zu dem angrenzenden Arbeitsraum erfasst. So entsteht der Eindruck einer respektablen Länge und Weite. Seitlich versetzt sind der Wohn- und Essbereich als offene Taschen angelegt. Dadurch werden diese Zonen zu einem durchwohnten, quer zu der Korridorachse angelegten zentralen Platz des Hauses. Die breiten Fenster geben von dort den Blick sowohl in den Vordergarten als auch in die Weite des Wiesengartens frei. Die lichte Helle des Raums erhält durch den Boden aus Eichendielen eine warme Tönung.

oriented toward the street. Much more than merely a prelude to entering the house, however, it is also a living space with breakfast terrace, conveniently placed adjacent to the kitchen.

The street elevation is dominated by the gable extending across the longitudinal façade. This lends the building a strong horizontal emphasis, with the garage also sheltered under the roof without any break in its line. One might be tempted to think that this is the stereotypical form of an Alpine chateau with barn at the side, were it not for the smooth, flat stucco façade, which eschews any folkloric ornament. And stout, protective walls are another element of that model that one seeks here in vain. The house was built of wood according to the architects' plans by a manufacturer of prefabricated homes, meaning that, while still complying with the KfW's Energy Standard 40, the walls are virtually cardboard-thin.

The low-slung, disproportionate character of the house is underscored further by closelyspaced rows of panoramic windows that emphasise its width. Almost athletically taut by contrast is the way the roof closes off the body of the building with hardly any overhang. And instead of doing so in the usual way these days with verge tiles at the edge of the gable, it takes the traditional route of a dentil moulding underneath what then appear to be razor-thin tiles.

Inside the entrance, a small vestibule leads to a short corridor that runs almost centrally along the longitudinal axis. This defines a sight line that first touches on the central cruciform support on the

Eine zentrale Kreuzstütze prägt den offenen Wohnbereich im Erdgeschoss.
A central cross-pillar dominates the open-plan living area on the ground floor.

Blick vom Treppenabsatz auf die bis zum Dachfirst offene obere Diele. Im Hintergrund rechts die vesetzt angeordnete Stiege zu dem Dachraum im 2. Obergeschoss.
View from stair landing of upper hallway, open up to roof ridge. In the background at the right are the offset stairs up to the 2nd-floor attic.

Essbereich und Küche mit Blick in den Vordergarten
Dining area and kitchen with view of front garden

Vordergarten mit Sonnenterrasse im Süden entlang der Stichstraße
Front garden with sun terrace on the southern side along the cul-de-sac

Mit Bedacht wurde die Fensterunterkante nicht bündig zum Boden ausgeführt, sondern ein wahrnehmbarer Sockelabstand belassen. Die raumabschließende Wand bleibt so noch erfahrbar und wird nicht in Scheiben fragmentiert. Die Deckenuntersicht des Holz-Fertigteilhauses wurde unverkleidet gelassen. Der auf der Stütze ruhende Längsträger betont die Linearität der Korridorachse, die quer dazu verlaufenden Balkenlagen rhythmisieren gleichzeitig die Raumwahrnehmung. Es sind diese kleinen Entscheidungen, die die Qualität des Hauses ausmachen. So entfaltet sich im Inneren eine ungezwungene, spielerische Komplexität und Offenheit.

Das gilt auch für die zweiläufige Treppe zum Obergeschoss. Auf der Höhe des Absatzes eröffnet sich eine unerwartete Perspektive: Die Treppe geht in eine Diele vor den Zimmern über, der Raum ist bis zum Dach geöffnet. Im Durchgang zum Schlafraum sieht man die ersten Stufe einer weiteren Stiege zu einem Raum direkt unter dem Dachfirst. Aus der Diele hat man einerseits einen erhöhten Panoramablick auf den Wiesengarten, zur anderen Seite aber sieht man auf die bis zum First reichende Wand vor den Zimmern – und erkennt nun das Umrissbild eines fünfseitigen Giebelhauses in der klassischen Proportionierung.

Das kleine Haus wartet mit einer überraschenden Differenziertheit an Raumsituationen auf, die durch die Bereitschaft der Bauherrenschaft zu einer offenen Lebensweise erst möglich wurde. Denn eine Abgeschottetheit gegenüber den Nachbarn entlang der Stichstraße im Süden ist nicht die Sache dieses Hauses.

ground floor and then takes in the wall closing off the room at the end and the passage to the adjacent office. An impression is created in this way of respectable length and breadth. The living and dining rooms are offset to the sides as open pockets. These zones thus become the central, open living area for the house, perpendicular to the axis of the corridor. The broad windows afford a view onto both the front garden and the expanse of the garden meadow to the rear. Oak floorboards lend the bright and airy rooms a warm tonality. With careful consideration, the lower edge of the windows was not set flush with the floor, but rather a perceptible area of wall was left below the ledge. This means that the wall remains tangible as an enclosure for the space and is not fragmented into slices. The ceiling of the prefabricated wooden house was left uncovered. The exposed longitudinal beam resting on the supporting pillars emphasises the linearity of the corridor axis, while the cross-joists give the room a visual rhythm. It is small decisions like this that make for the special quality of the house. Inside, a casual, playful complexity and openness unfold.

This also applies to the double-flight stairway to the upper floor. At the landing an unexpected perspective opens up: the stairs lead to a hallway giving onto the rooms that is open all the way up to the roof. Continuing into the bedroom one notices the first step of a further stairway leading up to a room directly under the roof ridge. From the upstairs hallway one has both an elevated panoramic view of the garden meadow as well as a full view of the wall soaring up to the roof – and suddenly the outline of a five-sided gable house of classic proportions becomes visible.

This small house offers a surprising diversity of spatial situations, made possible by the willingness of the clients to open themselves up to their surroundings. After all, the idea of the house was not to close itself off from the neighbours living on the street.

ARCHITEKT | ARCHITECT

FLORIAN NAGLER ARCHITEKTEN

GEBÄUDE | BUILDING

BESUCHERGEBÄUDE KZ-GEDENKSTÄTTE DACHAU

TEXT IRENE MEISSNER

07

ARCHITEKTEN | ARCHITECTS

Florian Nagler Architekten
Theodor-Storm-Straße 16
81245 München | Munich
www.nagler-architekten.de

MITARBEITER | TEAM

Florian Nagler, Matthias Müller, Stefan Lambertz

BAUHERR | CLIENT

Stiftung Bayerische Gedenkstätten

TRAGWERK | STRUCTURE

merz kley partner ZT GmbH, Dornbirn, Österreich | Austria

LANDSCHAFTSARCHITEKTEN LANDSCAPE ARCHITECTS

Latz + Partner GbR, Kranzberg

FERTIGSTELLUNG | COMPLETION

April 2009

STANDORT | LOCATION

Alte Römerstraße 75
85221 Dachau
www.kz-gedenkstaette-dachau.de

FOTOS | PHOTOS

Stefan Müller-Naumann, München | Munich

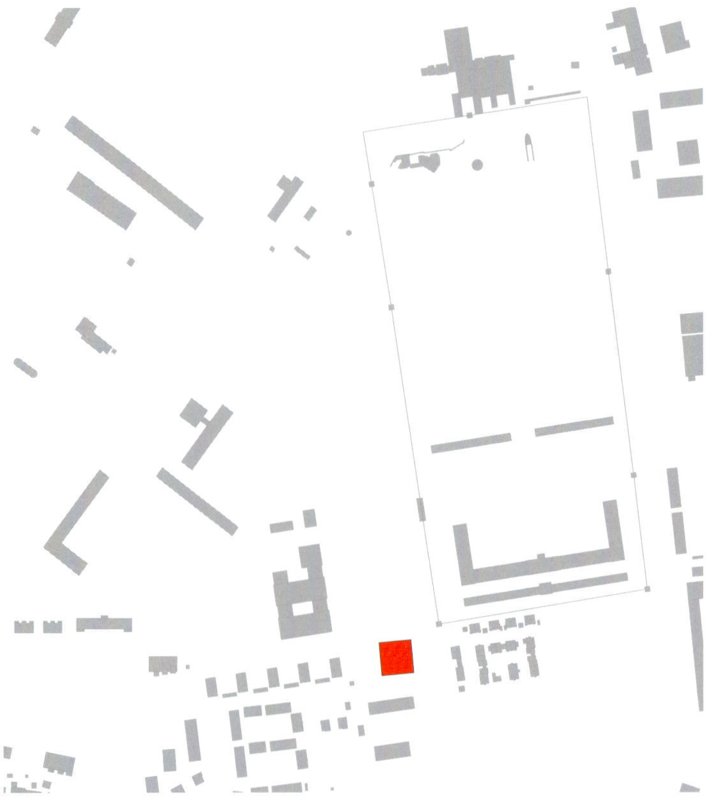

Lageplan | Site plan

Übersicht Nordost | Panoramic view from nort.east

Jährlich besuchen etwa 800 000 Menschen aus dem In- und Ausland die 20 Kilometer nördlich von München gelegene KZ-Gedenkstätte Dachau. Um den Besuchern einen ersten Überblick über das ausgedehnte ehemalige Konzentrationslager zu geben, war es längst an der Zeit, eine dem Ort angemessene Orientierungs- und Informationsstelle zu schaffen.
Während der Zeit des Nationalsozialismus waren im KZ Dachau 200 000 Menschen inhaftiert, mehr als 40 000 Häftlinge fanden im Stammlager und in den über 150 Außenlagern den Tod. Nach der Befreiung der Gefangenen im April 1945 wurde das Gelände als Internierungs- und Flüchtlingslager genutzt und baulich verändert. Da sich die Stadt Dachau und der Freistaat Bayern nicht weiter mit der Vergangenheit ‚belasten' wollten, entstand erst 1965 auf Initiative der überlebenden Opfer die KZ-Gedenkstätte Dachau.
Mitte der 1990er-Jahre erarbeitete ein wissenschaftlicher Fachbeirat ein neues Konzept für den Erinnerungs- und Lernort, in das die historische Bedeutung der vorhandenen Gebäude und Räume einbezogen wurde. Anstelle des bis dahin vorgegebenen Zugangs zur Gedenkstätte von der stadtabgewandten Straßenseite sollten die Besucher nun wieder über den „Weg der Häftlinge" das ehemalige Lager betreten. Dieser führte vom Bahnhof über das ehemalige SS-Übungsgelände zum Lagereingang, dem „Jourhaus". Seit 2005 ist dieser

Every year, some 800,000 people from Germany and abroad visit the Dachau Concentration Camp Memorial Site 20 kilometres north of Munich. In order to give these visitors an initial overview of the extensive grounds of the former concentration camp, a place for orientation and information was long overdue.
During the Nazi era, 200,000 people were imprisoned in the camp at Dachau; more than 40,000 prisoners met their deaths at the main camp and over 150 external sites. After the prisoners were liberated in April 1945, the complex was used as an internment and refugee camp, and the buildings were altered. As the Dachau authorities and the Free State of Bavaria subsequently did not wish to further "burden" themselves with the past, it was not until 1965 that survivors launched an initiative to establish a concentration camp memorial at Dachau.
In the mid-1990s a research council developed a new concept for a place of memory and learning that would incorporate the historical significance of the existing buildings and spaces. Instead of the previous route to the memorial site, leading from the

Fassadendetail Ost | Detail of eastern facade

Eingangsbereich Nordost | North-east entrance area

side of the camp opposite the town, the plan was for visitors now to follow the "path of the prisoners" to the former camp. This leads from the railway station past the former SS training grounds to the gate of the camp, the "Jourhaus". A "path of memory" was established here in 2005, with display panels explaining the various stations. That same year, the Stiftung Bayerische Gedenkstätten (Bavarian Memorials Foundation) announced a competition for a visitor centre, inviting four architecture offices to submit proposals. The Munich architect Florian Nagler was selected for his concept of creating not a building, but rather a place.

Nagler reacted with exceptional sensitivity to the complex situation. At the crossroads of the various access routes to the memorial site – the "path of memory" and the new pedestrian area extending from the car park over a new bridge and then onward to the Jourhaus, he designed a low, flat building, which is at first not perceived as a building at all, but rather seems to blend without fanfare into the stands of old trees before the camp complex. The outdoor spaces are laid out to flow freely: trees condense into groups, the paths dissolve into gravel areas and segue into patches of vegetation.

The structure is erected on a square plan measuring 36 by 36 metres and is articulated by three interior courtyards that provide natural lighting and ventilation. The look of the whole is dominated by the wooden pillars surrounding the enclosed space. The varying slants of these pillars stretched between the exposed concrete roof and floor slabs give rise to the impression that the birches all around continue into the building. A total of 460 pillars around the façade and an additional 189 inside carry the roof. For the contact points between the outside pillars and the concrete slabs a special connection was developed from a steel pipe with semi-spheres at the ends. It is mounted by means of a screw thread and can thus be used for both vertical and slanted pillars. This connection point enables both the later insertion of pillars and subsequent replacement.

The room is then actually closed off from the outside by glazing, usually large expanses, set behind the tree-pillars. Architecture and nature are in direct dialogue here. Depending on the direction in which visitors move, the building opens up and

„Weg des Erinnerns" eingerichtet und wird mit Schautafeln erklärt. Im selben Jahr schrieb die Stiftung Bayerische Gedenkstätten einen Gutachterwettbewerb für ein Besuchergebäude aus, zu dem vier Architekturbüros eingeladen wurden. Der Münchner Architekt Florian Nagler erhielt für sein Konzept, kein Haus, sondern einen Ort zu bauen, den Zuschlag.
Nagler reagierte in besonderer Weise auf die sensible Situation. Ausgehend von den verschiedenen Erschließungswegen, dem „Weg des Erinnerns" und dem neuen Fußgängerbereich, der sich vom Parkplatz über eine neue Brücke bis zum „Jourhaus" erstreckt, entwarf er an deren Kreuzungspunkt einen niedrigen Flachbau, der zuerst gar nicht als Gebäude wahrgenommen wird, da er sich wie selbstverständlich in den alten Baumbestand vor dem Lagergelände einfügt. Die Freiflächen sind fließend angelegt: Bäume verdichten sich zu Gruppen, die Wege lösen sich in Kiesflächen auf und gehen in Vegetationsbereiche über.
Der Bau ist über einem Quadrat von 36 mal 36 Metern errichtet und durch drei Innenhöfe gegliedert, die für eine natürliche Belichtung und Belüftung sorgen. Das Erscheinungsbild wird von einem mit Holzstützen verkleideten Raumkörper bestimmt. Die in unterschiedlichen Neigungen zwischen Dach- und Bodenplatte aus Sichtbeton aufgestellten Stützen rufen den Eindruck hervor, als gingen die Birken der Umgebung in den Bau über. Die insgesamt 460 Fassadenstützen und weitere 189 Stützen

closes again before their eyes, the rays of the sun generating an ever-changing play of light and shadow. Nature is guided gently into the geometry of the building and its flowing sequence of spaces. Visitors enter the building via a large entrance courtyard to the north-east. School classes or other visitor groups can gather here without interfering with the contemplative tranquillity of the memorial. A bright foyer, which can also be used as an event space, gives onto a bookstore and café that also offers an outdoor area protected from the elements.
The materials have been chosen with the utmost care. The pillars are made of rough-hewn Douglas fir stained a silvery grey, and the exposed concrete surfaces are sandblasted. The floors of polished, sand-coloured cement correspond with ceiling panels of light-coloured wood composite.
The building is reserved, developed out of the specific situation, and yet marked by individuality and a richness of spatial experiences. Florian Nagler has managed to achieve a synthesis: the visitor centre not only fulfils all the functional requirements; it also dovetails harmoniously with a difficult site without hiding itself.

Eingang, Foyer, Empfang | Entrance, foyer, reception area

im Inneren tragen das Dach. Für den Anschluss der Außenstützen an die Betonplatten wurde eine spezielle Verbindung aus einem Stahlrohr mit einer Halbkugel entwickelt, die mittels eines Gewindes montiert und sowohl für vertikale als auch geneigte Stützen verwendet werden kann. Dieser Knoten ermöglicht nicht nur den nachträglichen Einbau der Stützen, sondern bei Bedarf auch eine späteres Auswechseln.
Den eigentlichen Raumabschluss bildet eine hinter den Baumstützen liegende, meist großflächige Verglasung. Architektur und Natur korrespondieren miteinander. Je nach Bewegungsrichtung öffnet und schließt sich der Bau dem Betrachter und einfallendes Sonnenlicht erzeugt ein wechselndes Licht- und Schattenspiel. Die Natur wird sanft in die Geometrie des Hauses und dessen fließende Raumfolgen geleitet.
Der Besucher betritt das Gebäude über einen großen Eingangshof im Nordosten. Schulklassen oder andere Besuchergruppen können sich hier versammeln, ohne dass die Ruhe des Gedenkortes beeinträchtigt wird. An ein helles Foyer, das auch als Veranstaltungsraum genutzt werden kann, schließen sich ein Buchladen und eine Cafeteria an, die wiederum über einen nach außen abgeschirmten Freibereich verfügt.
Die Materialien sind feinfühlig eingesetzt. Für die Stützen wurde silbriggrau lasiertes, sägeraues Douglasienholz verwendet, die Sichtbetonflächen sind sandgestrahlt. Die Böden aus geschliffenem, sandfarbenem Zementestrich korrespondieren mit den Deckenverkleidungen aus hellen Holzwerkstoffplatten.
Der Bau ist zurückhaltend, aus der spezifischen Situation entwickelt und doch durch Individualität sowie einen Reichtum an räumlichen Erlebnissen gekennzeichnet. Florian Nagler ist eine Synthese geglückt; das Besuchergebäude genügt nicht nur den funktionalen Anforderungen, sondern es fügt sich in den schwierigen Ort harmonisch ein, ohne sich zu verstecken.

Fassade Innenhof | Façade of interior courtyard

Foyer, Empfang, Fassadenzwischenraum | Foyer, reception area, gap in façade

Übersicht Nord | Panoramic view from north

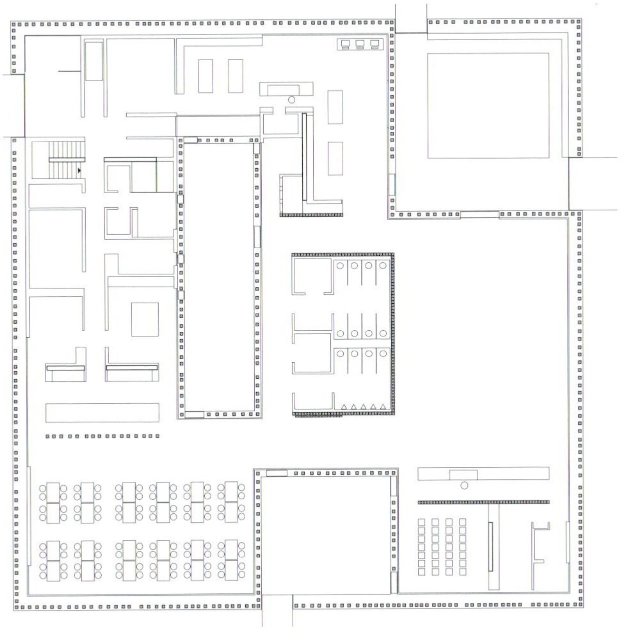

Grundriss | Floor plan

ARCHITEKT | ARCHITECT

GOETZ HOOTZ CASTORPH ARCHITEKTEN UND STADTPLANER

GEBÄUDE | BUILDING

STADTVILLEN IM HERDERPARK

TEXT WOLFGANG BACHMANN

08

ARCHITEKTEN | ARCHITECTS

Goetz Hootz Castorph Architekten und Stadtplaner GmbH Bäckerstraße 57 81241 München | Munich **www.goetzhootzcastorph.de**

WETTBEWERB UND ENTWURF COMPETITION AND SCHEMATIC DESIGN

Goetz Hootz Castorph Architekten und Stadtplaner GmbH

MITARBEITER | TEAM

Andrea Frank, Helene Kuithan, Diana Obermaier

BAUHERR | CLIENT

Herderparkpark GmbH & Co. KG, Bad Tölz

AUSSCHREIBUNG, OBJEKTÜBERWACHUNG | CALL FOR TENDERS, PROPERTY MANAGEMENT

baubar Architekten und Ingenieure, München | Munich

TRAGWERK | STRUCTURE

Buchner, Wehbe & Partner Ingenieurbüro, Bad Tölz

BAUPHYSIK | BUILDING PHYSICS

ACCON GmbH, Greifenberg

HAUSTECHNIK | M & E ENGINEERS

Franz Weber GmbH, Bad Tölz

PROJEKTSTEUERUNG PROJECT GUIDANCE

ALBA BauProjektManagement GmbH, Oberhaching

LANDSCHAFTSARCHITEKTEN LANDSCAPE ARCHITECTS

Studio RODEL, Lugano, Schweiz | Switzerland

FERTIGSTELLUNG | COMPLETION

November 2008

STANDORT | LOCATION

Buchenerstraße 3, 5 und | and **7 83646 Bad Tölz www.fontavia.de**

FOTOS | PHOTOS

Michael Heinrich, München | Munich

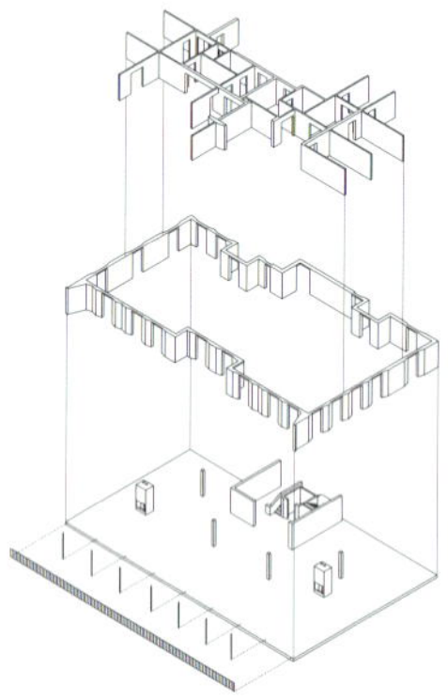

Isometrie Konstruktion Isometric drawing structure

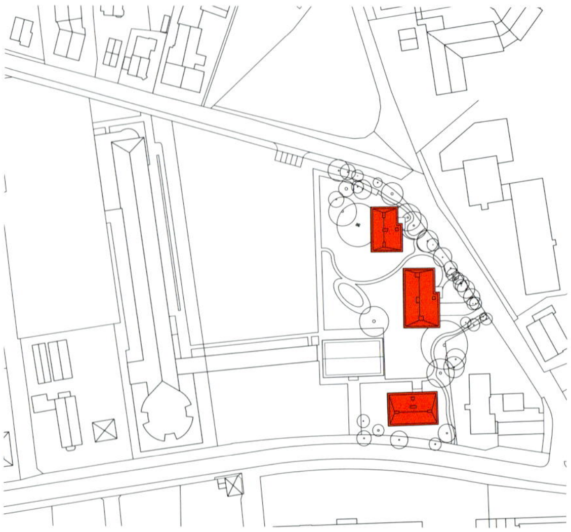

Lageplan | Site plan

Die Häuser wurden in den Park mit seinem altem Baum- und Baubestand integriert. | The houses were integrated into the park with its existing trees and buildings.

Bad Tölz, 50 Kilometer südlich von München gelegen, mit einer Privatbahn bestens angebunden, erstreckt sich zu beiden Seiten der Isar; das Skigebiet Brauneck befindet sich in Rufweite. 17 500 Einwohner teilen sich mehrere Barockkirchen, Kurkliniken und Sanatorien und eine romantische Marktstraße, die 1903 von dem heimatbegeisterten Gabriel von Seidl aufgehübscht wurde. Die Stadt hat einen weltberühmten Knabenchor und einen übergewichtigen Bullen.
Seine Zweitwohnung oder den Altersruhesitz nach hier zu verlegen, wäre also nicht die schlechteste Entscheidung, denn jetzt gibt es inmitten der vollfetten Oberbayern-Idylle sogar ansehnliche Architektur. Und das mitten an der Kurpromenade im Herderpark. Prominenter kann man nicht wohnen, bildet doch der Park als öffentlicher Raum ein vornehmes Passepartout für die vier- und fünfgeschossigen Stadthäuser, die die Architekten als „gestapelte Villen" beschreiben.

Bad Tölz, 50 kilometres south of Munich and with excellent connections into the city via a private railway, spreads out on both sides of the Isar River, and the Brauneck ski area is within earshot. The 17,500 inhabitants share several Baroque churches, resort clinics and sanatoria, along with a romantic market street that was prettied-up in 1903 by homeland enthusiast Gabriel von Seidl. The town boasts a world-famous boys' choir and an overweight TV cop.
This is not the worst spot to set up a second home or a retirement residence, because now there is even some appealing architecture in the midst of this voluptuous Upper Bavarian idyll. And it's located right on the spa promenade in the Herderpark. There is no more prominent place to live, with the

Die kubischen Baukörper einnern an klassische Bäderarchitektur.
The cubic houses recall classic spa architecture.

Die Fassaden werden durch Fenstertüren mit Klappläden aus Holz und abgeschrägten Laibungen gegliedert. | The façades are articulated by French doors with wooden louvre shutters that open into bevelled jambs.

Dass es sich nicht um Beispiele eines kosten- und flächensparenden Bauens handelt, ist offensichtlich, aber sogar als Zaungast darf man über diese drei Häuser froh sein. Es hätte vieles schief gehen können, bietet doch die in den letzten Jahrzehnten entstandene Umgebung keine Anhaltspunkte für ein Mindestmaß an Baukultur.

Was erfreulich ist: Diese Neubauten provozieren nicht als harsche Architektenmoderne, sondern finden eine wunderbare Balance zwischen funktional und gefällig, streng und verspielt – international und regional. Zunächst sind es weiße Kuben, deren Fassaden in durchlaufende, sich partiell in die Tiefe staffelnde Loggien aufgelöst oder durch regelmäßige französische Fenster perforiert sind. Man erinnert sich bei diesen Ansichten an die klassische Bäderarchitektur. Doch bei dieser rationalen Rasterung bleibt es nicht. Die weißen Lamellentüren schlagen in angeschrägte Laibungen auf, und beim Schließen stoßen sie stumpfwinklig vor dem ausgestellten Stabgeländer aneinander, sodass sie nie eine gerade Front bilden, sondern zum Garten hin eine Bewegung, wenn man so will eine Dialogbereitschaft signalisieren. Ein Rahmen fasst die Fensterstaffeln mit einem konservativen Schmuckmotiv zusammen. Dies taucht auch an den Hauskanten auf, ohne eine harmonische Symmetrie zu suchen, sondern ist eher ein ironischer Wink an die wohlhabende Klientel: Wir haben verstanden, ihr wohnt gerne etwas herrschaftlicher. Der Architekturbeflissene glaubt an einen weißen Kasten mit Flachdach, aber über dem Dachrand folgt ein unmerklicher Walm aus Zinkblech, der von braven Kaminen bekrönt wird. Der Heimatpfleger hingegen erkennt in den Geländern und schlanken Loggienstützen eine Nähe zu den 1950er-Jahren, wie sie damals das Hotel gegenüber eingeführt hat.

public garden forming a distinguished passepartout for the four- and five-storey townhouses that the architects describe as "stacked villas".
It is obvious that these residences are not prime examples of cost- and space-saving construction, but even as mere onlookers we can still delight in the sight of the three houses. Much could have gone wrong here, because when we look around there is little evidence of even the least effort at quality architecture in the past decades.
What is welcome in the new buildings is that they don't provoke us with a harsh brand of architectural modernism, but instead achieve a wonderful balance between being functional and agreeable, severe and whimsical – exuding both international flair and regional touches. At first glance, these are white cubes whose façades are dissolved by continuous loggias that are partially graduated in depth or perforated by regular French windows. These views summon pictures of classic spa architecture. But this rational gridwork is not all the buildings have to offer. The white louvre doors open into bevelled jambs, and when closed they abut each other at obtuse angles in front of the flared balcony railing, so that they never form a smooth front but rather convey a movement toward the garden, a willingness to enter into a dialogue, as it were. A frame unites the rows of windows with a conservative decorative motif. This design reappears at the edges of the buildings, without however seeking a harmonious symmetry. It's more like an ironic nod to the well-heeled clientele: we get it, you like to live in the grand manner. The architecture buff believes he is seeing here a classic white cube with flat roof, but above its edge there rises an inconspicuous hip of sheet zinc, crowned by ordinary chimneys. The guardian of homeland feeling on the other hand recognises in the balcony railings and slim loggia pillars echoes of the 1950s, once introduced by the hotel opposite.
This congenial coexistence of order and ornament recurs in the entrances. The white doors have a solid pushbar across their entire width, but it, too has a soft – and golden – profile. A gold parapet on the stairway landing responds to this – just to banish any fears on the part of the stacked villa

Die Villen wurden in einer zurückhaltenden, zeitlosen architektonischen Sprache entworfen. | The villas were designed in a reserved, timeless architectural idiom.

Dieses freundliche Nebeneinander von Ordnung und Ornament kehrt an den Hauseingängen wieder. Die weißen Türen haben einen soliden Stoßgriff über die ganze Breite, aber der ist weich profiliert und – gold. Ihm antwortet ein goldenes Brüstungsfeld auf dem Treppenpodest, als gelte es den gestapelten Villenbewohnern die Angst zu nehmen, sie könnten sich im Hausflur eines Mietshauses befinden. Das haben die Architekten durch funktionale Strenge und ein großzügiges Platzangebot gelöst. Die Briefkästen sind in die Treppenwange eingelassen, darunter befindet sich eine praktische Steinbank. Man wird vorzugsweise den Aufzug nehmen, eigentlich schade, denn die Patrouille der filigranen Geländerstäbe nimmt noch einmal die Außenmotive auf und bereitet auf die folgende zeitlose Wohnkultur vor. Die verkauft der Prospekt des Bauherrn als „die gelungene Transformation eines Raumkonzeptes der Gründerzeit in eine repräsentative und exklusive Architektur der Moderne". Er bietet aber lediglich Vorschläge, denn außer zwei notwendigen Stützpfeilern und dem (offenen) Kamin ist die Organisation frei wählbar. Die großzügige Befensterung bietet dafür alle Freiheiten. Die angebotenen Beispiele mit Bibliothek, Lese-, Kaminzimmer und Ankleide zeigen, dass man hier weniger an kinderreiche Lehrerehepaare gedacht hat. Eine Raumhöhe von 2,75 Metern, Zwischenflure, Flügeltüren, Holz- und Natursteinböden, Fußbodenheizung und stattliche Bäder zählen zum eleganten Standard der luxuriösen Wohnanlage. Der Park ist allseits im Blick und verbindet ungesäumt die weißen Villen, zwischen denen das alte Kurmittelhaus von 1861 gleichberechtigt stehen blieb. Wer es ganz bequem haben will und es sich leisten kann, wird vom benachbarten Hotel „Jodquellenhof" in jeder Hinsicht versorgt: wie ein Kurgast.
Es ist ein gelungenes Projekt, eine private Investition in Architektur und Stadtsanierung, um dem maroden Kurbetrieb und dem beliebigen Gebaue im Lokalkolorit eine andere Räson zu geben. Manchmal ist man dabei auf die Großkopferten angewiesen.

Durch das stupfwinklig angeschrägte Geländer vor dem Fenster und die schrägen Laibungen bilden die Fensterläden nie eine gerade Front. | Due to the obtuse angle of the flared railings in front of the windows and the slanted jambs, the window shutters never form a smooth front.

residents that they might find themselves here in the hallway of an apartment building. The architects have solved this problem through functional severity and generously proportioned rooms. The mailboxes are sunk into the stair string, and underneath them is a practical stone bench. Most residents will probably take the lift, which is a shame because the parade of filigree balusters once again takes up the exterior motifs, preparing the visitor for the timeless culture of fine domesticity to follow.
This form of living is sold to clients in the brochure as "the successful transformation of a late nineteenth-century spatial concept into prestigious and exclusive modern architecture". But the brochure offers only suggestions, because, apart from two necessary supporting pillars and the (open) fireplace, the interior layout can be designed at will. The generous fenestration offers every scope for creativity. The examples provided, with library, reading room, fireplace corner and walk-in closet, show that teacher couples with big families are not necessarily the targeted clientele. A ceiling height of 2.75 metres, interim hallways, double-wing doors, wood and stone floors, floor heating and sumptuous bathrooms are among the elegant appointments in these luxury residences. The park is in view from every room and seamlessly unites the white villas, amidst which the old Kurmittelhaus, a spa building from 1861, still holds its own. Anyone who can afford the utmost in comfort can rely on the neighbouring hotel, Jodquellenhof, to meet all daily needs: just like a spa guest.
This has been a successful project: a private investment in architecture and urban redevelopment designed to breathe fresh life into the ailing spa and the random local buildings with their forced quaintness. Sometimes you need to bring in the bigwigs.

Das Ensemble der drei Stadtvillen am Rand des Herderparks | The ensemble of three city villas at the edge of Herder Park

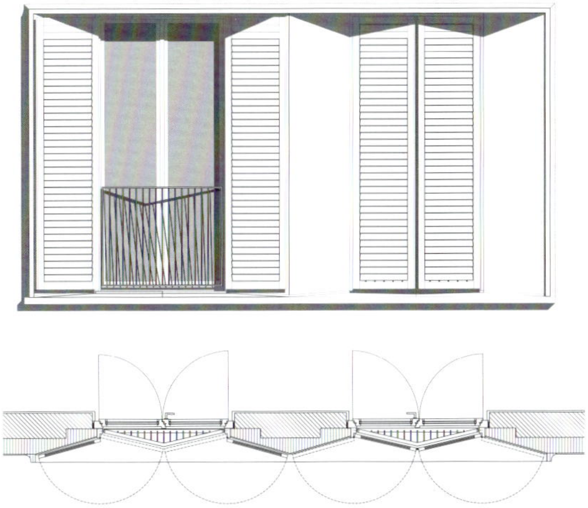

Fensterdetail | Window detail

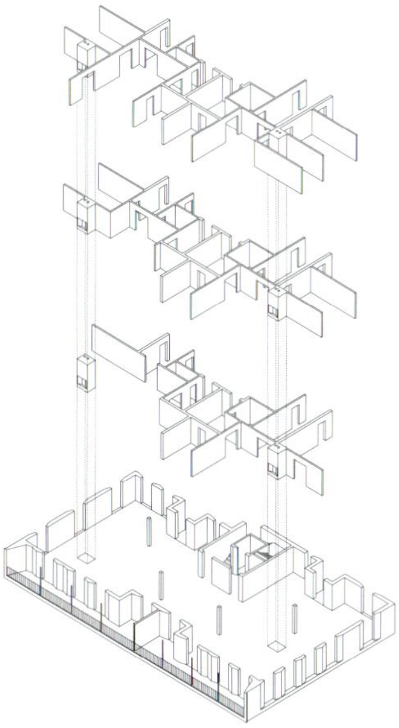

Isometrie von Grundrissvarianten für ‚gestapelte Villen'
Isometry of the floor plan variations for "stacked villas"

ARCHITEKT | ARCHITECT

HERZOG & DE MEURON

GEBÄUDE | BUILDING

VITRAHAUS

TEXT KARIN LEYDECKER

09

ARCHITEKTEN | ARCHITECTS

Herzog & de Meuron
Rheinschanze 6
4056 Basel,
Schweiz | Switzerland

MITARBEITER | TEAM

Partner | partner
Jacques Herzog, Pierre de Meuron, Wolfgang Hardt
Projektarchitekten
project architects
Guillaume Delemazure (Associate), Charlotte von Moos, Thomasine Wolfensberger (Associate)
Projektteam | project team
Katharina Rasshofer, Harald Schmidt, Sara Secci, Nicolas Venzin, Isabel Volkmar, Thomas Wyssen

BAUHERR | CLIENT

Vitra Verwaltungs GmbH,
Weil am Rhein,
Deutschland | Germany

AUSFÜHRUNGSPLANUNG
EXECUTION PLANNING

Mayer Baehrle
Freie Architekten bda, Lörrach,
Deutschland | Germany

TRAGWERK | STRUCTURE

ZPF Ingenieure AG,
Basel, Schweiz | Switzerland

LANDSCHAFTSARCHITEKTEN
LANDSCAPE ARCHITECTS

August Künzel
Landschaftsarchitekten AG,
Basel, Schweiz | Switzerland

HAUSTECHNIK | M & E ENGINEERS

Krebser und Freyler
Planungsbüro GmbH,
Teningen, Deutschland | Germany
Stahl + Weiß,
Büro für SonnenEnergie,
Freiburg, Deutschland | Germany

FERTIGSTELLUNG | COMPLETION

März 2010 | March 2010

STANDORT | LOCATION

Vitra Campus
Charles-Eames-Straße 2
79576 Weil am Rhein
www.vitra.com/de-de/campus/vitrahaus

FOTOS | PHOTOS

Iwan Baan, Amsterdam

Lageplan | Site plan

Das VitraHaus besteht aus zwölf Giebelhäusern, die sich durchdringend übereinander gestapelt sind. Der Anthrazitton der äußeren Putzhaut vereinheitlicht das Gebilde. | The VitraHaus consists of twelve stacked, interpenetrating gabled houses. The charcoal-grey tone of the outer stucco skin lends a uniform feel.

Die Basler Architekten Herzog & de Meuron sind begnadete Verpackungskünstler. Sie setzen die tracés régulateurs außer Kraft und suchen im assoziativen „Spielraum für Gestaltung …" nach der „jeweils individuellen Strategie".[1]
Bei der Bauaufgabe des Showrooms für die Möbelfirma Vitra in Weil am Rhein wählten sie das Prinzip Bricolage zu ihrem Spielplatz: Zwölf extrem lang gezogene Giebelhäuser stapelten sie in virtuoser Drehung und Durchdringung so übereinander, dass daraus eine dreidimensionale Collage entstand. Ein anthrazitfarbener Überzug gab dem aus Beton gegossenen Häuserhaufen die nötige Homogenität für das ganzheitliche Erfassen der expressiven Gestalt. Diese auf über 21 Meter Höhe gestapelte Dramatik mit bis zu 15 Metern auskragenden Hausvolumina

[1] Herzog & de Meuron, Minimalismus und Ornament, in: Arch+ 129/130, 1995, S. 18f.

Basel architects Herzog & de Meuron are talented packaging artists. They override the tracés régulateurs and search within an associative "creative scope" for "an individual strategy to fit the respective situation".[1]
Enlisted to create a showroom for the Vitra furniture company in Weil am Rhein, they chose the principle of bricolage as their playground, stacking twelve extremely elongated gabled houses one on top of the other in a virtuoso series of rotations and interpenetrations to form a three-dimensional collage. A charcoal-grey coating gave the poured concrete multi-part building the requisite homo-

[1] Herzog & de Meuron, Minimalism and Ornament, in: Arch+ 129/130, 1995, p. 115f. (summary)

Die durch den Häuserstapel gebildete offene Plaza des Eingangsbereichs
The open plaza formed at the entrance area by the stacked buildings

lässt alle übrigen Gebäude des Vitra Campus optisch schrumpfen und degradiert sogar Frank Gehrys strahlend weiße Museumsikone zur Marginalerscheinung. Damit definiert das VitraHaus nicht nur das neue Firmenentree, sondern es ist zugleich auch eine multisensuale Markeninszenierung für konsumrelevante Begegnungen mit den Vitra-Produkten.

Schon von Weitem sind die ausgestellten Möbel durch die mächtigen Schaufenster in den vollverglasten Giebelseiten der Stapelhäuschen zu sehen. In der Dämmerung verschmelzen die dunklen Gebäudekörper dann langsam mit der sie umgebenden Finsternis und verwandeln die Schaufenster zu schwebenden Laternen. Ein faszinierendes Bild! Als evokatives Äquivalent ist es markenpsychologisch ohnegleichen. So undogmatisch kann ein Haus nur agieren, wenn es an seinem Standort im Niemandsland zwischen Gewerbegebiet und Autobahn keine städtebaulichen Rücksichten nehmen muss.

Der neue Gebäudetyp aus Showroom, Museum und Erlebnisparcours präsentiert die „Home Collection" der Design-Firma Vitra, die an die Schöner-Wohnen-Emotionen von Privatleuten appelliert. Die konzeptionelle Inszenierung startet bereits in der Eingangszone, die den Besucher in einer intimen und zugleich zur Umgebung offenen Plaza umfängt. Für den Wohlfühlcharakter sorgt hier der Holzbelag, der sich sogar an die Sockelzone der Baukörper schmiegt und Sitzbänke ausbildet, die bis ins Gartencafé hinausführen. Auch das geräumige Entree knüpft mit seinem gefällig gestalteten Lobbycharakter an bekannte Sehgewohnheiten an. Dann beginnt der diskret gelenkte Erlebnisparcours im Raumlabyrinth des Hauses: Die komplexe Struktur der in sich verschachtelten Langhäuser schafft im Innern eine Vielfalt räumlicher Zonen, die im Entfalten ihrer Volumina den Blick wie von selbst führen. Obwohl nicht an jeder Schnittstelle zwischen Wendeltreppe und Körperkante ein spektakulärer Durchblick entsteht und auch der Fluss der Raumfolge im Eifer des Experiments hier und da staut, lustwandelt man gerne durch diese neue Heimat von Vitra.

Man genießt den Fernrohrblick durch die vollverglasten pentagonalen Stirnseiten, der markante Punkte der Umgebung fokussiert.

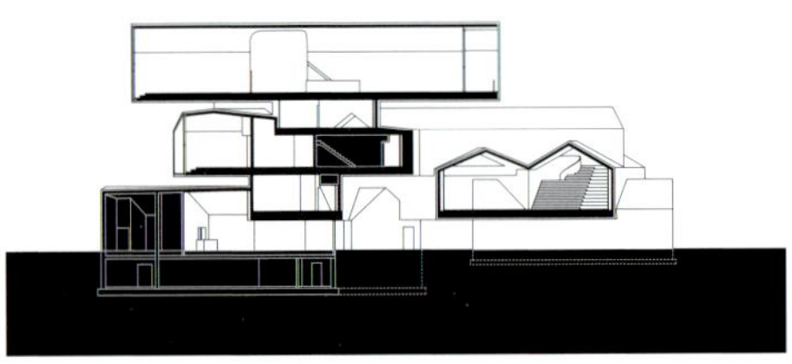

Schnitt 1 | Section 1

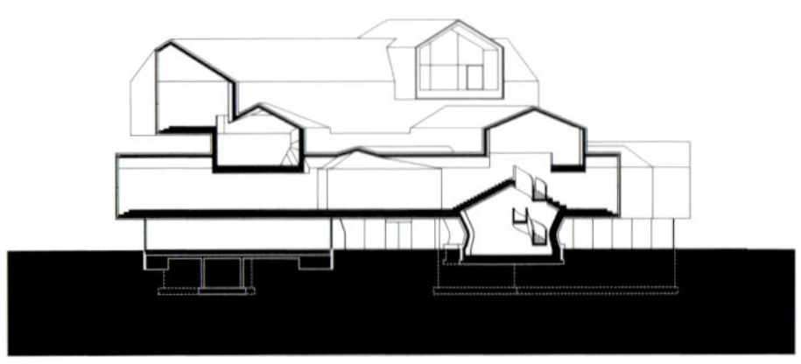

Schnitt 2 | Section 2

geneity to ensure that its expressive form can be comprehended holistically. This dramatic stack piled up at a height of over 21 metres, with volumes cantilevered out up to 15 metres, makes all the other buildings on the Vitra Campus optically shrink in its wake, even consigning Frank Gehry's radiant white iconic museum to the margins of perception.

The VitraHaus not only defines the new company entrance, but is at the same time a multisensual staging of the brand, setting the scene for consumption-relevant encounters with the Vitra products.

From a distance the visitor can already make out the furniture on display in the huge windows of the fully glazed gable ends of the stacked buildings. At twilight, the dark structures then gradually melt into the enveloping darkness and the display windows are transformed into floating lanterns. A fascinating sight! In terms of brand psychology this image is unparalleled as an evocative equivalent. A building can only unfold this kind of non-dogmatic effect when it is set in a no-man's-land between an industrial zone and the motorway and has no need to take urban planning into consideration.

The new building type made up of showroom, museum and discovery circuit presents the Home Collection from design firm Vitra, which appeals emotionally to the "exclusive lifestyle" aspirations of the private customer. The conceptual mise en scène already begins in the entrance zone, which enfolds the visitor in an intimate plaza that is at the same time open to its surroundings. Wood floors

Blick auf die Giebelfront mit dem Ausstellungsbereich für die Stuhlsammlung des Vitra Design Museums. In den Außenwänden befinden sich Holzbänke, die direkt in die Betonwände eingepasst sind. | View of the gable front with the exhibition area for the Vitra Design Museum's chair collection. On the exterior, wooden benches are built into the concrete walls.

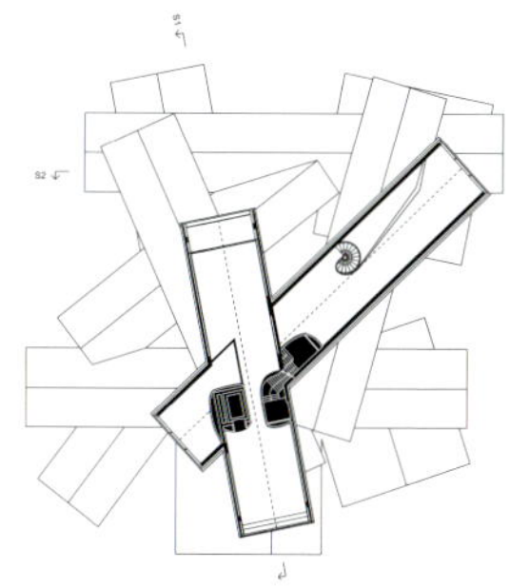

Grundriss Ebene 4 | Floor plan of Level 4

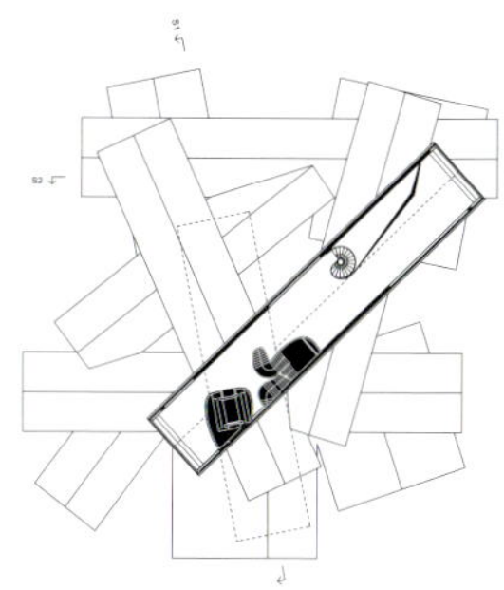

Grundriss Ebene 3 | Floor plan of Level 3

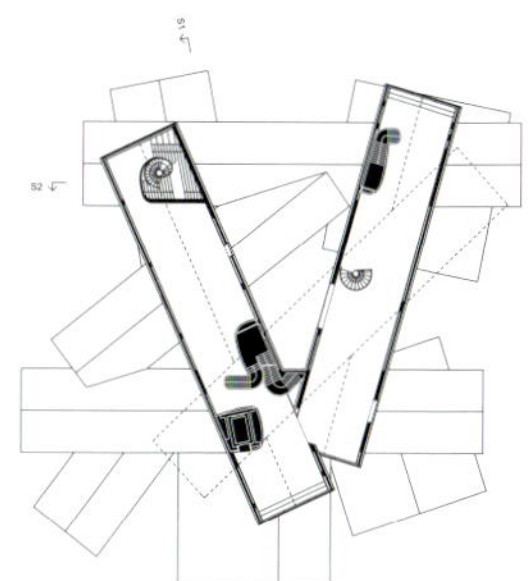

Grundriss Ebene 2 | Floor plan of Level 2

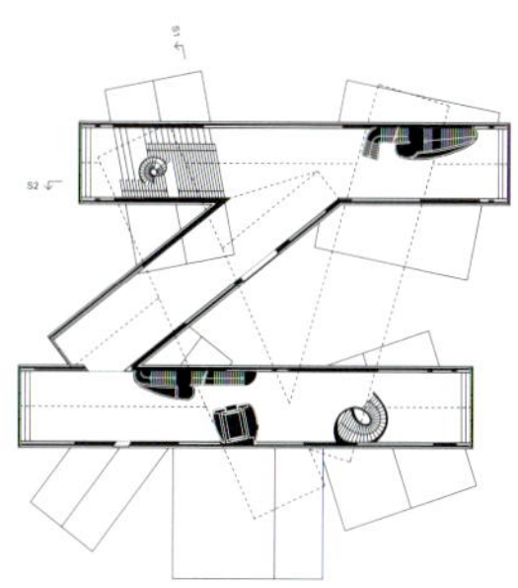

Grundriss Ebene 1 | Floor plan of Level 1

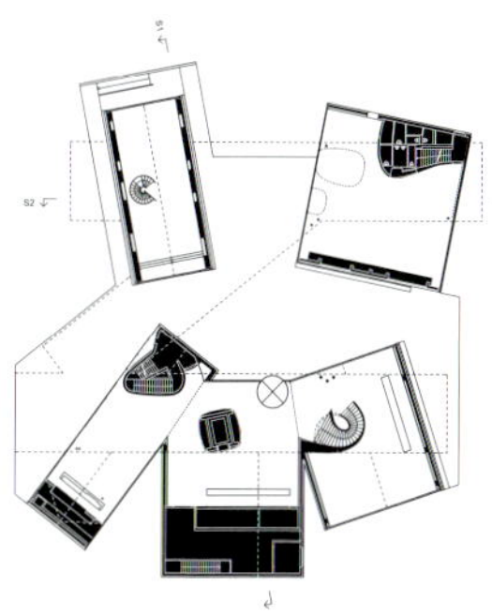

Grundriss Ebene 0 | Floor plan of Level 0

Die Komplexität im Inneren wird nicht nur durch die winkelförmige Verschneidung der einzelnen Häuser erzielt, sondern auch durch die organisch ausschwingenden Treppen zwischen den Ebenen. | The complex interiors are generated not only by the wedge-shaped overlaps between the various houses, but also by the organically undulating stairs between levels.

Die Ausrichtung der Häuser ist keinesfalls zufällig, sondern ist auf die Ausblicke abgestimmt. Die Proportionen und Dimensionen der Räume erinnern an vertraute, wohnlich konnotierte Raumsituationen. | The orientation of the houses is by no means random, but rather dictated by the views. The proportions and dimensions of the rooms recall familiar, domestic living spaces.

Von hier aus kann man auch den bunten baukünstlerischen Flickenteppich des Vitra Campus bewundern: Zaha Hadids Feuerwehrhaus, Alvaro Sizas Fabrikgebäude, Tadao Andos meditatives Konferenzzentrum und natürlich das Museumskleinod von Frank Gehry. Aber am schönsten ist die Aussicht auf die sanften Tüllinger Hügel von ganz oben im vierten Stock. Hier beginnt auch der Rundgang durch die in hedonistisches Stucco-Lustro-Weiß gekleideten Wohnszenarien, die von Boheme bis bürgerlich die gesamte Bandbreite der Vitra-Kollektion sinnlich aufblättern und der schließlich in einer tempelartig geschwungenen Vitrine mit den historischen Designklassikern der Vitra-Sammlung mündet. Inspiriert von der in Collage-Ästhetik präsentierten Möbel – der „Elephant" für Kinder von Charles & Ray Eames, der Verner Panton-Stuhl oder die Kombisysteme von Ronan & Erwan Bouroullec – kann man im VitraHaus per Chipkarte sein Lieblingsstück direkt beim Händler online ordern.

Schöner Shoppen in der Neuen Heimat der Vitra Home Collection! Herzog & de Meuron haben mit ihrer auf Synästhesie zielenden „Corporate Architecture" dazu den passenden Erlebnisrahmen geschaffen. Dabei zaubern sie mit einem Kunstgriff des Meisters Boullée, der dem Architekten als metteur de la nature en œuvre rät, aktiv in den Bereich der Empfindungen einzudringen und Gemütserregungen auszulösen. „Èmouvoir"[2] heißt das Zauberwort. Und wer wird sich dem entziehen.

promote a feeling of well-being, even clinging to the building's base zone and folding out to form benches that lead onward to the garden café. The spacious entry with its accommodating lobby character likewise caters to familiar visual habits. From there begins the discreetly guided discovery tour through the labyrinth of rooms: the complex structure of the nested longitudinal buildings results in the interior in a myriad of spaces that effortlessly lure the gaze forward as they unfold their volumes. Although not every intersection between the spiral staircases and building angles reveals a spectacular perspective, and the flow of rooms does not proceed smoothly here and there, it is a delight to wander through this new home for Vitra.

One can revel in telescopic views through the fully glazed pentagonal gable ends, which focus on the attractions in the building's environs. This is the perfect vantage point to admire the colourful architectural patchwork that is the Vitra Campus: Zaha Hadid's fire station, Alvaro Siza's factory, Tadao Ando's meditative conference centre and naturally the gem of a museum by Frank Gehry. But loveliest of all is the vista across the gently rolling Tüllinger Hills from high up on the fourth floor.

[2] Vgl. Werner Oechslin, Emouvoir – Boullée und Le Corbusier, in: Daidalos 30, 1988, S. 42f.

This is also where the discovery tour begins through hedonistic domestic scenarios arranged in their white stucco-lustro setting, treating the senses to the whole gamut of the Vitra collection from bohemian to bourgeois, culminating in a temple-like curved vitrine showcasing Vitra's historic design classics. Inspired by the collage aesthetic of the furniture presented here – the "Elephant" for children by Charles & Ray Eames, the Verner Panton chair or the combi-systems by Ronan & Erwan Bouroullec – visitors can immediately order their favourites directly from an online dealer via chipcard.

Shopping has never been more enjoyable than in the new home of the Vitra Home Collection! Herzog & de Meuron have created the perfect brand experience with their synaesthetic corporate architecture. They cast their spell using a magic trick advocated by the great master Boullée, who advised the architect, as metteur de la nature en œuvre, to actively delve into the realm of sensations in order to elicit an emotional response.

"Émouvoir"[2] is the magic word. And who can resist?

[2] See Werner Oechslin, "Emouvoir – Boullée and Le Corbusier", in: Daidalos 30, 1988, p. 42f.

Nachts werden die verglasten Stirnseiten der Häuser zu Vitrinen, die in die Umgebung leuchten.
At night, the glazed front sides of the houses turn into vitrines radiating their light into the surroundings.

ARCHITEKT | ARCHITECT

HILD UND K ARCHITEKTEN

GEBÄUDE | BUILDING

LOUIS HOTEL
AM VIKTUALIENMARKT

TEXT AXEL SIMON

10

ARCHITEKTEN | ARCHITECTS

Hild und K Architekten BDA
Andreas Hild, Dionys Ottl
Nikolaistraße 2
80802 München | Munich
www.hildundk.de

MITARBEITER | TEAM

Nina Großhauser (Projektleitung project management**), Katarzyna Kielkucka, Andrea Sommer, Stefanie Tröger**

BAUHERR | CLIENT

Grundbesitz - und Verwaltungsgesellschaft Viktualienmarkt 6 mbH, München | Munich

BAULEITUNG / PROJEKTSTEUERUNG
SITE MANAGEMENT / PROJECT GUIDANCE

Sieb Architekten, München | Munich

GENERALUNTERNEHMER
GENERAL CONTRACTOR

dh-PROJEKT Baubetreuungs- und Projektentwicklungsgesellschaft mbH, Chemnitz
Baresel GmbH, Grasbrunn

FERTIGSTELLUNG | COMPLETION

September 2009

STANDORT | LOCATION

Viktualienmarkt 6 / Rindermarkt 2
80331 München | Munich
www.louis-hotel.com

FOTOS | PHOTOS

Michael Heinrich, München | Munich
Stefan Braun, München | Munich

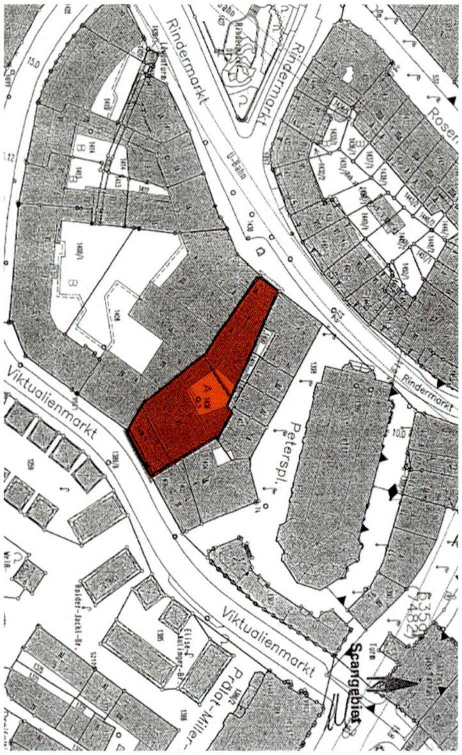

Lageplan | Site plan

Das Bestandsgebäude am Viktualienmarkt wurde zum Hotel mit Ladenpassage umgewandelt.
The existing building on Viktualienmarkt was converted into a hotel with shopping arcade.

Er war ein geübter Reisender. Immer auf der Suche nach der seltenen Mischung aus beiläufiger Selbstverständlichkeit, die entsteht, wenn kein Architekt im Spiel ist, und dieser Art Extravaganz, die nur egozentrische Architekten hinkriegen. Vor zehn Minuten hatte er noch im Menschenstrom des Viktualienmarkts gestanden, als ihm die mausgraue Fassade ins Auge stach. Hatte dort nicht noch vor wenigen Jahren ein türkises Bürohaus den Blick vom flunderplatten Peterskirchturm dahinter abgelenkt? Nun steigerten die französischen Balkone vor den Fenstern seine Vorfreude. Doch was war das: Hatten die Stuckateure die Fensterumrahmungen auf der rechten Seite vergessen? Den haushohen Schriftzug „HOTEL" haben sie jedenfalls in den Putz gedrückt.
Die Passage im Erdgeschoss führte den Reisenden, der Topografie folgend, eine Etage höher und bis ans andere Ende des Häuserblocks. Nicht die aufdringlichen Auslagen der Läden interessierten ihn (er dachte an den Handschuhmacher der

He was a seasoned traveller. Always on the lookout for that rare mixture of the casual, matter-of-fact quality that arises when no architect is involved, and the kind of extravagance that only egocentric architects are capable of producing. Just ten minutes ago, he was caught up in the crowds streaming through Munich's Viktualienmarkt when the mouse-grey façade caught his eye. Hadn't a turquoise-coloured office building once stood there, detracting from the view of the flounder-flat tower of the Church of St Peter behind it? The French balconies before the windows now quickened his

Schnitt | Section

Galerie Opera – ach, Paris!), sondern der barocke Schwung der Wände und Decken des Durchgangs. Am Ende der Passage dann der kleine Bruder des Hotels: grauer Putz, halbe Fensterrahmen. Nun verstand auch der Reisende den Sinn dieser Unvollständigkeit: Blickte er von links, verband sich die Fassade mit derjenigen des davorliegenden schlicht-barocken Hauses, blickte er von rechts, folgte sie derjenigen des dortigen Nachkriegsnachbarn. Nichts wie hinein!

Als er seine Zimmertür aufschloss, deren untere Hälfte mit Messing belegt war, erinnerte er sich, was ihn vor einigen Wochen auf das Hotel aufmerksam gemacht hatte: Die großen Räume, so stand es in einer Zeitschrift, wären wie das private Wohnzimmer von jemandem, der ein Händchen fürs Einrichten hätte. Innen begann er sogleich mit seiner rituellen Inspektion: Das Bett war ein richtiges Bett: massiver Nussbaum mit Beinen. Ein schmaler langer Schreibtisch mit brauner Ledereinlage stand im Zentrum des großen Raumes. Arbeitete man hier, ging der Blick hinüber zum Fenster und bis zu den Häusern am weiten Ende des Marktplatzes. Im Bad sah er durch ein großes Fenster zurück in den Raum. Mit Ratan bespannte Klappläden filterten den Blick – seine Großmutter besaß einst Stühle mit diesem ‚Wiener Geflecht', wie sie es immer genannt hatte. Auch die inneren Türen des Zimmers waren damit ausgefacht sowie die Lehnen von Sessel und Chaiselonge vor dem Fenster.

Er fühlte sich wohl. Mit seinen Widersprüchen hielt das Hotel seinen Geist auf Trab, lullte ihn nicht ein, wie es diese ewig gleichen Kettenfilialen rund um den Globus zu tun pflegen. Auch im Louis gab es schmiedeeiserne Lampen mit Stoffschirm, doch hier waren sie geometrisch-gradlinig. Die Sitzmöbel – auch sie,

anticipation. But, what's this? Did the stucco workers forget to complete the frames on the right sides of the windows? They at any rate pressed the huge letters "LOUIS" into the plaster.

The passage at ground level guides the traveller, following the topography, one floor higher and then to the other end of the block of buildings. The showy display windows of the shops inside are not what he's interested in (although they summoned memories of the glove maker at the Galerie Opéra – ah, Paris!), but rather the Baroque curvature of the walls and ceilings of this arcade. At the end of the walkway he then comes upon the little brother of the hotel: grey plaster, windows only half framed. Now the traveller suddenly comprehends the meaning of this incompleteness: when he looks from the left, the façade merges with that of the understated Baroque house before it; looking from the right, it harmonises with the front of its post-war neighbour on that side. Time to go inside!

When he unlocks the door to his room, the lower half of which is clad in brass, he remembers what initially drew his attention to the hotel a few weeks before: the large rooms, it said in a magazine, look like the private living room of someone who has a knack for interior decorating. Once inside, he immediately launches into his ritual inspection.

The bed is a real bed: solid walnut with legs. A long, narrow desk with a brown leather writing pad stands at the centre of the large space. Working

Die Fensterumrahmungen sind nur teilweise mit Stuckprofilen versehen. | The plaster window mouldings do not frame the windows on all sides.

Eine narrative Ästhetik bestimmt die Innenausstattung, die die Architekten entworfen haben. | The architects conceived a narrative aesthetic for the interior design.

Einheimische Hölzer ...
Native woods ...

... und Stoffe in Naturfarben ...
... and fabrics in natural shades ...

... sorgen für eine anheimelnde Atmosphäre.
... create a cosy atmosphere.

wie beinahe alles, vom Architekten entworfen – wirkten etwas steif, luden aber mit Polstern, Kissen und nur einer Armlehne zum gepflegten Fläzen ein. Nicht genug, dass die Polster der Sitzbänke mit moosgrünem Samtstoff bezogen waren: Stoffbänder banden sie ans Möbel. Farbige Berberteppiche bedeckten hier und da die geölten Eichendielen und die Schränke taten so, als seien sie Behälter aus der Pionierzeit des Reisens. Ihr feiner Wollstoff und ihre ledernen Griffe ließen den Reisenden über den Hotelnamen spekulieren: eher Louis Vuitton als Luis Trenker. Er blickte zur Decke. Schmucklose Stuckbänder rundeten den Übergang von Wand zur Decke und umschlossen in beiden Richtungen den Raum wie Kofferbeschläge, die für den physischen Schutz des Gastes zuständig waren. Noch nie, so dachte er, als beim Verlassen des Raumes sein Blick die Fliesen des Bades streifte, hatte er in der Pariser Metro gebadet.

Er entspannte sich in einem der Lobby-Sessel vor dem Restaurant und betrachtete die Wand. Holzrahmen, mit verschiedenen Geweben und Furnieren gefüllt, umgaben ein großes hellblaues Bild, schräg gegenüber ein rotes, was nach Feng-Shui-Berater

Passagenzugang vom Rindermarkt. Die Fassade eines bestehenden Ärztehauses wurde im Rahmen des Umbaus ebenfalls saniert. | Passageway to Rindermarkt. The façade of an existing medical building was also renovated during the reconstruction.

here, one can gaze out of the window all the way to the buildings at the far end of the market square. In the bathroom he can look through a large window back into the room. Rattan-covered shutters filter the view – his grandmother once had chairs with this kind of "Viennese canework", as she called it. The inside doors in the room also feature these cane panels, as do the backrests of the armchair and chaise longue set before the window.

He feels at home. With its contradictions the hotel keeps his mind alert, doesn't lull him into boredom like those cookie-cutter hotel chains around the globe. Here at the Louis there are also wrought-iron lamps with fabric shades, but now they have clear-cut geometric lines. The seating furniture – which, like almost everything here, has been designed by the architect – looks a bit stiff, but its upholstery, cushions and one-sided armrests nonetheless invite the traveller to indulge in some refined lounging. Not only are the seats upholstered in moss-green velvet: bands of the fabric also bind the cushions to the furniture. Coloured Berber rugs are scattered here and there on the oiled oak floorboards, and the cabinets pretend to be trunks from the pioneering days of travel. Their fine wool fabric and leather handles induce the traveller to speculate about the name of the hotel: more Louis Vuitton than Luis Trenker. He looks up at the ceiling. Plain stucco mouldings round off the transition between wall and ceiling and envelop the room in both directions like

Die Fliesen der Pariser Metro dienten als Vorbild.
The tiles in the Paris Metro were the model here.

roch. Tischchen aus Ulmenstämmen wie Elefantenfüße. Eine Dame in Schwarz führte ihn ins Restaurant. Seidenvorhänge, die den Viktualienmarkt rahmten, waren wie Segel gerafft. Wie könnte man den Stil der Stühle beschreiben? Louis XIV. oder Ludwig II.? Der folgende, nicht endende Fluss sonderbarer Speisen und deren Namen versetzte ihn und seinen Magen in einen tranceähnlichen Zustand. Sein Blick ging zur Decke, sah über Lampen gespannte Ziegenhäute, fragte sich, ob dazu ein Ponzu-Sesam-Dip passe. Beim Absacker-Sake an der Bar sagte er Pfau und Hase Gute Nacht. Bald sank er in der ägyptischen Baumwolle seines Bettes in tiefe Träume. Ein Architekturkritiker mit ergrautem Schnäuzer und Pailettenkleid sprang hin und her und rief „Klorollenhalter!".
Als er am Morgen erwachte, drang zartes Marktgemurmel an sein Ohr. Er war glücklich.

the fittings at the edges of a suitcase – only here they seem charged with the physical protection of the guest. Casting a glance at the tiles in the bathroom as he leaves the room, it suddenly comes to mind that he has never had a bath in the Paris Metro.
He relaxes in one of the lobby armchairs in front of the restaurant and looks at the wall. Wooden frames, filled with various fabrics and veneers, surround a large light-blue picture, diagonally opposite it a red one, which smacks of a feng shui adviser. A little table rests on elm trunks that look like elephant feet. A woman in black leads him into the restaurant. Silk curtains framing the Viktualienmarkt are gathered like a sail. How to describe the style of the chairs? Louis XIV or Ludwig II? The never-ending flow of exquisite delicacies that follows and their exotic names put him and his stomach into a trance-like state. He casts his eyes up to the ceiling, sees goatskins stretched over lamps, wonders if a ponzu sesame dip would be the right thing to go with them. With a sake nightcap at the bar he says goodnight to the peacock and the hare. Soon he sinks into the Egyptian cotton sheets and is off to dreamland.
An architecture critic with greying moustache and sequinned dress leaps back and forth crying out "toilet paper holder!"
When he awakens the next morning, the gentle murmurings of the market drift up to his ears. He is content.

Abendansicht vom Viktualienmarkt aus | Evening view from Viktualienmarkt

Restaurant im 1. Obergeschoss | 1st-floor restaurant

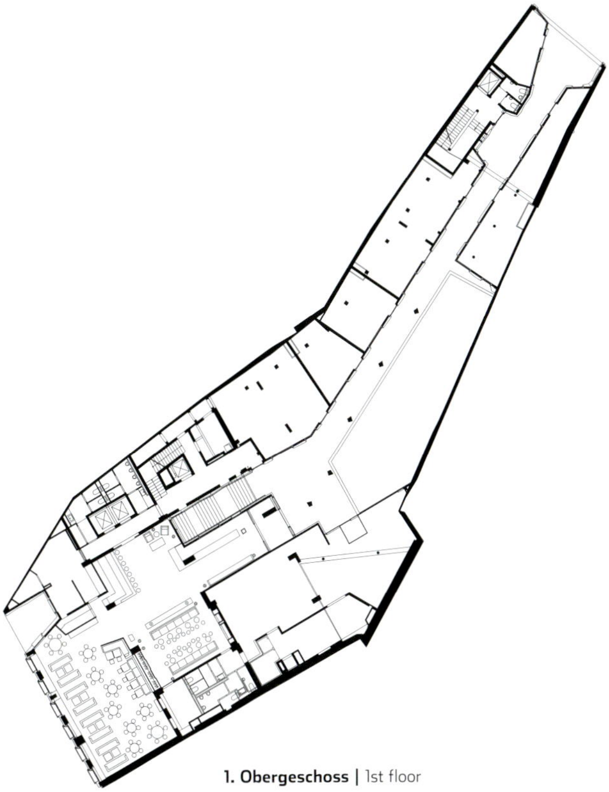

1. Obergeschoss | 1st floor

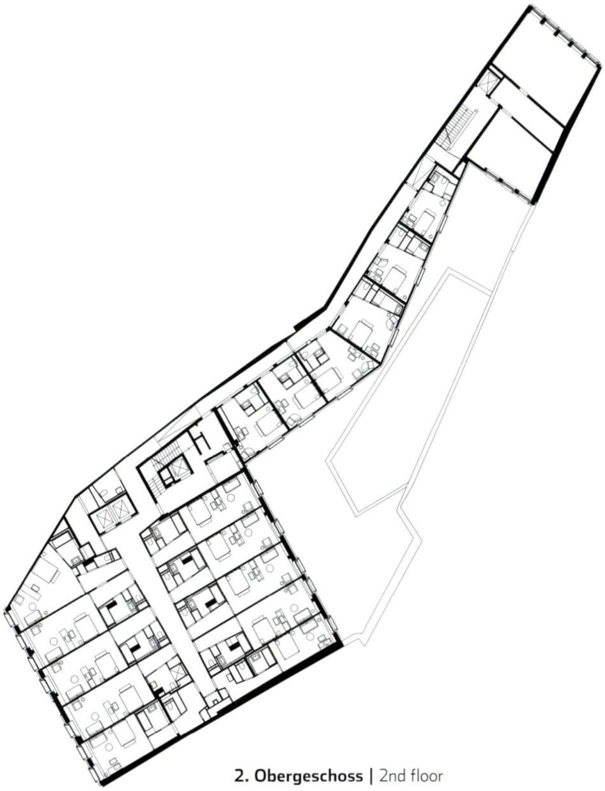

2. Obergeschoss | 2nd floor

ARCHITEKT | ARCHITECT

KARO* ARCHITEKTEN ANTJE HEUER, STEFAN RETTICH, BERT HAFERMALZ

GEBÄUDE | BUILDING

LESEZEICHEN SALBKE

TEXT FRIEDERIKE MEYER

ARCHITEKTEN | ARCHITECTS

KARO* architekten, Antje Heuer, Stefan Rettich, Bert Hafermalz
Pfaffendorfer Straße 26b
04105 Leipzig
www.karo-architekten.de

STÄDTEBAULICHER RAHMENPLAN UND PROZESSBEGLEITUNG IN ARGE MIT | URBAN MASTER PLAN AND PROCESS GUIDANCE IN CONSORTIUM WITH

Architektur+Netzwerk, Magdeburg
www.eling-saalmann.com

MITARBEITER | TEAM

Christian Burkhardt, Gregor Schneider, Mandy Neuenfeld

BAUHERR | CLIENT

Landeshauptstadt Magdeburg

PROJEKTFÖRDERUNG PROJECT FUNDING

Bundesministerium für Verkehr, Bau und Stadtentwicklung/ Bundesamt für Bauwesen und Raumordnung, Abteilung ExWoSt

PROJEKTPARTNER PROJECT PARTNER

Bürgerverein Salbke-Fermersleben-Westerhüsen e. V.

BAULEITUNG | SITE MANAGEMENT

Ingenieurbüro Schröder, Magdeburg

TRAGWERK | STRUCTURE

Michael Kurt, Leipzig

LICHTKONZEPT UND HAUSTECHNIK | LIGHTING CONCEPT AND M & E ENGINEERS

Jürgen Meier, architektur&medien, Leipzig

FERTIGSTELLUNG | COMPLETION

Juni 2009 | June 2009

STANDORT | LOCATION

Alt Salbke 37
39122 Magdeburg

FOTOS | PHOTOS

Anja Schlamann, Köln/Leipzig | Cologne/Leipzig

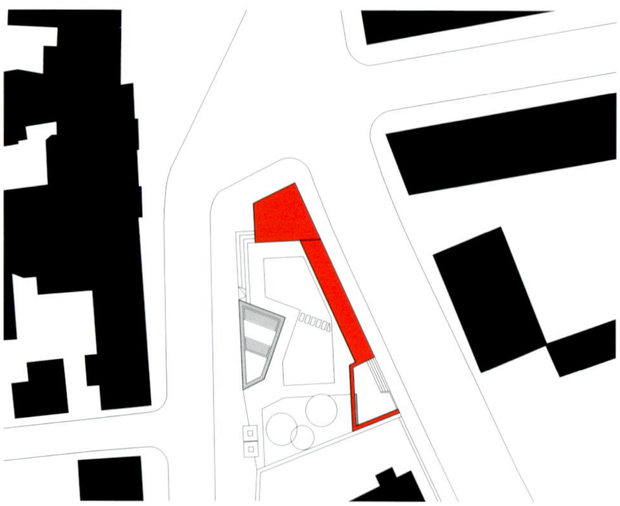

Lageplan | Site plan

Aus dem Beteiligungsprozess mit den Bürgern ging die Idee eines ‚grünen Wohnzimmers' hervor, das geschützt vom Straßenlärm eine Ruhezone im Stadtteil bieten soll. | Citizen participation in the planning process gave rise to the idea of a "green living room" protected from street noise, which would offer a tranquil oasis for the city district.

Salbke ist kein attraktiver Ort. Als nach der Wende die Schwerindustrie zusammenbrach, gingen hier, im Südosten von Magdeburg, 6000 Arbeitsplätze verloren. Entsprechend vernachlässigt wirken die Häuser an der Durchfahrtsstraße, das Angebot der wenigen Geschäfte beschränkt sich auf Lebenswichtiges. Sein Schicksal teilt der Stadtteil mit vielen anderen, vom demografischen Wandel gebeutelten Gebieten in Deutschland. Doch für die Bewohner, organisiert in einem rührigen Verein, war dies kein Grund zu resignieren. Mit der Hilfe von Architekten haben sie eine Freiluftbibliothek eingerichtet, die viel mehr geworden ist als eine Anlaufstelle für Lesende. Das „Lesezeichen Salbke" ist Treffpunkt und Ortsmitte, Schulaula und Konzertbühne, Spielplatz und Garten zugleich.

Salbke is not an attractive spot. When heavy industry collapsed following reunification, 6,000 jobs were lost here in the south-eastern part of Magdeburg. The buildings lining the through-road look correspondingly run-down, and the goods on offer in the few shops are limited to the necessities of life. This city district shares its fate with many areas of Germany that are likewise suffering from demographic change. But for the residents, organised into an enterprising civic association, this is no reason for resignation. Enlisting the aid of architects, they have established an open-air library that has become much more than just a centre for

Auffälligstes Merkmal des Objekts ist die Fassade aus tiefgezogenen Aluminiumformteilen.
The structure's most conspicuous feature is the façade of deep-drawn moulded aluminium panels.

readers. The "Lesezeichen Salbke" (Salbke Bookmark) is a meeting point and town square, school auditorium and concert stage, playground and garden.

At the behest of the town planning office, Sabine Eling-Saalmann from the firm Architektur + Netzwerk and Stefan Rettich from KARO* came to Salbke for the first time in 2004. They were asked to supply ideas for derelict areas, and for a 500-square-metre plot at the edge of the through-road where the district library had burned down in the mid-1980s. Their proposal to take up the theme of reading again led to a workshop. For one week, suggestions were collected, children made models, and people brought along books. Finally, they came up with the idea of giving Salbke a kind of communal green living room, shielded from street noise, with a stage and seating, cabinets for books and a tower as signal.

On a dark, cloudy day in October 2005, a beverage service in Salbke unloaded 1,000 empty beer crates at the site. After two days they had been transformed into a sculpture with the help of cable ties. Everyone pitched in – the residents, the architects and a few employees from the town planning office – to give shape to their idea on the empty plot of land. The reading festival was attended by authors from Berlin and Dresden, and in the evening a band played. People had once again brought books with them. But everyone realised that the beer crates were no long-term solution.

The architects could have simply added the beer crate action to their portfolio and moved on to the

Weil die Baustelle bereits nach zwei Tagen beschmiert war, entstand die Idee, den Betonsockel von Graffiti-Künstlern gestalten zu lassen. Einzige Vorgabe für den Wettbewerb war die Reduzierung auf die Farben Schwarz, Weiß und Chrom. | As the building site was already "tagged" after two days, the planners came up with the idea of having grafftti artists design the concrete base. The only competition specification was a reduction of the palette to black, white and chrome.

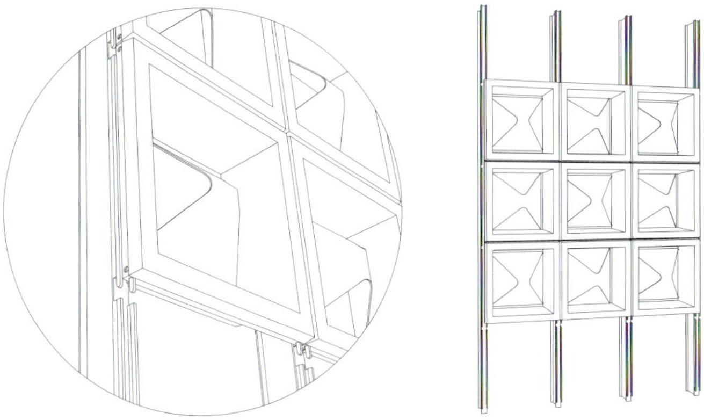

Fassadensystem aus Aluminiumformteilen
Façade system of moulded aluminium panels

Im Auftrag des Stadtplanungsamtes kamen Sabine Eling-Saalmann von Architektur + Netzwerk und Stefan Rettich von KARO* im Jahr 2004 erstmals nach Salbke. Ideen für Brachflächen sollten sie liefern, auch für jene 500 Quadratmeter am Rand der Durchfahrtsstraße, wo Mitte der 1980er-Jahre die Stadtteilbibliothek abgebrannt war. Ihr Vorschlag, das Thema Lesen wieder aufzunehmen, führte zu einem Workshop. Eine Woche lang wurden Vorschläge gesammelt, die Kinder bastelten Modelle, manche brachten Bücher vorbei. Schließlich stand fest: Salbke soll eine Art grünes Wohnzimmer bekommen, abgeschirmt vom Straßenlärm, mit Bühne und Sitzgelegenheiten, mit Schränken für Bücher und einem Turm als Signal.

An einem trüben nebligen Tag im Oktober 2005 lud ein Getränkelieferant in Salbke 1000 leere Bierkästen ab. Nach zwei Tagen waren sie, dank Kabelbindern, zu einer Skulptur geworden. Alle gemeinsam, die Bewohner, die Architekten und einige Mitarbeiter des Stadtplanungsamts, hatten ihre Idee auf das Grundstück gebaut. Zum Lesefest kamen Autoren aus Berlin und Dresden, am Abend spielte eine Band. Wieder hatten Leute Bücher vorbeigebracht. Dass die Bierkisten nicht dauerhaft stehen bleiben konnten, war allen klar.

Die Architekten hätten die Bierkistenaktion in ihr Portfolio aufnehmen und sich einem anderen Projekt widmen können. Doch sie stellten die geplante Freiluftbibliothek beim Bundesamt für Bauwesen und Raumordnung vor. Dessen Förderprogramm „ExWoSt“ versprach Geld für experimentellen Wohn- und Städtebau. Zum Empfang der Vertreter des Bundesamtes an einem heißen Sommertag mähten die Salbker ein paar Quadratmeter Wiese, kochten Kaffee und stellten einen Sonnenschirm auf. „Sie haben gesehen, wir meinen das ernst“, erinnert sich Rainer Mann vom Bürgerverein.

next project. But instead they presented the plans for the open-air library to the Federal Office for Building and Regional Planning. Its "ExWoSt" promotion programme promised funds to experimental residential and urban building projects. To prepare for the visit by representatives from the federal authority, the people of Salbke mowed a few square metres of meadow, made coffee and put up a sunshade. "They could see we mean business," Rainer Mann from the civic association remembers. The federal government ended up supplying 325,000 euros for the construction, and Magdeburg contributed 20,000 euros for purchasing the land. The Lesezeichen rose again, but this time as a steel-framed structure on a concrete base, with display cases on the street side and seating niches

In der äußeren Fassade sind gläserne Aluminiumvitrinen eingelassen, die als Info-Boards des Stadtteils dienen.
Aluminium-framed glass display cases are incorporated into the façade to serve as info boards for the district.

72
71

325 000 Euro stellte der Bund für den Bau bereit, 20 000 Euro die Stadt Magdeburg für den Erwerb des Grundstücks. Das Lesezeichen entstand erneut, nun aber auf einem Betonsockel, als Stahlrahmenwandkonstruktion, mit Vitrinen auf der Straßenseite und Sitznischen mit Bücherregalen auf der holzverkleideten Innenseite. Eine 30 Meter lange Bank spannt davor, ein Dach am Turm schützt die kleine Bühne.
Während der Planungsphase erfuhr Stefan Rettich vom Abriss des ehemaligen Horten-Warenhauses im westfälischen Hamm, das, wie andere Warenhäuser seiner Zeit, mit einer ornamentalen Fassade verkleidet war. Die Verwaltung von Hamm verkaufte einige Hundert der Hortenkacheln aus Aluminium zu Preisen unter Materialwert, um das Projekt in Salbke zu unterstützen. Die Module wurden chemisch entlackt und mit einer neuen Pulverbeschichtung überzogen; für die Verwendung der 40 Jahre alten Bauteile ohne Zertifikat gab es schließlich eine „Zustimmung im Einzelfall". Die Kommunikation von Stefan Rettich mit den Fachbehörden der Stadt füllt unverhältnismäßig viele Ordner. Sie zeugen einerseits von seiner Beharrlichkeit, andererseits aber auch von den hohen Genehmigungshürden, die ungewöhnlichen Bauwerken hierzulande häufig in den Weg gerückt werden.
„Bei dem Projekt", schreibt der Architekt, „geht es um Bewusstseinsveränderung und um die Arbeit an der Gemeinschaft. Darum, die Möglichkeit von Stadt auch an vermeintlichen Unorten zu testen und unerwartete Handlungsoptionen aufzudecken – wir nennen das ‚situativen Urbanismus'."
Seit der Eröffnung des Lesezeichens im Sommer 2009 ist im unmittelbaren Umfeld einiges passiert. Salbke hat eine neue Haltestelle bekommen, zwei leer stehende Häuser sind an Einheimische mit Sanierungsabsicht verkauft worden, die beiden vietnamesischen Lokale haben ihre Fassaden renoviert. Ein Einzelfall seien die eingeschlagenen Scheiben der Sitzecken, heißt es, das Verfahren gegen die Täter läuft. Die Jugendlichen haben das Lesezeichen als Freiraum entdeckt, die Schule verabschiedet ihre Schüler auf dessen Bühne, der Verein organisiert Konzerte und freut sich über den regen Bücheraustausch. Ehrenamtlich hält er zusätzlich ein Ladenlokal mit mittlerweile rund 34 000 Büchern geöffnet.

with bookshelves in the wood-panelled interior. A 30-metre bench stretches along the front, and a roof on the tower shelters the small stage.
During the planning phase Stefan Rettich learned that a former Horten department store was to be torn down in the Westphalian city of Hamm – one that, like other department stores of its era, had an ornamental façade. The municipal administration in Hamm sold a few hundred of the Horten aluminium façade tiles at a price below their material value to support the project in Salbke. The modules were chemically stripped of their paint and given a new powder coating; despite the lack of a certificate, the use of the 40-year-old components was approved on an "individual case basis". Stefan Rettich's correspondence with the municipal authorities fills many more binders than the usual project. They attest both to his persistence and to the high approval hurdles that are frequently placed in the way of unusual structures in this country.

Aluminiumformteilfassade zur Straße, Holzverkleidung zum geschützten Freiraum. Sitznischen in der Wand vermitteln dazwischen, mit Sicherheitsglas sind sie gegen den Straßenlärm geschützt. | Moulded aluminium panel façade on the street side, wooden panelling in the protected outdoor space. Seat niches are built into the wall in between, protected by safety glass from street noise.

"This project", writes the architect, "is all about a change in awareness and working for the good of the community. It's about a city testing out the potential of supposed non-locations and uncovering unexpected options for taking action – we call it situational urbanism."
Since the opening of the Lesezeichen in summer 2009 a great deal has happened in its vicinity. Salbke now has a new bus stop, two vacant houses have been sold to locals who plan to refurbish them, and the two Vietnamese restaurants nearby have renovated their façades. The smashed windows of the seating areas are an isolated incident, people say, and the offenders are being prosecuted. Young people have discovered the Lesezeichen as a hangout, graduation ceremonies take place on its stage, and the civic association organises concerts and is gratified to witness the lively exchange of books. Volunteers from its ranks also run a shop that today offers some 34,000 books for sale.

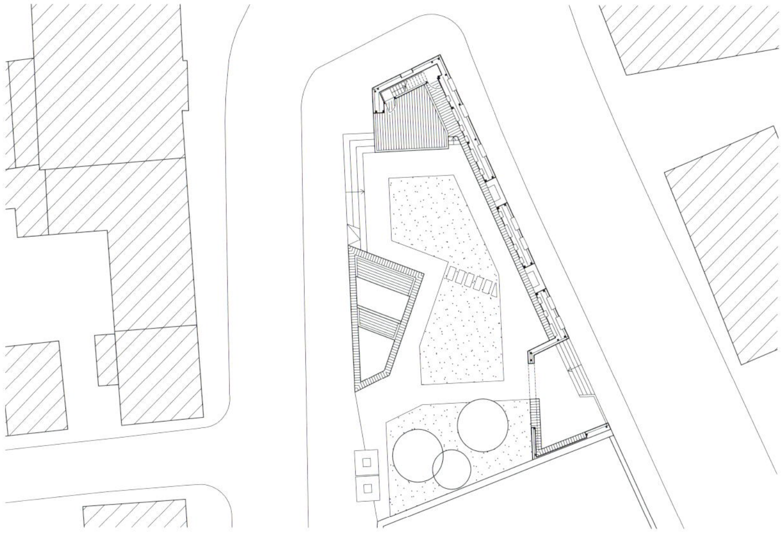

Grundriss | Floor plan

Das Lesezeichen steht heute als neues „Village Icon" für den Aufbruch des Stadtteils nach Jahren starker demografischer Schrumpfung. | The open-air library as new "village icon" stands today for a reawakening of the district after years of strong demographic shrinkage.

ARCHITEKT | ARCHITECT

LEDERER + RAGNARSDÓTTIR + OEI

GEBÄUDE | BUILDING

KLOSTER HEGNE MARIANUM
ZENTRUM FÜR BILDUNG UND ERZIEHUNG

TEXT CHRISTIAN HOLL

12

ARCHITEKTEN | ARCHITECTS

Lederer + Ragnarsdóttir + Oei
Kornbergstraße 36
70176 Stuttgart
www.archlro.de

WETTBEWERB UND ENTWURF
COMPETITION AND SCHEMATIC DESIGN

Lederer + Ragnarsdóttir + Oei

MITARBEITER | TEAM

Thilo Holzer, Matthias Schneider

BAUHERR | CLIENT

Kongregation der Barmherzigen Schwestern vom Heiligen Kreuz von Ingenbohl in Hegne, Provinz Baden-Württemberg, Allensbach-Hegne

TRAGWERK | STRUCTURE

Ingenieurbüro Baur, Singen-Hausen

HAUSTECHNIK | M & E ENGINEERS

Planungsbüro Sütterlin + Partner GbR, Freiburg i. Br.

LANDSCHAFTSARCHITEKTEN
LANDSCAPE ARCHITECTS

Helmut Hornstein, Überlingen / Bodensee

FERTIGSTELLUNG | COMPLETION

Dezember 2008 | December 2008

STANDORT | LOCATION

Konradistraße 16
78476 Allensbach-Hegne
www.marianum-hegne.de

FOTOS | PHOTOS

Zooey Braun, Stuttgart

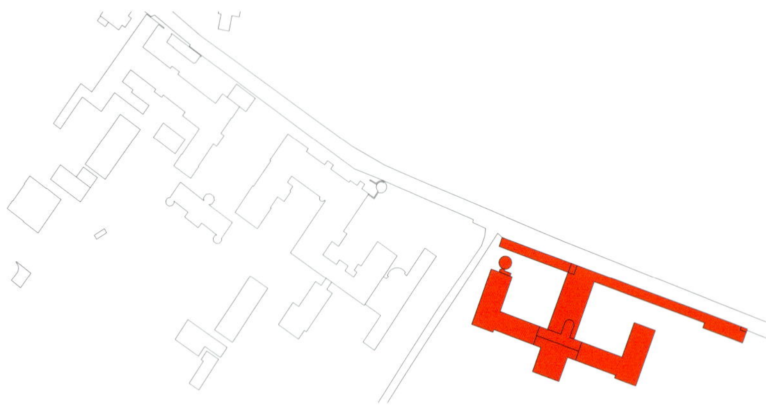

Lageplan | Site plan

Der Entwurf thematisiert die Kontinuität des Ortes, der Gestalt und der Geschichte.
The theme of the design is the continuity of the place, its form and its history.

Der einleitende Satz, mit dem das Kloster Hegne auf seiner Internetseite die Schule charakterisiert, könnte die Architektur nicht besser beschreiben: „Alles hat sein Eigenleben, aber nichts lebt nur für sich allein." Gebaut hat diese Schule das Büro Lederer Ragnarsdóttir Oei Architekten. Den Altbau von 1927 hatte man in den 1960er-Jahren erweitert, doch der Neubau war zu sehr mit Schadstoffen belastet gewesen, als dass man ihn hätte erhalten können. Den Wettbewerb für einen abermaligen Neubau gewannen LRO Architekten mit dem Vorschlag, das bestehende Gebäude zu spiegeln und die so entstehende, zweiflüglige Anlage mit einer schmalen, die Straße begleitenden, eingeschossigen Bebauung im Charakter einer Mauer zu schließen. In der Mittelachse zwischen den Schulhäusern vervollständigen eine Mensa, ein gedeckter Eingangsbereich, Foyer und Musikraum sowie die im

The introductory sentence with which Hegne Monastery characterises its school on its website could not describe the architecture any better: "Everything has its own life, but nothing lives for itself alone." The school was built by the firm of Lederer Ragnarsdóttir Oei Architekten. The original 1927 building had been extended in the 1960s, but it was later discovered that the new sections contained too many harmful substances to be retained. LRO Architekten won the competition to replace the 1960s annexe by presenting a proposal to mirror the existing building, closing the resulting two-wing complex with a narrow one-storey structure along the street that has the character of a wall. In the central axis between the two school

Den nördlichen Abschluss der Anlage bildet eine breite Mauer. Ein Hackschnitzelkraftwerk und dessen Schornstein markiert die Grenze zur Landschaft. | The northern border of the complex is formed by a broad wall. A wood-chip power plant and its smokestack mark the boundary with the landscape.

In der Mitte der neuen Anlage liegen die gemeinsamen Verpflegungs- und Veranstaltungsräume. | In the middle of the new annexe are the common dining and event rooms.

Mensa, Eingangsbereich und Loggien sind mit flachen Kappen überwölbt, deren Konstruktionsmaterial sichtbar bleibt. | Cafeteria, entrance area and loggias are vaulted with shallow domes whose construction material remains visible.

Untergeschoss in den leicht abfallenden Hang eingeschobene Turnhalle das Ensemble. Es entstand ein Komplex aus zwei Höfen.
Die Anlage greift die das Kloster prägenden Themen der Symmetrie sowie der Höfe auf und verbindet sie in einer dem Kloster adäquaten Form eines übersichtlichen Schutzraums, der jene Distanz zur Welt schafft, derer es bedarf, um ihr gelassen gegenübertreten zu können. In diesem Sinne werden Offenheit und Geschlossenheit als ein aufeinander bezogenes Paar von Raumqualitäten gestaltet. Nie ist die Anlage so weit geschlossen, dass der Bezug zur Landschaft verloren ginge. Das hätte man ihr hier, so direkt am Bodensee, mit Blick auf die Insel Reichenau, auch nicht verziehen. Umso schöner, wie Landschaft, Weg, Haus und Funktion zueinander in Beziehung gesetzt werden. Wer über den Hof das zwischen beiden Schulhäusern liegende Foyer betritt, sieht hinaus zum See, die beiden Gebäude, das eine für die Berufs-, das andere für die Realschule, sind untereinander mit einer offenen, mehrgeschossigen Loggia verbunden. Und von allen Stockwerken ist der See zu sehen. Gedanken, wie man Räume erlebt, benutzt und sich ihrer bewusst wird, werden miteinander verknüpft. So muss man durch einen gedeckten, aber offenen Bereich gehen, um in die Mensa zu gelangen: Zwischen Schule und Essen wird eine Zäsur gesetzt, die es erlaubt, Abstand zu nehmen.
Am besten lässt sich die besondere Qualität aus Offen und Geschlossen an der den nördlichen Abschluss bildenden, breiten Mauer zeigen. Sie ist zur Straße, zur Richtung, aus der man sich der Schule nähert, geöffnet. Es schließen sich ein Glockenturm und die Nebenräume der in der Mittelspange untergebrachten Mensa an. Anschließend wird die Mauer in durchlässige Scheiben aufgelöst: Hier sind Parkplätze untergebracht. Über den zweiten Hof hinaus leitet die Mauer in die Landschaft über. Ein Hackschnitzelkraftwerk und dessen Schornstein markiert Grenze und Übergang zwischen dem Raum der Schule und dem der Landschaft.
Mensa, Eingangsbereich und Loggien sind mit flachen Kappen überwölbt, deren Konstruktionsmaterial (Ziegelelemente) sichtbar bleibt; sie stehen für die Sorgfalt im Umgang mit der Einfachheit. Alle die beiden Haupthäuser verbindende Bauten changieren zwischen landschaftlichem, architektonischem,

houses, a cafeteria, a covered entrance area, a foyer and a music room now complete the ensemble, together with a gymnasium inserted in the lower storey, which is set on a slight slope. The result is a complex with two courtyards.
The ensemble takes up the themes of symmetry and courtyards that shape the monastery's design and combines them with the idea of a compact sheltered refuge that is integral to monastic life, creating that modicum of distance from the world outside needed to face it with assurance. In this spirit, openness and closure are conceived here as an interrelated pair of spatial qualities. The complex is never so self-contained that it loses its dialogue with the surrounding landscape. This would indeed be inexcusable in this lovely setting, directly on Lake Constance, with a view of Reichenau Island. The way landscape, pathways, building and function have been related here is hence all the more admirable. Proceeding through the courtyard and entering the foyer between the two school buildings, one can look out toward the lake. The two buildings, one housing a vocational school and the other a secondary school, are united by an open, multi-storey loggia. And lake vistas can be enjoyed from every floor. Thoughts of how people experience, use and become conscious of spaces are linked here. It is therefore necessary to walk through a covered, yet open, area to reach the cafeteria: this creates a caesura between school and dining, allowing students and teachers to first gain a little distance.
The best place to get an impression of the special quality of openness and closure here is at the stout wall closing off the complex to the north. It opens onto the street, to the direction from which one approaches the school. Adjacent are a bell tower and the auxiliary spaces of the cafeteria that is housed in the middle, connecting, section. The wall then breaks up into permeable slices: this is where the parking spaces have been integrated. Beyond the second courtyard the wall leads out into the landscape. A wood-chip power plant and its smokestack mark the border and transition between school and landscape.
Cafeteria, entrance area and loggias are covered with shallow vaults whose construction material (brick elements) is left visible. They stand for the careful simplicity that has been aimed at here. All of the structures connecting the two main buildings oscillate between landscape, architectural, integrated and object-like character. Their look is achieved through light-coloured, variegated clinker bricks which have been laid to leave their base sides visible, enlivening

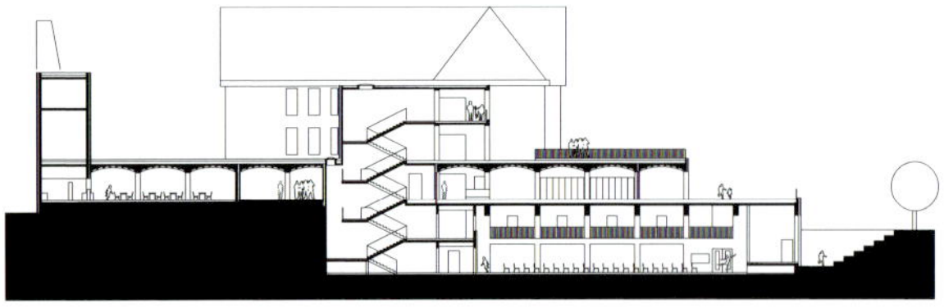

Schnitt | Section

Nie ist die Anlage so weit geschlossen, dass der Bezug zur Landschaft direkt am Bodensee verloren ginge.
The ensemble is never so self-contained that it loses sight of its relationship with the landscape setting directly on Lake Constance.

integriertem und objekthaftem Charakter. Sie sind von einem hellen, bunt geflammten Klinker geprägt, deren Fußseiten als Sichtseite eingemauert sind und so die Flächen beleben. Dazu im Kontrast stehen die beiden weiß verputzten, dunkelgrau eingedeckten Schulhäuser. Sie können so ebenfalls ihr Eigenleben bewahren – der Neubau paraphrasiert den Altbau, ohne ihn zu kopieren.
Auch im Inneren wechseln sich offene und geschlossene Räume ab, Gruppenarbeit und offener Unterricht lassen sich integrieren; die Lehrer haben Arbeitsplätze in den Klassenzimmern. Weiße Wände kontrastieren mit solchen aus dem bunten Klinker – das Thema der die Funktionen zusammenbindenden Mauer kehrt wieder. Unter Bänken in Nischen können Taschen verstaut werden; die oberen Öffnungsflügel der Fenster werden durch Manschetten geschützt, sodass bei jedem Wetter gelüftet werden kann.
Konzentriert findet sich die Haltung der Architekten zwischen Neuerfindung, Erweiterung und Verwandlung des Bestandes im Raum der Stille, der direkt an das Nordende des bestehenden Baues angefügt wurde und von einem mit Rosen bepflanzten Umgang eingefasst wird. Der Raum der Stille ist ein Zentralraum in einer einfachen, innen schwarz gestrichenen Holzkonstruktion. In sie wurden die Glasfenster der Kappelle des Vorgängerbaus aus den 1960er-Jahren eingesetzt. Die Glasfenster wurden neu nach Farben gruppiert und verleihen dem Ort je nach Licht und Tageszeit eine jeweils eigene, besondere Atmosphäre – ein Eigenleben eben, das nicht nur für sich alleine lebt.

the surfaces. Contrasting with the brick masonry are the two white stucco schoolhouses with their dark grey roofs. They are thus likewise allowed to maintain their own life – the new construction paraphrases the old, without copying it.
Inside as well, open and closed rooms alternate, making space for both group work and open instruction; the teachers have offices within the classrooms. White walls contrast with multicoloured brick masonry – the theme of the wall that connects different functions returns. Bags can be stowed under benches set in niches, and the upper opening wings of the windows are protected by sleeves so that the rooms can be aired even in inclement weather.
The architects' strategy of invention, extension and transformation of the existing building fabric can be found in concentrated form in the Room of Silence, which was added directly onto the northern end of the existing building, enclosed by a rose-covered bower. The Room of Silence, in a plain wooden structure painted black inside, has a central ground plan. The stained-glass windows of the chapel from the previous 1960s building have been set into this framework. These windows have been rearranged according to colour and lend the scene a special atmosphere depending on the light and time of day – it then truly takes on its own life, while yet not living for itself alone.

Die Materialität des bunten Klinker (hier im Foyer mit Pforte) wechselt ... | The material properties of the multicoloured bricks (here in the foyer with portal) alternate ...

... mit weißen Wänden (hier im Lehrerzimmer).
... with white walls (here in the teachers' room).

Der Raum der Stille im Bibliothekshof nördlich des Bestandsgebäudes. Die Fenster der alten Kapelle wurden integriert. | The Room of Silence in the library courtyard north of the previously existing building. The windows of the old chapel were integrated here.

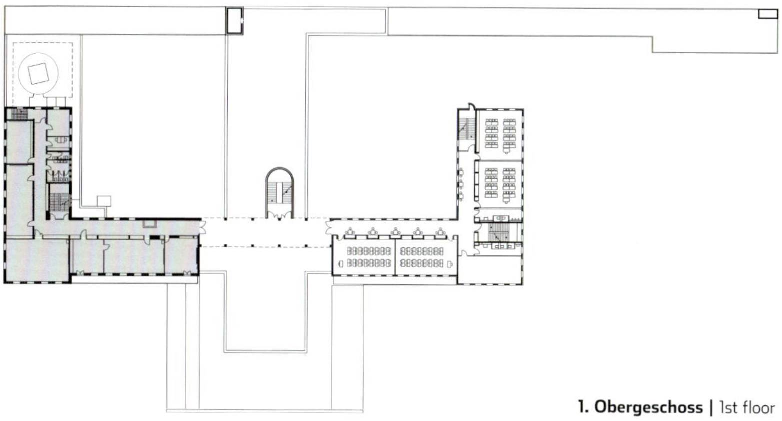

1. Obergeschoss | 1st floor

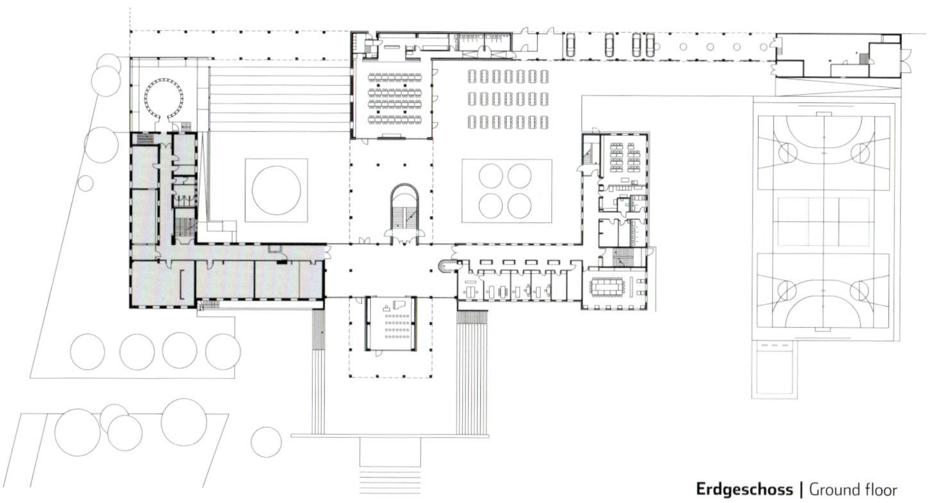

Erdgeschoss | Ground floor

ARCHITEKT | ARCHITECT

MAX DUDLER

GEBÄUDE | BUILDING

JACOB-UND-WILHELM-GRIMM-ZENTRUM
HUMBOLDT-UNIVERSITÄT ZU BERLIN

TEXT OLIVER ELSER

13

ARCHITEKTEN | ARCHITECTS

Max Dudler
Oranienplatz 4
10999 Berlin
www.maxdudler.de

STÄDTEBAULICHER RAHMENPLAN, BAUANTRAG GESAMTENSEMBLE
URBAN MASTER PLAN, BUILDING APPLICATION FOR COMPLETE ENSEMBLE

Max Dudler

WETTBEWERB UND ENTWURF
COMPETITION AND SCHEMATIC DESIGN

Max Dudler

MITARBEITER | TEAM

Jochen Soydan, Andreas Enge (Projektleitung project management**), Andrea Deckert, Gesine Gummi**

BAUHERR | CLIENT

Humboldt-Universität zu Berlin, vertreten durch ihre Technische Abteilung Baudienststelle: Senatsverwaltung für Stadtentwicklung, Abteilung V

BAULEITUNG / PROJEKTSTEUERUNG | SITE MANAGEMENT / PROJECT GUIDANCE

ProCon Ingenieurgesellschaft für wirtschaftliches Bauen mbH

TRAGWERK | STRUCTURE

Leonhardt, Andrä und Partner, Berlin

ENERGIEKONZEPT
ENERGY CONCEPT

ZWP Ingenieur-AG, Berlin

HAUSTECHNIK | M & E ENGINEERS

ZWP Ingenieur-AG, Berlin

LANDSCHAFTSARCHITEKTEN
LANDSCAPE ARCHITECTS

Max Dudler mit | with **Lützow 7 Landschaftsarchitekten, Berlin**

KUNST AM BAU | ART

Arun Kuplas, R. Wickert

FERTIGSTELLUNG | COMPLETION

Oktober | October **2009**

STANDORT | LOCATION

Geschwister-Scholl-Straße 1
10117 Berlin-Mitte
www.grimm-zentrum.hu-berlin.de

FOTOS | PHOTOS

Stefan Müller, Berlin

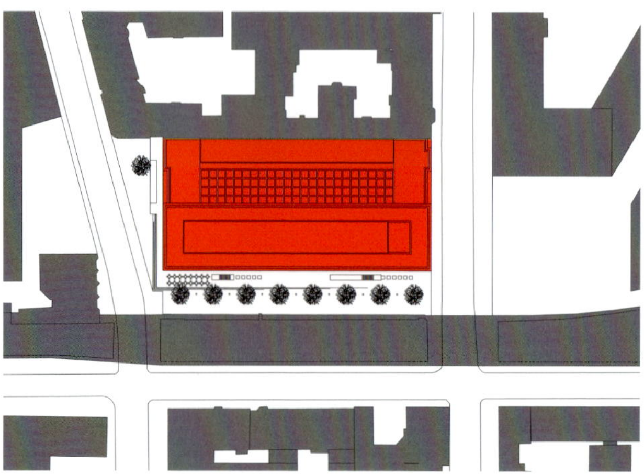

Lageplan | Site plan

Haupteingang | Main entrance

Das Foto des großen Lesesaals der neuen Zentralbibliothek der Humboldt-Universität zählt zu den betörendsten Architekturaufnahmen der vergangenen Jahre. Doch so schwer es auch fällt, sich der Sogwirkung des hölzernen Raumgitters zu entziehen – am realen Bauwerk scheiden sich die Geister: Gilt es den einen als „Gesamtkunstwerk" (FAZ), wird andernorts im Feuilleton die äußere Erscheinung als „übergeometrisierte Apotheose des Friedrichstraßen-Stils" (Süddeutsche Zeitung) in Zweifel gezogen oder die Organisation der Betriebsabläufe infrage gestellt (FAZ und Süddeutsche Zeitung).
Tatsächlich kann sich der Benutzer, wenn er denn als Leser kommt, zunächst also Mantel und Tasche loswerden muss, darüber wundern, dass ihn der Weg als Erstes über mehrere Treppenwindungen zu den Schließfächern in den Keller führt. Andererseits herrschte beim Probebesuch im März, also vier Monate nach Eröffnung, gerade dort, tief unten inmitten von

The view of the big reading room in the new central library at Humboldt University in Berlin is among the most beguiling architectural photographs of recent years. But no matter how hard it is to escape the mesmerism of the room's wooden grid – opinions are nonetheless divided on the structure itself. While some regard it as a "total work of art" ("Frankfurter Allgemeine Zeitung" newspaper), elsewhere arts and review pages look askance at this "over-geometricised apotheosis of the Friedrichstrasse style" ("Süddeutsche Zeitung") or call into question how day-to-day operations are organised here ("FAZ" and "Süddeutsche Zeitung"). And in fact visitors who come here to read, and hence must first check in their coats and bags, might be quite surprised to find they have to descend a long

Blick von Südosten | View from the south-east

Blick aus der Universitätsstraße | View from Universitätsstrasse

Highschool-Stahlschränken, eine herzliche, geradezu aufgekratzte Stimmung. Bevor es wieder hinaufgeht in die Flüsterzonen der heiligen Lesehallen werden laut schnatternd letzte Alltagsdinge besprochen. Vielleicht muss das so sein: Die Umkleidekabinen im Stadion von Bayern München sind schließlich auch kein architektonisches Highlight, sondern nur Durchgangsstation zum großen Auftritt. Diesen erleben die Leserinnen und Leser im Jacob-und-Wilhelm-Grimm-Zentrum bereits knapp hinter der Sicherheitsschleuse. Denn entgegen aller Erwartungen ist die Bibliothek ein transparentes, geradezu luftiges Haus, in dem, nicht nur im großen Lesesaal, ein Spiel des Durchschreitens und der Durchblicke inszeniert wird. Nicht wenige der Studentinnen und Studenten sehen aus, als wären sie gerade vom Laufsteg einer Modenschau herabgestiegen. Deutschlands größte Freihandbibliothek mit 1,5 Millionen offen zugänglichen Bänden und circa 1250 Leseplätzen ist dank eines so einfachen wie bezwingenden Prinzips kein hermetischer Bücherspeicher geworden. Max Dudler hat das bereits bei seiner Diözesanbibliothek in Münster (2002–2005) erprobte System, die Architektur bis ins letzte Detail auf die Breite eines beidseitig zugänglichen Bücherregals abzustimmen, in Berlin zur Vollendung gebracht. Sämtliche Stützen, Gänge, Fenster, Durchgänge und Blickachsen sind in das allumfassende Raster der Bücherregale eingespannt.

Wirkt das nun aufgeräumt oder schlägt es um ins Manische, in eine Geometrie-Obsession, für die Max Dudler als einstiger Meisterschüler von Oswald Mathias Ungers gewiss prädestiniert wäre? Es dürfte schwerfallen, an dieser Stelle die Skeptiker vom Gegenteil zu überzeugen, zeigt sich doch auf den Architekturfotos, bei aller Faszination, eine gewisse Vergatterung des Blicks. Doch das Gegenteil ist der Fall: Wer die Bibliothek

Eingangshalle | Entrance hall

stairway over several turns to reach the lockers in the basement. On the other hand, at a test visit in March, four months after the opening, a mood of warmth, even high-spirited excitement still prevailed down below amongst the high-schoolish lockers. Before ascending to the whispering zones of the sacred reading halls, students take advantage of this last chance to discuss everyday matters in a loud chatter. Perhaps this is just the way it should be: after all, the locker rooms at the stadium where the Bayern München football team plays are not exactly an architectural highlight either, but merely a way-station before the grand entrance. Readers at the Jacob and Wilhelm Grimm Centre experience this entrée as soon as they pass through the security gates because, against all expectations, the library is a transparent, even airy building in which a game of passing through and looking through is staged, not only in the huge reading room. More than a few of the students look as though they have just alighted from a fashion-show catwalk.
Thanks to a principle that is both simple and compelling, Germany's largest open-stack library, with 1.5 million volumes available to the public and some 1,250 seats for readers, has become anything but a hermetic book warehouse. Max Dudler has perfected here in Berlin a system that he already tested out in his Diocese Library in Münster (2002–2005), which calls for reconciling the architecture down to the last detail with the width of a bookshelf that is accessible on both sides. All

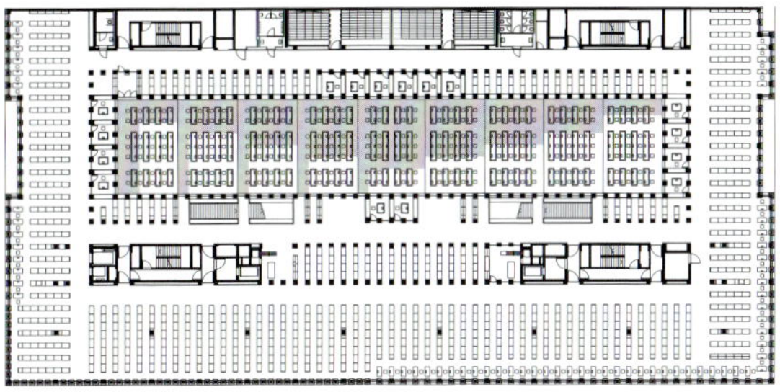

5. Obergeschoss | 5th floor

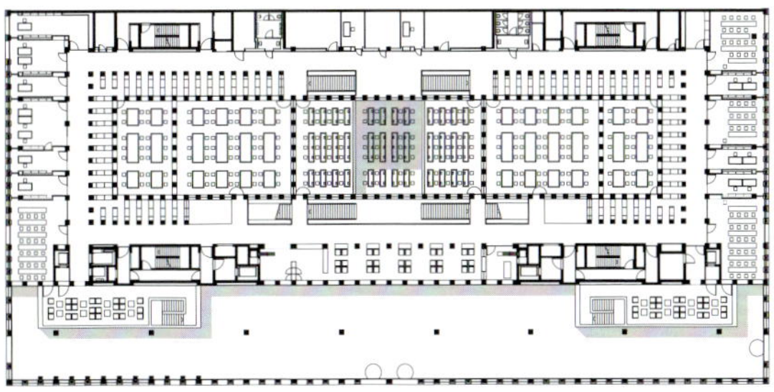

1. Obergeschoss | 1st floor

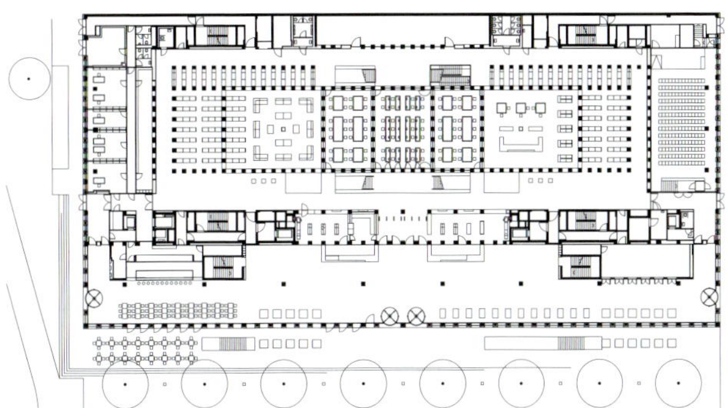

Erdgeschoss | Ground floor

Treppenaufgang am Lesesaal | Stairs in reading room

Treppenaufgang am Lesesaal | Stairs in reading room

besucht, wird an den Punkt gelangen, wo sich die Architektur verblüffenderweise als Kippfigur erweist. Man nimmt mit einem Mal nicht mehr die harte, unverrückbare Baumasse wahr und folgt mit den Augen nicht mehr der schier endlosen Reihung und Tiefenstaffelung, sondern erlebt die Zwischenräume, sieht, aus der Tiefe des Lesesaals heraus, auf die vorbeirauschenden ICEs und S-Bahnen und bemerkt das Gewusel zwischen den Regalen. Die Blickrichtung lässt sich auch umkehren: Wer mit dem Zug durch Berlins Zentrum fährt, der erlebt, vor allem bei Nacht, kurz hinter dem Bahnhof Friedrichstraße, die Bibliothek im Daumenkinoeffekt: Als blättere man schnell durch die Seiten eines Buches, fächern sich die Bücherregale auf. Bis schließlich um Mitternacht die letzten Leser ihre tagsüber zäh verteidigten Plätze verlassen müssen und das Licht gelöscht wird.

Eine Kippfigur ist die Bibliothek auch noch in anderer Hinsicht: Lebt doch ein Lesesaal bei allen ‚klassischen' Vorbildern – von den Klosterbibliotheken bis zu den großen Nationalbibliotheken in Paris und London oder Asplunds Bibliothek in Stockholm – von den endlosen Regalmetern der Werke, die ihn und damit die Leser als ein Bollwerk des Wissens umschließen. In Dudlers zentralem Lesesaal hingegen ist kein einziger Buchrücken direkt zu sehen. Die geballte Buchmasse tritt bei Dudler gewissermaßen strukturell in Erscheinung. Die Regale scheinen das Haus zu tragen, die Architektur, so dominant sie zunächst erscheinen mag, ist hier so sehr in den Dienst der Bücher gestellt, dass es nicht falsch wäre zu sagen: Diese Bibliothek ist in erster Linie ein riesiges Bücherregal und die Architektur, sie dient, anstatt selbst Kapriolen zu schlagen.

Die vielfältigen Durchblicke in Längs- und Querrichtung haben noch einen weiteren Effekt. Zwar konnte nicht jede Stelle des Hauses in so kostbare Materialien gehüllt werden wie der Lesesaal. Doch dieser schimmert selbst zu den eher prosaischen Gängen auf der Nordseite des Gebäudes hindurch und sorgt für Orientierung und etwas Glanz noch im entferntesten Winkel.

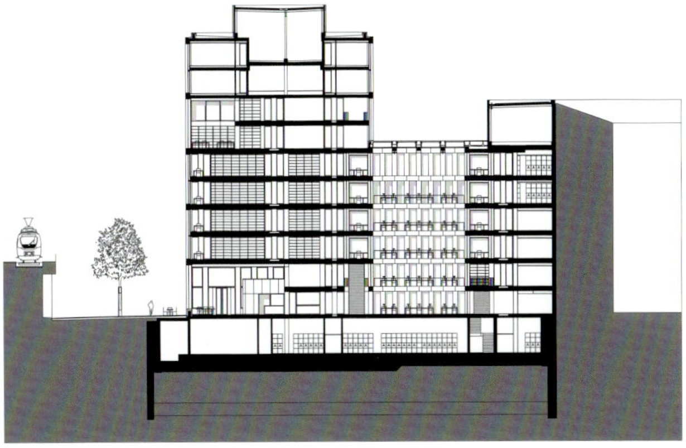

Querschnitt | Cross-section

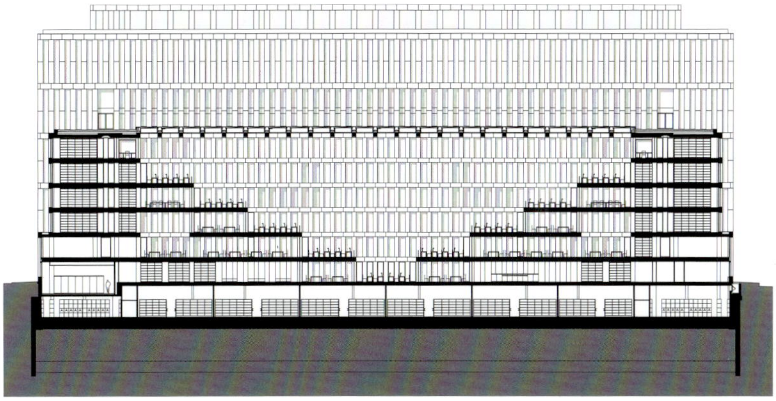

Längsschnitt | Longitudinal section

supports, corridors, windows, passageways and sight axes are conceived within the all-encompassing grid of the bookshelves.
Does this look orderly, or does it verge on mania, on an obsession with geometry for which Max Dudler as erstwhile master student of Oswald Mathias Unger was understandably predestined? At this point, it will probably be difficult to convince sceptics of the contrary, the architectural photos attesting, despite all their fascination, to a certain fencing in of the gaze. Actually, however, the opposite is true: anyone visiting the library will reach a point where the architecture astoundingly proves itself to be like one of those optical illusions where a figure magically reverses to produce a different image entirely. All at once, one no longer sees the hard, immovable structural mass; the eye no longer follows the virtually endless rows and gradations into depth, but experiences instead the interim spaces, looks out from the depths of the reading room onto the intercity and commuter trains rushing past, and notices the bustling life amongst the shelves. This viewpoint can also be reversed: those travelling by train through the centre of Berlin will experience the library shortly after passing through Friedrichstrasse Station, and particularly at night, in a kind of flip-book effect: the bookshelves file by as if one were quickly leafing through the pages of a book. Until finally, around midnight, the last readers must

Arbeitskabine (mit Blick in den Lesesaal) | Work cubicle (with view of reading room)

Leseplätze im Freihandmagazin
Reading desks in the open stacks

Freihandmagazin | Open stacks

Zentraler Lesesaal | Central reading room

relinquish the seats they defended tooth and nail by day, and the lights are switched off.

The library is also a reversible figure in another sense, because in all the "classical" models – whether monastery libraries, the grand national book repositories in Paris and London, or Asplund's library in Stockholm – a reading room takes its life from the endless metres of books that enclose it and thus the readers as a bulwark of knowledge. In Dudler's central reading room, by contrast, not a single book spine is to be seen directly. The concentrated mass of works is, so to speak, a structural component instead: the shelves seem to carry the weight of the building. The architecture, dominant as it might first appear, is put at the service of the books here to such an extent that it would not be wrong to say: this library is first and foremost a gigantic bookshelf and the architecture is subservient to it rather than pulling any capers of its own.

The multiple perspectives in both longitudinal and crosswise directions have yet a further effect. Although not every spot in the building could be clad in such costly materials as the reading room, this room nonetheless shimmers through even into the rather prosaic hallways on the northern side of the building, providing orientation and a touch of splendour in the remotest corners.

Südfassade am Abend | Southern façade in the evening

ARCHITEKT | ARCHITECT

PETER KULKA ARCHITEKTUR DRESDEN

GEBÄUDE | BUILDING

ÜBERDACHUNG KLEINER SCHLOSSHOF

RESIDENZSCHLOSS DRESDEN

TEXT FALK JAEGER

14

ARCHITEKTEN | ARCHITECTS

Peter Kulka Architektur Dresden
Peter Kulka / Philipp Stamborski
Werner-Hartmann-Straße 1
01099 Dresden
www.peterkulka.de

MITARBEITER | TEAM

Pit Dörrwächter, Christoph Goeke, Egbert Heller, Thorsten Mildner, Eva Trebin

BAUHERR | CLIENT

Freistaat Sachsen / Staatsministerium der Finanzen vertreten durch: SIB – Staatsbetrieb Sächsisches Immobilien und Baumanagement, Niederlassung Dresden 1

BAULEITUNG / PROJEKTSTEUERUNG SITE MANAGEMENT / PROJECT GUIDANCE

Objektüberwachung site supervision
AES Ingenieurgesellschaft mbH, Dresden
Projektsteuerung | project guidance
Kaiser Baucontrol Ingenieurgesellschaft mbH, Dresden

TRAGWERK | STRUCTURE

Entwurfsstatik structural engineering design
ahw Ingenieure, Münster

Genehmigungsstatik und Ausführungsplanung structural engineering approval and execution planning
Leonard, Andrä & Partner, Dresden

Verstärkungen im Bestand reinforcements of building fabric
Kröning / Ulbrich / Schröter / Ingenieure Tragwerksplanung, Dresden

Prüfstatik | structural engineering inspection
Prof. Dr. Bernd Dressel, Dresden

HAUSTECHNIK | M & E ENGINEERS

Heizung-Lüftung-Sanitär-Elektro HVAC, plumbing and electrical
Dresdner ÖKOTHERM GmbH, Dresden

BAUAUSFÜHRUNG CONSTRUCTION EXECUTION

Stahlbau Traggitterschale steel support grid for roof
MBM Metallbau Dresden GmbH, Dresden

ETFE Folie-Kissenmembran ETFE cushion membrane
CENO TEC GmbH, Greven

FERTIGSTELLUNG | COMPLETION

Januar 2009 | January 2009

STANDORT | LOCATION

Residenzschloss Dresden
Staatliche Kunstsammlungen Dresden
Taschenberg 2
01067 Dresden
www.skd-dresden.de

FOTOS | PHOTOS

Jörg Schöner, Dresden

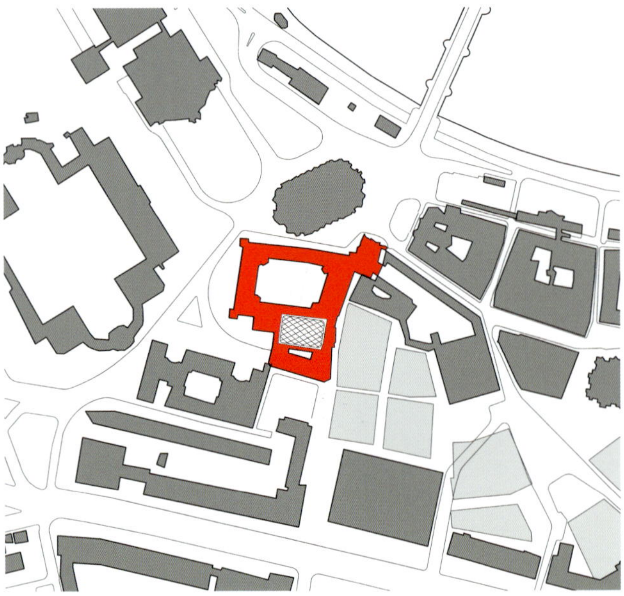

Lageplan | Site plan

Ostflügel des Dresdner Schlosses mit der Kuppel über dem Kleinen Schlosshof
East wing of Dresden Royal Palace with the dome over the Small Courtyard

Manchmal geschieht Unerhörtes. Zum Beispiel beim Dresdner Residenzschloss. Der Generaldirektor der Staatlichen Kunstsammlungen Dresden, Martin Roth, rechnet mit der Vollendung des Wiederaufbaus bereits im Jahr 2014. Wo doch ursprünglich 2017 geplant war. Noch harren die im Krieg ausgebrannten Paraderäume der Rekonstruktion, baut man am Riesensaal und versieht man den Großen Schlosshof mit frisch entworfenen Renaissance-Sgraffitos (nicht ganz unumstritten übrigens, diese Neuinszenierung der vor 300 Jahren verlorenen höfischen Pracht).

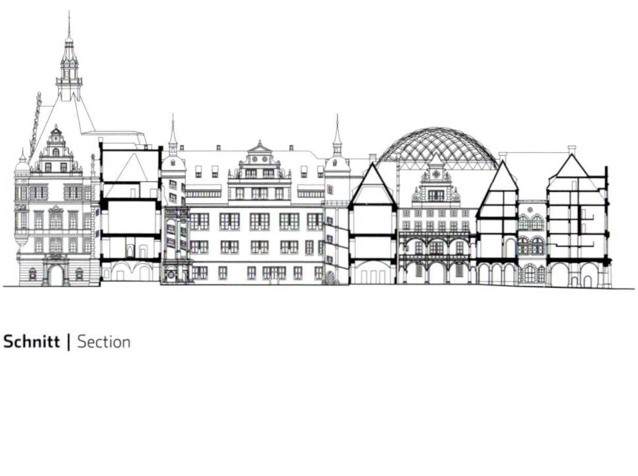

Schnitt | Section

Sometimes unheard-of things happen. At the Royal Palace in Dresden, for example. The general director of the State Art Collections housed there, Martin Roth, anticipates that its reconstruction will be complete by 2014. Even though 2017 was originally forecast. The state rooms, burned out in the Second World War, are still awaiting restoration, the Grand Hall is under construction, and the Great Courtyard is being furnished with freshly conceived Renaissance-style sgraffitos (not entirely uncontroversial incidentally, this re-enactment of a courtly splendour that vanished 300 years ago).
Martin Roth is the master of the house and the general overseeing four museums that have their new or traditional homes in the palace. The legendary Grünes Gewölbe (Green Vault) is among them, also the Münzkabinett (Coin Cabinet), the Kupferstichkabinett (Collection of Prints, Drawings and Photographs) and the Rüstkammer (Armoury), along with the Türckischen Cammer (Turkish Chamber), whose opening in March was attended by a host of major political figures.

Die Eindeckung der Kuppel erfolgte mit 265 pneumatischen Kissen aus leichter und witterungsbeständiger ETFE- Folie. | The dome was roofed with 265 pneumatic cushions made of lightweight, weatherproof ETFE film.

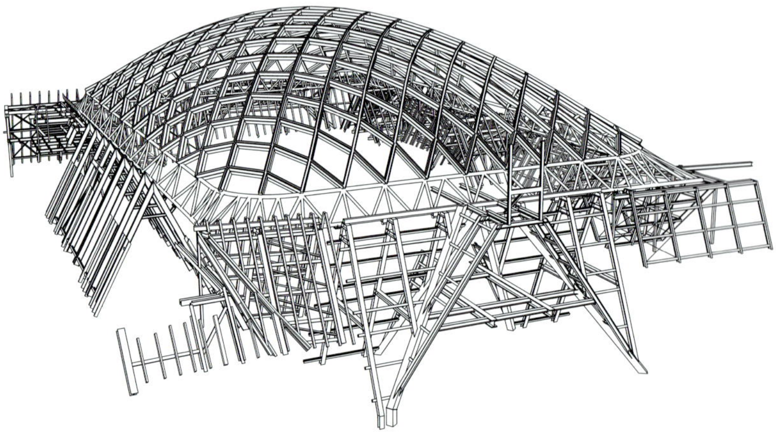

Stabgitterschale | Space grid structure

Martin Roth ist Hausherr und General von vier Museen, die im Schloss ihre neue oder angestammte Heimat haben. Das legendäre Grüne Gewölbe ist darunter, aber auch das Münzkabinett, das Kupferstichkabinett und die Rüstkammer mit der erst im März unter Aufbietung von Politprominenz eröffneten „Türckischen Cammer".
Roth hatte sich sehnlichst eine Lösung für die prekären räumlichen Verhältnisse seiner Museen gewünscht: ein zentrales Foyer mit Platz für die Busladungen auswärtiger Besucher und für all die peripheren Funktionen vom Kassentresen bis zum Museumsshop, ohne die ein zeitgemäßer Museumsbetrieb nicht auskommt.
Raum dafür gab es eigentlich nur im Kleinen Schlosshof. Kann man den Hof denkmalverträglich überdachen, so lautete die entscheidende Frage.
Es gab verschiedene Vorschläge, etwa den, eine leichte Glasdecke auf halber Höhe in den Hof einzuziehen, die jedoch an den statischen Verhältnissen, an den Entwässerungsproblemen und wohl auch an der fragwürdigen Ästhetik scheiterte.

Roth longed for a solution to the precarious spatial relationships between his museums: a central foyer with room to hold the busloads of visitors and all the peripheral functions from admission desk to museum shop which a modern-day museum cannot do without.
The only place with enough space for this purpose was the Kleiner Schlosshof (Small Palace Courtyard). The question was whether this courtyard could be roofed over in a way compatible with the demands of historical preservation.
Various proposals were made, for example to put a lightweight glass roof halfway up the façades, but these solutions came up against difficult structural engineering issues, drainage problems and presumably questionable aesthetic value. Ultimately, Peter Kulka saved the day with his idea to vault the courtyard with a transparent dome at the height of the roof ridges. The plan seemed appealing, and yet the traditionalists among Dresden's citizenry were immediately up in arms, viewing the bubble of pumped-up ETFE cushions as an outrageous disfigurement of their palace. The architect argued that the roof would hardly be visible from outside and presented various visualisations to prove it.
Now the roof is in place, and it can in fact be seen from outside, from various directions. The question is: does it disrupt the cityscape? It's a little bit like the dome of the Reichstag in Berlin. Because it's so alien-looking, the viewer tends not to associate the dome with the palace, getting more the impression that it's part of the building behind it.
More serious is the question as to its impact inside the courtyard. And this effect is astounding. The courtyard still feels like an outdoor space, the walls and roofs (complete with gutters and snow guards!) signalising exterior façade. The membrane sky is hardly perceived at all against the light pouring in from its zenith, at least by day.
All the same, the architect had little chance of making the roof disappear completely. The flatter the vault, the greater the forces it exerts outward and downward, and therefore the stronger the steel framework must be. The curvature of the steel skeleton therefore had to exceed a certain rise, or it would look clumsy. Moreover, for structural reasons a broad metal apron lining the lower edge of the new roof was unavoidable. The reasons lie in the building and planning history of the reconstruction. By the time the decision was made to roof over the courtyard, the roofs all around had already been completed, their interiors filled with building services. Thus it took skill to engineer the considerable load and attendant forces of this additional domed roof through the extant buildings.
When designing the geometry of the dome, the architect was confronted with a further problem.

Letztlich durchgesetzt hat sich Peter Kulka mit seiner Idee, den Hof mit einer transparenten Kuppel auf Höhe der Dachfirste zu überwölben. Die Idee schien bestechend, rief aber sofort die Traditionalisten unter den Dresdner Bürgern auf den Plan, die in der Blase aus aufgepumpten ETFE-Kissen eine ungeheure Verschandelung ihres Schlosses sahen. Das Dach werde man von außerhalb kaum sehen, argumentierte der Architekt und präsentierte diverse Schaubilder.
Inzwischen ist das Dach montiert, und man sieht es doch, aus verschiedenen Richtungen. Die Frage ist, stört es? Ein wenig ist es wie mit der Reichstagskuppel in Berlin. Weil sie so fremd und andersartig ist, bringt man die Kuppel mit dem Schloss nicht in Verbindung, hat den Eindruck, als gehöre sie zu einem dahinter liegenden Gebäude.
Schwerer wiegt die Frage nach der Wirkung im Inneren des Hofes. Und die ist verblüffend. Der Hof bleibt Freiraum, die Wände und Dächer (samt Dachrinnen und Schneefanggitter!) signalisieren Außenfassaden. Der Folienhimmel wird im Zenitgegenlicht kaum wahrgenommen, zumindest nicht bei Tag.
Dabei hatte der Architekt wenig Chancen, das Dach optisch verschwinden zulassen. Je flacher die Wölbung, desto größer die Kräfte, desto stärker auch die Stahlprofile. Die Wölbung der Stabgitterschale konnte also eine gewisse Stichhöhe nicht unterschreiten, ohne zu plump auszufallen. Zudem ließ sich aus konstruktiven Gründen ein starker unterer Rand des neuen Daches nicht vermeiden. Die Gründe liegen in der Bau- und Planungsgeschichte des Wiederaufbaus. Als die Überdachung des Hofes beschlossen wurde, waren die Dächer rings um den Hof bereits geschlossen, die Dachkonstruktionen fertig, die Dachräume mit Haustechnik angefüllt. Da war es eine Kunst für sich, die erheblichen Lasten und Kräfte aus dem zusätzlichen Kuppeldach hindurchzufädeln.
Beim Entwurf der Geometrie der Kuppel sah sich der Architekt mit einem weiteren Problem konfrontiert. Die Dachkörper der den Hof umgebenden Schlossflügel haben keineswegs übereinstimmende Trauf- und Firsthöhen. Dennoch gelang es, eine geeignete Position im Firstbereich zu finden, bei der alle Zwerchgiebel überwölbt werden und lediglich ein Quergiebel angeschnitten wird. Der lugt über die Kuppel hinaus und macht deutlich, dass die Bereiche innerhalb und außerhalb des Daches zusammengehören.
Leider ist der Natursandsteinplattenboden zu glatt geraten, mehr Pflastercharakter hätte den Außenraumeindruck des Kleinen Schlosshofs gestärkt. Die Kuppel ist indes nur der erste Punkt, an dem der Besucher, der in ein vermeintlich intaktes historisches Schloss tritt, mit moderner Formensprache konfrontiert wird. Diese Erfahrungen gehen weiter, beim Treppenhaus aus DDR-Zeiten, aber auch bei den von Kulka in fast zu harter und kompromissloser Moderne neu gestalteten Sälen. Und nur bei der Englischen Treppe ist er sich ein wenig untreu geworden – die hat er nach den Kriegszerstörungen weitgehend rekonstruiert, freilich nicht bis hin zur letzten Stuck-Kartusche und den barocken Kandelabern. Doch mehr war von ihm an Rekonstruktionen nicht zu haben. Zum Glück für den Bau, wenngleich der Architekt sich damit in Dresden nicht nur Freunde gemacht hat.

Für die Überdachung musste eine Konstruktion gefunden werden, die die verschiedenen Fassaden des Renaissanceschlosshofes mit den unterschiedlichen Gesimshöhen und Ziergiebeln in Gänze erlebbar lässt.
A roof structure had to be found that would allow the various façades lining the Renaissance palace courtyard with their varying eaves heights and decorative gables to be experienced in full.

The roof structures of the palace wings surrounding the courtyard by no means have the same eave and ridge heights. And yet the architect succeeded in finding a suitable position in the ridge area at which all the transverse gables could be vaulted over and only one side gable needed to be transected. This single gable peeks out above the dome and makes it evident that the areas inside and outside the roof belong together.
Unfortunately, the sandstone floor is too smooth; a texture more like flagstones would have underscored the impression of the Small Courtyard as outdoor space. The dome is incidentally only the first element that confronts visitors to the ostensibly intact historic palace with modern formal idiom. This experience continues as he ascends a stairway from GDR days, but also in rooms newly designed by Kulka in a modern style that is almost too hard and uncompromising. Only in the English Stairs has he been a bit untrue to himself – he reconstructed them as they were before their destruction in the war, admittedly not down to the last plaster cartouche and Baroque candelabra. But more reconstruction than this was not to be had from him. Which is a good thing for the building, although the architect has not made only friends in Dresden with his approach.

ARCHITEKT | ARCHITECT

PROF. CHRISTOPH MÄCKLER ARCHITEKTEN

GEBÄUDE | BUILDING

OPERNTURM

TEXT DIETER BARTETZKO

15

ARCHITEKTEN | ARCHITECTS

Prof. Christoph Mäckler Architekten
Platz der Republik 6
60325 Frankfurt am Main
www.chm.de

MITARBEITER | TEAM

Henry Hess (Projektleiter | project manager), Sonja Bockemühl, Mischa Bosch, Cornelius Boy, Larissa Chinenaya, Martin Eichholz, Dieter Hassinger, Nadja Hellenthal, Nadine Lorius, Damian Paris, Christian Schmidt, Christian Wiechers, Stephanie Wymer

BAUHERR | CLIENT

Eigentümer | owner
Opernplatz Property Holdings GmbH & Co. KG
c/o Tishman Speyer Properties Deutschland GmbH
Projektentwickler | project developer
Tishman Speyer Properties Deutschland GmbH

TRAGWERK | STRUCTURE

B+G Ingenieure
Bollinger und Grohmann GmbH, Frankfurt am Main;
Grontmij BGS Ingenieurgesellschaft mbH, Frankfurt am Main

ELEKTROINGENIEURE
ELECTRICAL ENGINEERS

Ebener & Partner AG
Planungsgesellschaft für Elektrotechnik, Frankfurt am Main

INGENIEURE FÜR TECHNISCHE GEBÄUDEAUSRÜSTUNG
TECHNICAL BUILDING EQUIPMENT ENGINEERS

TechDesign Gesellschaft für Technische Ausrüstung und Energietechnik mbH, Frankfurt am Main

FASSADENBERATER
FAÇADE CONSULTANTS

Emmer Pfenninger Partner AG, Münchenstein, Schweiz | Switzerland

BAUPHYSIK | BUILDING PHYSICS

vRP Bauphysik Ingenieurbüro von Rekowski und Partner, Weinheim

BRANDSCHUTZ
FIRE PREVENTION

BPK Brandschutz Planung Klingsch GmbH, Frankfurt am Main

LICHTPLANUNG | LIGHTING DESIGN

LICHTVISION GmbH, Berlin

VERKEHRSPLANER
TRAFFIC PLANNER

Prof. Dr.-Ing. Rudolf Eger, Darmstadt

LANDSCHAFTSARCHITEKTEN
LANDSCAPE ARCHITECTS

Gräfin Adelheid von Schönborn, München | Munich

KUNST AM BAU | ART

Gemälde | painting „AHAB“
Julian Schnabel
Kunstwerk | artwork „VOID“
Manfred Peckl
Kunstwerk | artwork „Phänomenom“
Manfred Peckl

FERTIGSTELLUNG | COMPLETION

2009

STANDORT | LOCATION

Bockenheimer Landstraße 2–4
60306 Frankfurt am Main
www.opernturm.com

FOTOS | PHOTOS

Thomas Eicken, Mühltal
Klaus Helbig, Frankfurt am Main
Christian Richters, Münster

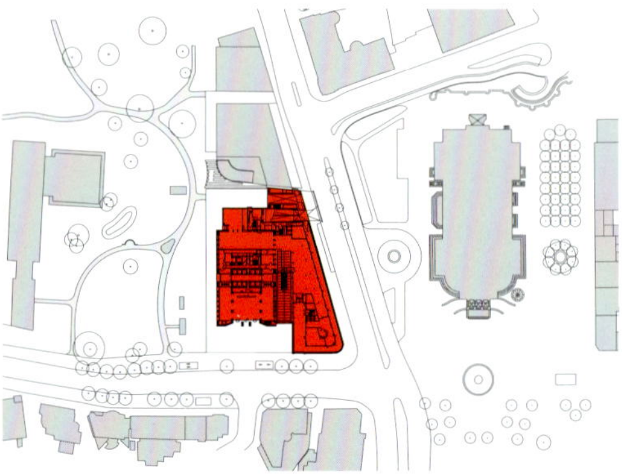

Lageplan | Site plan

OpernTurm mit Blockrandbebauung zur Alten Oper, im Hintergrund das Bankenviertel. | OpernTurm with perimeter block development toward the Alte Oper, with the banking district in the background.

„Es kommt nichts Besseres nach" – Christoph Mäcklers neuer OpernTurm hat diese derzeit uneingeschränkte Grundregel des abrisswütigen Frankfurt bravourös durchbrochen. Sein Hochhaus ersetzt das Zürichhochhaus, das 1962 als erstes europäisches Exemplar der neuen amerikanischen ‚Sandwich'-Architektur – alle Fassadenelemente wurden nur noch in das Stahlbetonskelett eingehängt und verschraubt – an der Alten Oper errichtet worden war. Sofort als reizvoller moderner Kontrast zum Opernhaus geschätzt (das damals noch den makaberen Titel „Deutschlands schönste Kriegsruine" trug), wurde das Zürichhaus 1985, zwei Jahre nach dem Wiederaufbau der Alten Oper, unter Denkmalschutz gestellt – und 2002 gegen den Willen der Bürger abgerissen.

"Nothing better will replace it" – this ground rule, which is currently being voiced everywhere in demolition-happy Frankfurt, has been boldly and masterfully overturned by Christoph Mäckler's new OpernTurm. His high-rise replaces Zurich House, which was erected next to the Alte Oper in 1962 as the first European example of the new American "sandwich" architecture in which all façade elements were simply hung into a skeleton of steel-reinforced concrete and screwed in place. Immediately appreciated as an appealingly modern contrast to the old-fashioned opera house (which at the time bore the macabre title of "Germany's loveliest war ruin"),

Der 170 Meter hohe OpernTurm mit seiner siebengeschossigen Blockrandbebauung zum Opernplatz
The 170-metre-high OpernTurm with its seven-storey perimeter block development toward Opernplatz

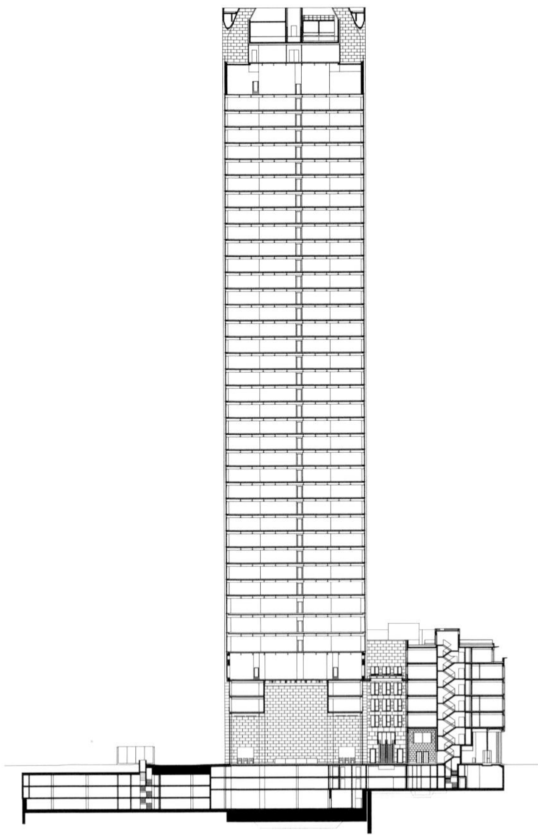

Schnitt | Section

Mit 170 Metern fast zweieinhalb Mal höher als sein Vorgänger, und mit einer massiv wirkenden Verkleidung aus weiß-beigem portugiesischem Kalkstein die Antithese zu dessen schwebeleichten Fassaden aus blau emailliertem Glas und silbrigem Blech, wirkt Mäcklers Gigant dennoch integrativ, ja geradezu taktvoll. Denn sein siebengeschossiger Podiumsbau, der den Schaft trapezoid einfasst, schließt die letzte Lücke der Platzbebauung rings um Richard Lucaes Opernhaus von 1880.
Frei von plumpem Imitat greift Mäcklers Sockelarchitektur mit axialer Symmetrie – einer ‚gerundeten Ecke', einem oberen, eingezogen umlaufenden Fensterband und einer zwei Geschosse übergreifenden Pfeilerarkade – Charakteristika der Gründerzeitbauten an der Südseite des Platzes, aber auch den Monumentalismus des Fin de Siecle in Wien, Mailand oder Barcelona auf. Der Alten Oper erweist die Steinverkleidung, die der des Altbaus stark ähnelt, ihre Reverenz. Die Bürger honorieren all dies mit regem Besuch der Restaurants und Läden im Sockel des OpernTurms.
Der Hauptzugang des Hochhauses öffnet sich an der Westseite. Mit 18 Metern Höhe bietet er sich außen als pathetisches, zwischen altägyptischen Tempelpylonen und Art déco oszillierendes Doppel aus markanten, hochkant gestellten Rechtecken dar. Um mehrere Meter hinter die Fluchtlinie des Sockelbaus zurückgesetzt, blickt dieser Eingang auf einen aufwändig gefliesten Vorhof, der zusätzliche Noblesse ausstrahlt. Das gilt auch für die bemerkenswert schlanken Profile aus Baubronze, die die riesigen Glasflächen der Stirn- und Seitenwände halten. Durch sie schaut man in die gleichfalls steinverkleidete Lobby

Zurich House was made a protected monument in 1985, two years after the rebuilding of the Alte Oper – only to be torn down against the will of the citizenry in 2002.
At 170 metres nearly two-and-a-half times as tall as its forerunner, and with a solid-looking cladding of white-beige Portuguese limestone the antithesis of the lightweight floating façade of blue-enamelled glass and silvery sheet metal on Zurich House, Mäckler's giant nonetheless integrates itself almost tactfully into its surroundings. This is partly because its seven-storey podium section, a trapezoid wrapped round the shaft, closes the last gap in the development all round Richard Lucae's opera house of 1880. Free of any clumsy attempts at imitation, Mäckler's podium architecture with its axial symmetry – a rounded corner, an upper concave moulding surrounding the windows and a two-storey colonnade – takes up features of the Wilhelminian buildings on the south side of the plaza, but also recalls the monumentalism of fin-de-siècle Vienna, Milan or Barcelona. The stone surface, which strongly resembles that of the Alte Oper, shows reverence for the older building. Frankfurt's residents honour all of this by frequenting the restaurants and shops in the base of the OpernTurm.
The main entrance to the high-rise opens up on the west side. With a hight of 18 metres its striking rectangular columns make a lofty impression oscillating between ancient Egyptian temple pylons and Art Deco. Set back several metres behind the frontage of the podium building, the entrance looks onto an elaborately tiled forecourt, which lends additional noblesse. This can also be said of the admirably sleek profiles of structural bronze that hold the enormous glass expanses of the front and side walls. Through these windows one looks into the lobby, also stone-clad, with its eccentric monumental painting by Julian Schnabel.
In the lobby a further glass wall opens to the south to afford a view of a passage of equal height that traverses the tower, holding lifts, shops and a cafeteria. Polished stone, stairways, escalators and

UBS
BHF-BANK

Im Sinne des typisch städtischen Stilelements aus dem 19. Jahrhundert befinden sich in der Blockrandbebauung zweigeschossige Arkaden mit Läden und Gastronomie. | Echoing typical urban style elements from the 19th century, the perimeter block development features two-storey arcades with shops and restaurants.

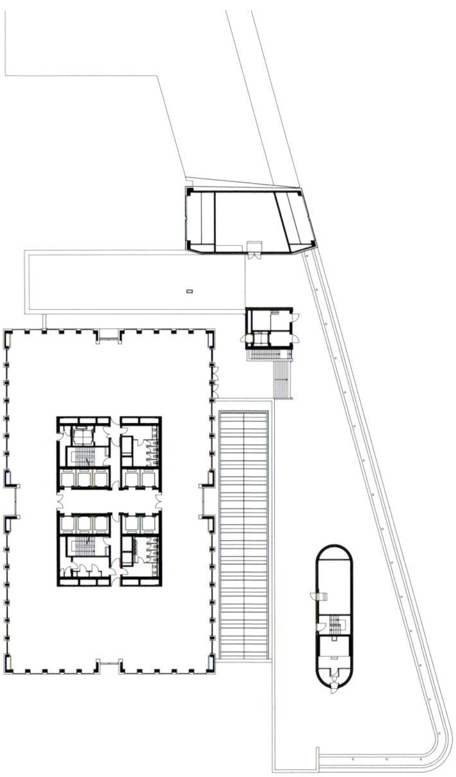

Regelgeschoss mit Dachterrasse der Blockrandbebauung
Standard storey in the perimeter block development, with rooftop terrace

mit einem exzentrischen Monumentalgemälde von Julian Schnabel.
Beim Aufenthalt in der Lobby öffnet sich südlich durch eine weitere Glaswand der Blick in eine gleich hohe Passage, die, Lifts, Läden und eine Kantine erschließend, den Turm durchquert. Polierter Stein, (Roll)Treppen und Rampen strahlen eine ähnlich suggestive Feierlichkeit aus wie die benachbarte Eingangshalle.
Der Turm selbst besteht aus vier Hochkanten, deren Einzelstellung außen durch die eingetieften Fensterachsen der Treppenhäuser erkennbar ist. Wie diese geben auch die kantigen Fensterlaibungen sowie die öffnungslosen und damit ins Auge springenden Ecken der Vierkante dem Baukörper Tiefenstaffelung, straffe Struktur und ausdrückliche Solidität. Dass dieses für Mäckler charakteristische, skulpturale Element momentan noch vom schimmernden Weiß des frisch gebrochenen portugiesischen Kalksteins in den Hintergrund gedrängt wird, dürfte sich bald ändern: Einige Jahre Witterung, gepaart mit der an Schadstoffen nicht armen Luft der Metropole, werden für Patina und damit für zunehmende Körperlichkeit des OpernTurms sorgen.
Im Inneren kehrt sich der Eindruck um: statt Masse prägt Transparenz die Atmosphäre. Alle Räume, selbst die innen liegenden Flure, haben Tageslicht. In den Büros, Besprechungszimmern und Lounges sind die Fenster bis auf Bodenhöhe herabgezogen, die unvermutete lichte Weite kulminiert in der Hochhausspitze. Hier, wo man das Kapitell jenes kannelierten Vierkantpfeilers verortet, dem der OpernTurm in der Fernsicht gleicht, befindet sich ein riesiger, zwei Geschosse übergreifender Veranstaltungssaal. Terrassen umgeben ihn, auf deren federnden Pfeilern kreissegmentförmige Unterzüge gleich gotischen Travéen oder Segeln eines Flugschiffs á la da Vinci aufsetzen.
Wer einen direkten Blick hinunter zum Hochhausfuß riskiert, bemerkt den angrenzenden Rothschildpark – Rest des einst in ganz Europa berühmten Parks der Bankiersfamilie, deren Palais hier bis zur Kriegszerstörung stand. Die Ruine wurde abgerissen, große Teile des Gartens parzelliert. Mäckler und sein Bauherr Tishman Speyer haben auch hier Frankfurter Usancen durchbrochen: Dem Park wurden fünfeinhalbtausend Quadratmeter Fläche zurückgegeben.
Das wiederum ist nur Teil eines ehrgeizigen ökologischen Bauprogramms, an dessen Ende 23 % weniger Energieverbrauch als der von der Energiesparverordnung EnEV 2007 festgelegte stehen. Man kann dies getrost vorbildlich nennen. Das eigentlich Wegweisende am OpernTurm ist aber die Tatsache, dass er das Hochhaus, sonst der schlimmste Feind aller städtebaulichen Kontinuität, zum Musterbeispiel für einfühlsames „Bauen im Bestand" gemacht hat.

Sockel des OpernTurms mit Zugang zur Eingangshalle von der Bockenheimer Landstraße aus.
Base of the OpernTurm with access to the entrance hall from Bockenheimer Landstrasse.

Blick quer durch die 18 Meter hohe Eingangshalle | View through the 18-metre-high entrance hall

ramps exude the same suggestive ceremoniousness as the neighbouring entrance hall.

The tower itself consists of four vertical rectangles that are visibly separated outside by the recessed window axes of the stairwells. Like these, the angular window reveals and the continuous and hence prominent corners of the four rectangles that make up the building's body give it a strong relief with multiple gradations into depth, a taut structure and expressive solidity. Although this sculptural look, characteristic for Mäckler, is at the moment outshone by the gleaming white of the freshly hewn Portuguese limestone, this can be expected to change soon: one year of weathering, coupled with the not quite pollutant-free air of the city will serve to lend surface patina and thus increasing corporeality to the OpernTurm.

Inside, this impression is reversed: transparency rather than massiveness marks the atmosphere. All rooms, even the inside hallways, enjoy daylight. In the offices, conference rooms and lounges there are floor-length windows, and these unexpected bright expanses then culminate in the top of the high-rise. Here, in the "capital" of the fluted, four-sided column that the OpernTurm resembles from afar, a gigantic event hall occupies two storeys. It is surrounded by terraces, from whose resilient pillars arc-shaped girders spring like gothic travées or the sails of a flying ship à la da Vinci.

Risking a dizzying glance directly down to the base, one notices the adjacent Rothschild Park – the remains of the once-famous grounds of the palace of the banking family, which was destroyed in the war. The ruins were torn down, and large stretches of the gardens carved up into plots. Here as well, Mäckler and his client, Tishman Speyer, have broken with Frankfurt custom: an area of five-and-a-half thousand square metres was given back to the park.

That in turn was only part of this ambitious ecological building programme, at the end of which 23 per cent less energy will be consumed than required by the EnEV 2007 Energy Conservation Ordinance. We can confidently call this exemplary. But what is really forward-looking about the OpernTurm is the fact that it makes the high-rise, otherwise the worst enemy of all urban planning continuity, into a paragon of sensitive "construction based on the existing building stock".

Stadtloggien bilden den markanten Kopf des Hochhauses. City loggias form the striking crowning element for the high-rise.

Blick auf eine der Stadtloggien im 41. OG | View of a loggia on the 41st floor

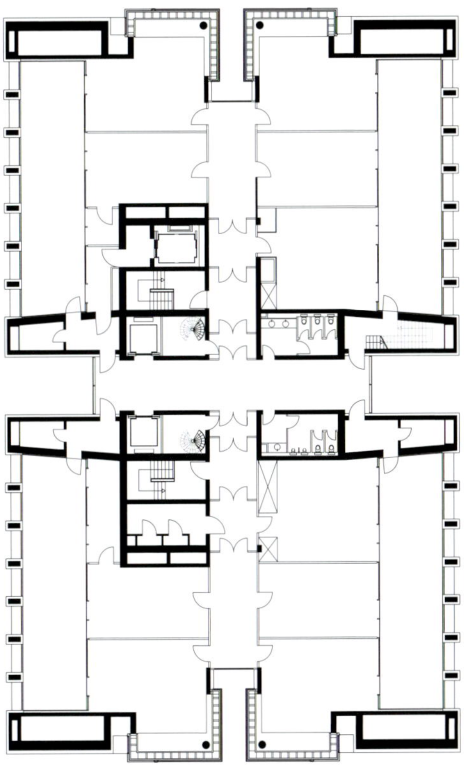

41. Obergeschoss | 41st floor

ARCHITEKT | ARCHITECT

ROBERTNEUN™ BAECKER BUSCHMANN FRIEDRICH

GEBÄUDE | BUILDING

FRISCHE PARADIES LINDENBERG

PRENZLAUER BERG

TEXT OLIVER G. HAMM

16

ARCHITEKTEN | ARCHITECTS

ROBERTNEUN™ BAECKER BUSCHMANN FRIEDRICH ARCHITEKTENPARTNERSCHAFT
Straßburger Straße 6–8
10405 Berlin
www.robertneun.de

MITARBEITER | TEAM

Johannes Gramse, Linda Hasselmann, Claudia Heger, Hjördis Klein, Max Dengler, Ingo Nolte, Frank Häberer, Markus Theel, Katharina Benz, Phillip Rudzinski

BAUHERR | CLIENT

Frische Paradies Lindenberg & Co. KG, Berlin

AUSSCHREIBUNG / VERGABE CALL FOR TENDERS / AWARDING OF CONTRACT

Beusterien + Eschwe, Berlin

GENERALUNTERNEHMER GENERAL CONTRACTOR

Ingenieurbau GmbH, Berlin

TRAGWERK | STRUCTURE

Assmann Beraten + Planen GmbH, Hamburg

HAUSTECHNIK | M & E ENGINEERS

Eneratio Ingenieurbüro für rationellen Energieeinsatz GbR, Hamburg

HOLZFASSADE | WOODEN FAÇADE

Ingenieur-Holzbau Cordes GmbH, Rotenburg an der Wümme

GLASFASSADEN | GLASS FAÇADES

AluStahl Kostyra, Berlin

LADENBAU STORE CONSTRUCTION

Körling Interiors GmbH, Dortmund

FERTIGSTELLUNG | COMPLETION

April 2009

STANDORT | LOCATION

Hermann-Blankenstein-Straße 48
10249 Berlin
www.frischeparadies.de

FOTOS | PHOTOS

Annette Kisling, Berlin

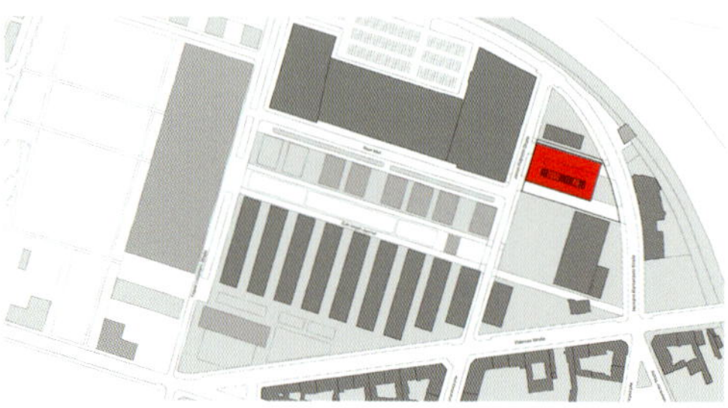

Lageplan | Site plan

Die Form des Daches basiert auf der großmaßstäblichen Übersetzung einer Art Corporate Icon – der Europalette.
The roof form is based on the translation to a large scale of a kind of corporate icon – the europallet.

Vom Paradies hat sicher jeder so seine ganz eigene Vorstellung. Doch manchmal muss man schon viel Fantasie aufbringen, damit sich das Bild im Kopf mit dem real vom Auge erfassten Bild zur Deckung bringen lässt. Zum Beispiel am äußersten östlichen Ende des Berliner Stadtbezirks Prenzlauer Berg: Nichts als zahlreiche schuhboxartige Discounter, größtenteils wenig gepflegte Backsteinbauten aus der Zeit der vorletzten Jahrhundertwende, Wohntrutzburgen, Hochspannungsmasten, viel freies Feld, ein offener S-Bahngraben und dahinter hohe Plattenbauwohnhäuser. Und Straßennamen wie „Neue Welt" und „Zum Langen Jammer", die mehr nach Aufbruch und Angst als nach Ankommen und mußevollem Verweilen (im Paradies) klingen. Der Betreiber eines Delikatess-Einkaufsmarkts hat sich dennoch für diesen Standort

Everyone has his own idea of paradise. But sometimes you need a vivid imagination to make the image in your head match what you actually see before your eyes. For example at the far eastern end of the Berlin district of Prenzlauer Berg, where the view is nothing but shoebox-like discount stores, run-down brick buildings from the turn of the last century, houses like fortresses, electricity pylons, plenty of empty fields, an open cutting for commuter trains and behind it apartment high-rises of pre-cast concrete. Street names like "Neue Welt" (New World) and "Zum Langen Jammer" (The Long Lament) tell more of decampment and anxiety than arrival and leisurely lingering (in paradise).

Die Raumstruktur erzeugt eine maximale Transparenz. Die Telefoneinkäufer im Obergeschoss können von ihrem Arbeitsplatz verfolgen, wie die gerade georderten Waren verpackt werden, … | The room structure generates maximum transparency. Telephone purchasers on the upper floor can look down and see the goods they have just ordered being packed, …

… wie auch die Kunden Einblick in die Kommissionierungshalle und die Warenanlieferung erhalten. | … while customers get a glimpse of the order assembly hall and incoming goods area.

entschieden – am Schnittpunkt der beiden Szenebezirke Prenzlauer Berg und Friedrichshain mit dem traditionellen Arbeiterbezirk Lichtenberg.

Jahrzehntelang wurden auf dem riesigen Areal täglich Tausende von Rindern zur Schlachtbank geführt. Nach der Wiedervereinigung wurde es zum Entwicklungsgebiet Eldenaer Straße – und durch allzu ambitionierte Planungen eher lahmgelegt als in der Entwicklung vorangebracht. Schließlich überließ man diese „innere Peripherie" den „üblichen Verdächtigen": den Discountern, die zahlreiche ausdruckslose Riesenkisten abwarfen, und den Projektentwicklern, die auf den verbleibenden Restflächen scheinbar wahllos allzu kleinformatige und nach außen weitgehend abgeschottete Reihenhäuschen einstreuten.

Da erscheint es schon beinahe trotzig, dass das Frische Paradies Lindenberg Ost am Rande dieser Zwischenstadt sein Lager aufschlug – und dann auch noch mit ambitionierter Architektur den gesichts- und belanglosen Nachbarbauten etwas entgegenhält. Wer nach all den Zumutungen, die sich dem Auge des die Hermann-Blankenstein-Straße entlangfahrenden Betrachters bieten, plötzlich das wohlproportionierte und fein detaillierte Gebäude erblickt, muss zwangsläufig an das berühmte gallische Dorf denken.

Das Frische Paradies Lindenberg Ost ist der erste Neubau des Berliner Architekturbüros ROBERTNEUN™, das sich zuvor bereits mit mehreren An- und Umbauten für den gleichen Bauherrn bewährt hatte. Dessen Qualitätsansprüche nicht nur an die von ihm angebotenen Produkte, sondern auch an die Architektur, die lange gemeinsame Erfahrung von Bauherr und Architekten sowie deren Verständnis für die komplexen Funktionszusammenhänge eines Einkaufsmarkts mit Kommissionierungsbetrieb kommen dem Bauwerk bis ins letzte Detail zugute – vor allem auch deshalb, weil die Architekten die (heute seltene) Chance hatten, sogar die komplette Inneneinrichtung

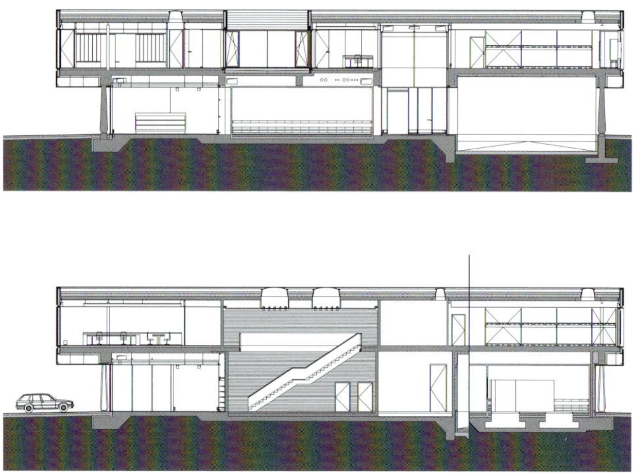

Schnitte | Sections

The operator of a wholesale/retail delicatessen has nonetheless chosen to set up shop here – where the two hip districts Prenzlauer Berg and Friedrichshain meet the traditional workers' borough of Lichtenberg.
For decades, thousands of cattle were daily led to the slaughterhouse across this enormous plot. Following reunification it became a development area called Eldenaer Strasse – but instead of being propelled forward was virtually paralysed by all-too-ambitious planning. Finally, this "inner periphery" was left to the whims of the "usual suspects": the discount retailers, who put up numerous huge, expressionless boxes, and the developers, who strewed seemingly at random across the remaining land row houses that were much too modestly dimensioned and for the most part walled off from the outside world.
It would thus appear to be almost an act of defiance that the Frische Paradies Lindenberg Ost set up camp at the edge of this urban sprawl – and, what's more, challenged the bland neighbourhood buildings with some ambitious architecture. After all the eyesores that assault the senses driving along Hermann Blankenstein Strasse, you suddenly come upon this pleasingly proportioned and finely detailed building, and will inevitably be reminded of that famous Gallic village that stood up to an empire.
The Frische Paradies Lindenberg Ost is the first new building designed by Berlin architecture office ROBERTNEUN™, which has previously demonstrated its capabilities with several extensions and conversions for the same client. The exacting demands that this client places not only on the products it offers but also on the architecture representing its image, together with the long working relationship between client and architects, as well as their understanding of the complex functional requirements of a retail market that also supplies the restaurant and catering trade, benefited the structure down to the last detail – especially because the architects had the chance, rarely encountered today, also to design the complete interior. ROBERTNEUN™ fortunately did not fall prey here to the temptation to rely too much on a "building kit" of forms and materials for their first new building. Instead, industrial materials such as wood, asphalt, sheet metal and aluminium were merely lent fine finishes. These textures, together with a comparatively large proportion of glass in the

Industrielle und lediglich durch Oberflächenbehandlung veredelte Materialien wie Holz, Asphalt, Blech und Aluminium sowie Glas prägen den Raumeindruck. | Industrial materials such as wood, asphalt, sheet metal and aluminium, refined solely through surface finishing, as well as glass dominate the interiors.

Die Kunden erwartet eine Folge von Räumen, die auf Warengruppen abgestimmt sind: Die Fischabteilung wird durch handbemalten Fliesen geprägt, … | Awaiting customers is a sequence of rooms tailored to the respective product groups: the fish counter, for example, features hand-painted tiles, …

… während sich in anderern Bereichen die bunte Welt der Produkte spiegelt. … while other areas reflect the colourful variety of products on offer.

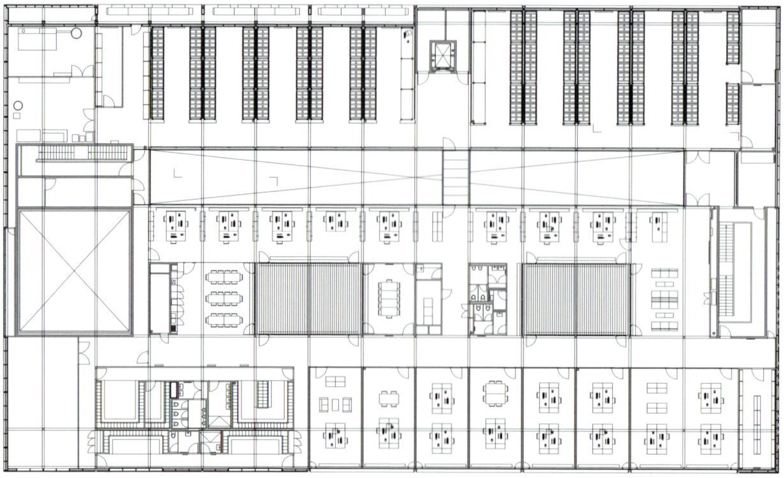

1. Obergeschoss | 1st floor

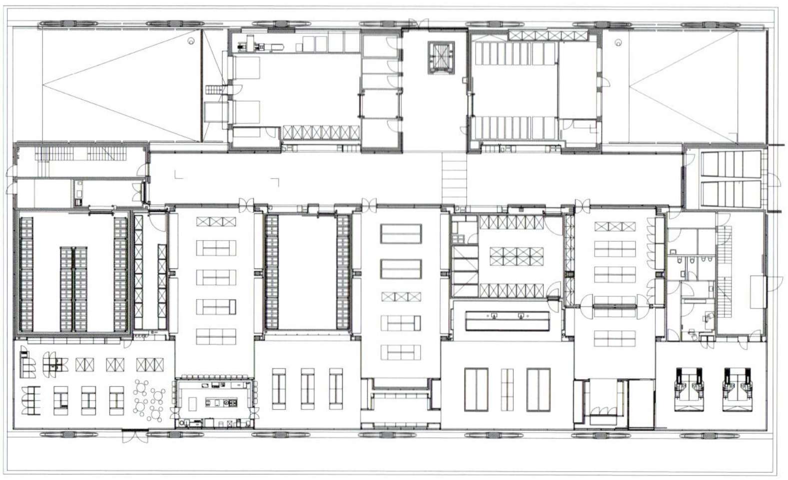

Erdgeschoss | Ground floor

Intention des Projekts war es, alltägliche Gewerbearchitektur über den Zweckbau hinaus zu entwickeln. | The aim of the projects was to develop en everyday commercial architecture that goes beyond purpose-built structures.

selbst zu entwerfen. Der Gefahr, sich beim Erstlingswerk allzu sehr des Formen- und Material-„Baukastens" zu bedienen, ist ROBERTNEUN™ zum Glück nicht erlegen: Industrielle und lediglich durch Oberflächenbehandlung veredelte Materialien wie Holz, Asphalt, Blech und Aluminium sowie ein vergleichsweise großer Glasanteil in den Fassaden prägen die äußere Erscheinung und auch den inneren Raumeindruck.

Die Lasten des auskragenden, an eine Holzpalette erinnernden Obergeschosses (mit den um einen Lichthof mit Blick in die zentrale Kommissionierungshalle im Erdgeschoss bzw. um zwei Patios angeordneten Büro-, Personal- und Technikräumen sowie dem Trockenlager des Betreibers) werden von grazilen V-förmigen Betonträgern abgefangen. Sie und das in raumbildenden Wänden ‚versteckte' sonstige Tragwerk ermöglichen erst die maximale Transparenz des Gebäudes nach außen – und nach innen: Sowohl den Mitarbeitern als auch den Kunden wird Einblick selbst in den Kommissionierungs- und Lieferbereich gewährt. Im Verkaufsbereich erwartet die Kunden eine Folge von Räumen, die auf die jeweiligen Warengruppen abgestimmt sind: Die Fischabteilung wird durch das traditionelle Bild von – allerdings handbemalten – Fliesen geprägt, die Obst- und Gemüseabteilung spiegelt im wahrsten Sinne des Wortes die bunte Welt der Produkte, während die Fleisch- und Geflügelabteilung schwarz gestrichen ist, damit das Rot des Fleisches gut zur Geltung kommt. Über dem gesamten Verkaufsbereich mit einem geschliffenen Asphaltboden ‚schwebt' eine Holzdecke.

Wahrscheinlich gibt es nirgendwo weniger Prenzlauer-Berg-Feeling als in diesem Zipfel des Stadtbezirks. Dank des Frische Paradieses lohnt er dennoch einen Besuch – und lädt zum Sinnieren über die Möglichkeiten ein, wenn die „inneren Peripherien" von Städten ambitionierten Bauherren und Architekten überlassen werden.

façades, dominate the look of both exterior and interior.

The loads from the cantilevered upper storey, reminiscent of a wooden shipping pallet (and containing offices, staff and services rooms as well as an area for dry storage, all arranged around an atrium, i.e. around two patios, with views down into the central order assembly hall) are taken up by graceful V-shaped concrete supports. These, and the remaining support framework "hidden" in the walls that shape the interior spaces, allow for maximum transparency in the building toward both the outside and the inside: employees as well as customers are granted a glimpse even of the order assembly and delivery area. Awaiting the customer on the sales floor is a sequence of rooms that are geared toward the various merchandise groups: the fish counter is dominated by the traditional tile decoration – here hand-painted; the produce department literally reflects the colourful world of fruit and vegetables; and the meat and poultry section is painted black to bring out the red of the meat. Over the entire sales area with its polished asphalt floor "floats" a wooden ceiling.

It would be hard to find a place where there is less Prenzlauer Berg feeling than right here in this spot. Thanks to the Frische Paradies, though, it's certainly worth a visit – if only to ponder the possibilities if we were to entrust the "inner peripheries" of our cities to the capable hands of ambitious clients and architects.

ARCHITEKT | ARCHITECT

SPRINGER ARCHITEKTEN

GEBÄUDE | BUILDING

WOHNQUARTIER ALTENHAGENER WEG

TEXT URSULA KLEEFISCH-JOBST

17

ARCHITEKTEN | ARCHITECTS

Springer Architekten
Gesellschaft von Architekten mbH
Erkelenzdamm 11–13
10999 Berlin
www.springerarchitekten.de

MITARBEITER | TEAM

Jörg Springer, Arnold Brückner, Jana Kluge, Sabine U. Miedlich, José Primo, Torsten Richter, Helmut Riemer, Ulrich Russ, Frank Vaupel

BAUHERR | CLIENT

Helvetia – Schweizerische Versicherungsgesellschaft AG
Direktion für Deutschland, Frankfurt am Main

TRAGWERK | STRUCTURE

Ingenieurbüro Rüdiger Jockwer GmbH, Berlin

LANDSCHAFTSARCHITEKTEN | LANDSCAPE ARCHITECTS

SPRINGER ARCHITEKTEN, Berlin
mit | with
Georg v. Gayl
Landschaftsarchitektur, Berlin

HAUSTECHNIK | M & E ENGINEERS

pin Planende Ingenieure GmbH, Berlin

FARBKONZEPT INNENRÄUME | INTERIOR COLOUR CONCEPT

Friederike Tebbe, Berlin

FERTIGSTELLUNG | COMPLETION

September 2009

STANDORT | LOCATION

Altenhagener Weg 1–5, 2–6;
Farmsener Zoll 9, 15, 19;
Am Knill 18
22147 Hamburg-Rahlstedt
www.altenhagener-weg.de

FOTOS | PHOTOS

Bernd Hiepe, Berlin

Wohnanlage am Altenhagener Weg, Zustand 2004
Housing estate on Altenhagener Weg, as of 2004

Lageplan | Site plan

Teilansicht der diagonal auf dem Grundstück angeordneten Zeilen des sanierten Bestandes und der Neubauten an den Grundstücksrändern
Partial view of the diagonally arranged blocks of renovated buildings and the new houses on the edges of the plot

Immer öffentlicher und heftiger wird die Diskussion um den Umgang mit den Bauten der späten 1950er- und 1960er-Jahre geführt. In die Jahre gekommen, vielfach vernachlässigt, sind viele dieser Bauwerke dringend sanierungsbedürftig. Es sind zurzeit vor allem die Bürger, die sich für den Erhalt der wichtigen Zeitzeugnisse aus den frühen Jahren der Bundesrepublik einsetzen, wie es der erfolgreiche Kampf der Kölner Bürger für ihr Opern- und Schauspielhaus oder das Engagement für die Sanierung der Bonner Beethovenhalle beweisen. Diese Inkunabeln sind aber nur die Spitze des sanierungsbedürftigen Bestandes, der vor allem im Bereich des Wohnungsbaus liegt.
In den 1960er-Jahren war der Bedarf an modernem Wohnraum in der Bundesrepublik immer noch sehr hoch, zum einen als Folge der Kriegszerstörungen, zum anderen wegen der

The debate on how to deal with Germany's remaining building stock from the late 1950s to 60s is increasingly being conducted in the public eye and with growing vehemence. Run down and often neglected, many of these structures are urgently in need of renovation. Nowadays, it is mostly the citizens themselves who plead for the preservation of important buildings bearing witness to the early years of the Federal Republic, as demonstrated by the successful battle of Cologne's residents for their Opera House, or the great dedication shown to restoring Bonn's Beethovenhalle. But these incunabula are only the tip of the iceberg of building, primarily in the area of housing, that is in dire need of rehabilitation.

Freiraum zwischen den südlichen Zeilen. Zustand vor dem Umbau 2004. | Free space between the southern blocks. Before the reconstruction in 2004.

Die Zeilen erhielten eine Dämmung und neue Ziegelfassaden in konventioneller Ausführung. | The housing blocks were given a layer of insulation and new brick façades in conventional style.

anhaltenden Flüchtlingsströme aus dem Osten bis zum Bau der Mauer, aber auch verstärkt durch die Anwerbung von Gastarbeitern seit der Mitte der 1950er-Jahre. Märkisches Viertel in Berlin, Neuperlach in München, Neue Vahr in Bremen, Köln Chorweiler oder Düsseldorf Garath sind nur einige der großen Wohnungsquartiere, die auf der grünen Wiese entstanden.
Für viele sind sie heute Synonym für einen städteplanerischen und architektonischen Irrweg. Die Menschen sind damals mit Begeisterung in diese Quartiere gezogen, einige von ihnen leben noch heute dort, oftmals auch ihre Kinder und Enkel. Diese Kontinuität zeugt von hoher Identifikation und gewachsenen nachbarschaftlichen Strukturen. Was die Bewohner an diesen Quartieren schätzen, ist die aufgelockerte Bebauung mit ihren grünen Freiflächen, die Anbindung an die nahe gelegenen Stadtzentren mit öffentlichen Verkehrsmitteln und die hellen Wohnungen.
So verhält es sich auch mit dem Wohnquartier in Hamburgs Nordosten rund um den Altenhagener Weg, das in den späten 1950er-Jahren begonnen wurde. Der von Springer Architekten sanierte Teil der Anlage, sechs unterschiedlich lange, ursprünglich zwei- und dreigeschossige Zeilen, gehört einem Schweizer Versicherungsunternehmen. Die Hamburger Anlage ist weder in ihrer Gesamtkomposition noch in der Gestaltung der einzelnen Zeilen eine herausragende baukünstlerische Leistung, also kein Fall für den Denkmalschutz, aber eine zeittypische, solide Wohnbebauung mit Qualitäten. Hierzu zählt die Einbettung der Zeilen in begrünte Freiflächen, ihre Ausrichtung in südwestliche Richtung zur optimalen Besonnung. Die Wohnungen weisen lichte Raumhöhen von 2,60 Metern auf. Diese Qualitäten sowie die langjährige Mieterbindung veranlassten die Bauherren und Architekten zu einer umfassenden Sanierung und sogar Verdichtung.
Die Verdichtung erfolgte zum einen durch die teilweise Aufstockung der Zeilen, zum anderen durch vier fünfgeschossige Punkthäuser auf Restflächen, auf denen sich Garagen befanden. Die benötigten Stellplätze sind nun in zwei Tiefgaragen der Punkthäuser gebündelt. So beschneiden die neuen Wohnhäuser nicht die Grünflächen, sondern geben ihnen am südlichen Grundstücksrand vielmehr eine deutliche Begrenzung. In den Neubauten und den neuen oberen Geschossen wurden insgesamt 48 Drei- bis Viereinhalbzimmerwohnungen geschaffen. Diese größeren Wohnungszuschnitte ermöglichten es, in den Zeilen ansonsten die ursprünglichen Zwei- bis Zweieinhalbzimmerwohnungen zu erhalten.

In the 1960s the demand for modern living space in West Germany was still extremely high, both as a consequence of war-time destruction and streams of refugees who still poured in from the East until the borders were closed, but also because of the increasing recruitment of foreign workers starting in the mid-1950s. The Märkisches Viertel in Berlin, Neuperlach in Munich, Neue Vahr in Bremen, Cologne Chorweiler or Düsseldorf Garath are just a few of the huge housing estates that sprang up on green city outskirts during this era. To many people today, they are synonymous with misguided urban planning and architecture. But back then, the first residents enthusiastically embraced these estates, and some of them live there still, in many cases with their children and grandchildren. This continuity attests to the way people identify with these places, and to the neighbourhood structures that have grown up. What their inhabitants value about these estates is the lack of urban crowding, with plenty of green areas but good public transport to the nearby city centres, and of course the light-filled apartments.
All these qualities can be found in the housing estate around Altenhagener Weg in north-east Hamburg, for which ground was broken in the late 1950s. The section of the complex that has now been refurbished by Springer Architekten, comprising six rows of what were originally two- and three-storey blocks of various lengths, belongs to a Swiss insurance company. Neither in its overall composition nor in the design of the individual blocks could the Hamburg estate be called an outstanding architectural achievement, so there was certainly no call for historic preservation. It is however solid residential building typical of its time, with certain qualities. These include the way the rows are embedded in open green spaces, and their south-west orientation for optimum sun. The apartments also have relatively high ceilings of 2.60 metres. These qualities, as well as the long-term tenancies, prompted the clients and architects to undertake a comprehensive rehabilitation and even to add more living space.

Der umfangreichste Eingriff erfolgte am Außenbau. Die Zeilen erhielten eine Dämmung und neue Ziegelfassaden in konventioneller Ausführung. Vermauert wurden die gleichen hellen Ziegel, die auch schon die ursprüngliche Anlage prägten. Die neuen Ziegelwände nutzten die Architekten, um die einzelnen Häuser und Wohnungen durch „Schildwände" deutlicher voneinander zu trennen und zwischen ihnen durchlaufende Balkone anzubringen. Die Wohnungen öffnen sich jetzt mit raumhohen Fenstern zu diesen Balkonen. Durch diese Eingriffe wurde das ursprüngliche Erscheinungsbild der Zeilen grundlegend verändert. Die nun viel flächiger wirkenden Fronten mit einer Akzentuierung der Vertikalen verhehlen ihre Inspiration an der Architektur des Bauhauses nicht.

Es ist sinnvoll, auch im Zeichen der Nachhaltigkeit, Bausubstanz weiter zu „verwerten". Springer Architekten sind hier einen radikalen Weg gegangen, indem sie nicht Kosmetik am Bau betrieben, sondern die ihnen qualitätvoll erscheinende Substanz für eine gänzlich neue Interpretation nutzten. Sofern es sich nicht um Zeitzeugnisse handelt, deren charakteristisches Erscheinungsbild weitestgehend gewahrt bleiben sollte, ist dies ein nachahmenswertes Vorgehen. Hierzu gehört auch die Freiheit, wie in der Hamburger Siedlung zu verdichten oder – was wohl in Zukunft häufiger vorkommen wird – Teile zurückzubauen, wie es mit Erfolg bereits in der Neuen Stadt Wulfen bei Dorste geschehen ist oder in Köln Chorweiler zurzeit diskutiert wird.

New apartments were created by adding more storeys to some of the housing blocks and by erecting four new five-storey tower blocks on areas formerly occupied by garages. The required parking spaces are now bundled in two underground car parks beneath the tower blocks. The new apartment buildings hence do not reduce the green areas, but merely give them a more distinct boundary at the southern edge of the estate. A total of 48 three- to four-and-a-half-room apartments were created in the new buildings and new upper storeys. These larger layouts allowed the original apartments of two to two-and-a-half rooms to otherwise be retained in the existing blocks.

The most extensive changes were made on the exterior. The apartment houses were given a layer of insulation and new conventional-style brick façades. The same light-coloured bricks were used that were already found in the original masonry. But the architects also made use of the new brickwork to separate the individual houses and apartments more distinctly through "shielding walls" and to attach balconies running between them. The apartments now open onto these balconies with floor-to-ceiling windows. These interventions fundamentally transformed the way the buildings

Südliches Bestandsgebäude nach Umbau. Unsaniertes Gebäude im Hintergrund, Zustand 10/2007.
Existing building to the south after renovation. Unrenovated building in the background, as of 10/2007.

Die neuen Punkthäuser und die sanierten Bestandsbauten sind gestalterisch weitgehend angeglichen. | The exterior design of the new tower blocks dovetails with that of the renovated buildings.

look. The now much flatter-seeming façades with their accentuation of the vertical make no effort to hide their inspiration in Bauhaus architecture.

It makes good sense to "recycle" building stock in this way, not only with a view to sustainability. Springer Architekten chose a radical path by not merely making cosmetic changes, but rather taking advantage of what they found worth preserving in the existing structures in order to conceive a complete re-interpretation. In cases like this, which are not time capsules whose characteristic look is to be preserved as far as possible, this is an approach worth emulating. It includes taking the liberty, as here in the Hamburg housing estate, to augment or – something which will presumably come up more often in future – to scale back certain parts, as has already been done successfully in the Neue Stadt Wulfen near Dorste and is currently being considered in Cologne Chorweiler.

Eine Nachverdichtung erfolgte zum einen durch die teilweise Aufstockung der Zeilen, zum anderen durch fünfgeschossige Punkthäuser.
New apartments were created by adding more storeys to some of the housing blocks and by erecting new five-storey tower blocks.

Siedlungsgrundriss | Layout of housing estate

Die atmosphärische Veränderung ist auf den Südwestseiten mit den neuen durchlaufenden Balkonplatten und den raumhohen Fenstern besonders augenfällig.
The change in atmosphere is most conspicuous on the south-west sides with their new continuous balconies and floor-to-ceiling windows.

ARCHITEKT | ARCHITECT

SUNDER-PLASSMANN ARCHITEKTEN

GEBÄUDE | BUILDING

MUSEUM KUNST DER WESTKÜSTE

TEXT MICHAELA BUSENKELL

18

ARCHITEKTEN | ARCHITECTS

Sunder-Plassmann Architekten
Gregor Sunder-Plassmann BDA
Am Hafen 3
24376 Kappeln
www.sunder-plassmann.com

MITARBEITER | TEAM

Projektleiter | project manager
Gregor Sunder-Plassmann
Projektteam | project team
Dörte Bünning, Bettina Jastrembski, Gesche Kötting, Sven Kotulla, Cristina Treiber, Kai Stender

BAUHERR | CLIENT

Gemeinde Alkersum
Amt Föhr-Amrum, Wyk
und | and
NESOS GmbH, Alkersum
Prof. Dr. Frederik Paulsen

BAULEITUNG | SITE MANAGEMENT

Sunder-Plassmann Architekten mit Thomas Paulsen, Wyk

TRAGWERK | STRUCTURE

Wetzel & von Seht, Hamburg

HAUSTECHNIK | M & E ENGINEERS

Ingenieurgesellschaft Ridder-Meyn-Nuckel mbH, Norderstedt

LICHTPLANUNG LIGHTING DESIGN

Studio Dinnebier – Dinnebier Blieske GbR, Berlin

FERTIGSTELLUNG | COMPLETION

Juni | June **2009**

STANDORT | LOCATION

Hauptstraße 1
25938 Alkersum / Föhr
www.mkdw.de

FOTOS | PHOTOS

Frank Grießhammer

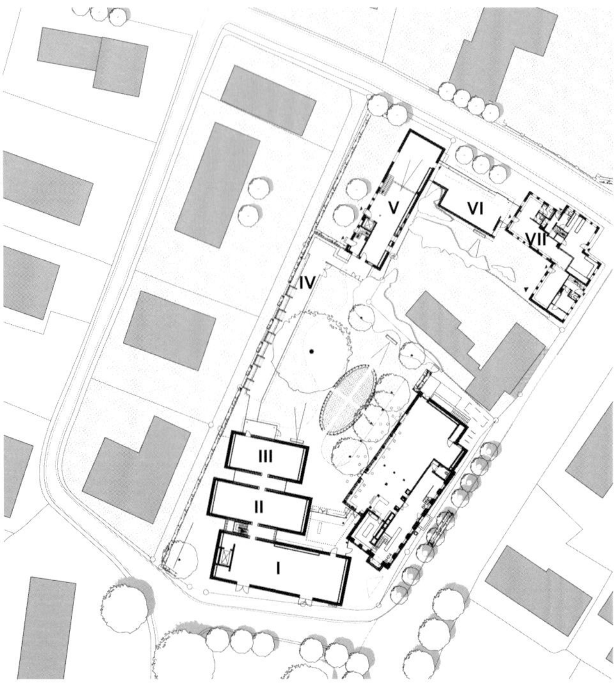

Lageplan | Site plan

I, II, III Ausstellungssäle exhibition galleries

IV Gartensaal (Passerelle) garden room (passerelle)

V für Ausstellungszwecke zum Teil umgebautes und erweitertes Wohnhaus mit integrierter Wohnnutzung house with integrated residential use, extended and converted for exhibitions

VI Museumspädagogischer Raum mit Panoramafenster museum education room with panoramic window

VII Museumspädagogischer Raum museum education room

Als motivische Zitate von Historie und Tradition bestimmen die ‚Ausstellungsscheune' und der Gasthof im Stil eines skandinavischen Herrenhauses aus dem 19. Jahrhundert den ersten Blick auf das Museumsensemble. | The restaurant and "exhibition barn" in the style of a 19th-century Scandinavian manor house, quoting historical and traditional motifs, dominate the visitor's first impression of the museum ensemble.

„Strandlandschaft bei beginnender Flut", „Schiffe in der Brandung", „Badende Knaben" und „Friesinnen im Garten" – von jeher sind diese Motive den Einwohnern der nordfriesischen Insel Föhr vertraut. Im Museum der Westküste, das im Sommer 2009 eröffnet wurde, gehen Kunst, Landschaft und Leben eine unmittelbare Verbindung ein, die Gemäldesammlung des 19. und frühen 20. Jahrhunderts spiegelt Dasein und Alltag der Menschen an der Nordseeküste wieder.
So erscheint auch die Übereinkunft von Museumsarchitektur und Lebenswelt nur folgerichtig. Als vielgliedriges Gefüge wurde das Museumsensemble mit etwa 900 Quadratmetern Ausstellungsfläche in die kleinteilige Struktur des Föhrer Dorfes Alkersum eingewoben. Sechs Museumsbauten und „Grethjens Gasthof" gruppieren sich in der Dorfmitte um den bestehenden Garten mit fünf alten Linden.
Den reetgedeckten Ziegelbau, der sich neben dem Gasthof zu ducken scheint, könnte man auf den ersten Blick für eine ortsübliche Scheune halten. Zunächst verweisen nur zwei raumhohe Fenster und ein versteckter Museumseingang auf die eigentliche Nutzung. In den Innenräumen wird das Zitat der Scheune abstrahiert: Das Foyer öffnet sich zum Garten; der

"Beach Landscape with Tide Coming In", "Ships in the Surf", "Bathing Boys and Frisian Women in Garden" – motifs like these have been familiar to the inhabitants of the North Frisian island of Föhr from time immemorial. At the Museum Kunst der Westküste, which opened in summer 2009, art, landscape and life enter into a symbiosis, because the collection of paintings from the 19th and 20th centuries mirrors the everyday lives of people on the North Sea coast.
The way the architecture of the museum responds to its coastal surroundings thus seems only natural here. A four-wing complex with some 900 square metres of exhibition space, the museum is woven into the intricate structure of the Föhr village of Alkersum. Six museum buildings and the café Grethjens Gasthof are grouped in the middle of town around an existing garden with five old lime trees.
The brick building with thatched roof that seems to cower next to the restaurant might at first glance be

Mit verglasten Übergängen schließen zwei Ziegelbauten an das scheunenähnliche Haupthaus an und abstrahieren deren Form zum Garten hin mit Flachdächern zu Rechteckkörpern. | Glazed walkways connect two brick wings with the barn-like main building, abstracting their form into simple rectangles on the garden side by means of flat roofs.

Ausstellungssaal mit einem offenen Dachraum ist als klassischer ‚white cube' ausgebildet, Boden, Fenster- und Türelemente sind aus heller Eiche. Durch den verglasten Firststreifen fällt Tageslicht ein. Sonne und Wolken in schnellem Wechsel, charakteristisch für die nordischen Küstenlandschaften, treiben auch in der Ausstellung ein Spiel mit Licht und Schatten. In Salonhängung werden die Gemälde aus der Sammlung des Stifters und Bauherrn Frederik Paulsen präsentiert – niederländische, skandinavische und deutsche Maler, große Namen wie Max Beckmann, Johan Christian Clausen Dahl, Edvard Munch oder Peder Severin Krøyer neben regionalen friesischen Künstlern.

Vom Hauptgebäude ausgehend, entwickeln sich die weiteren Ausstellungssäle in und um den Garten. Mit verglasten Übergängen schließen zwei Ziegelbauten an die ‚Scheune' an und abstrahieren deren Form mit Flachdächern – als Tageslicht-Glasdecken – zu Rechteckkörpern. In den Innenräumen werden der historisch orientierten Gemäldesammlung auch zeitgenössische Sonderausstellungen gegenübergestellt – eine Filmcollage der Künstlerin Fiona Tan beispielsweise, die Wasseraufnahmen von idyllischen Impressionen bis hin zu entfesselten Naturgewalten aufeinanderfolgen lässt.

Eine lang gestreckte Glaspasserelle – der Gartensaal – begrenzt das Areal nach Süden und erscheint, von der Nutzung her unspezifisch und vieldeutig, wie eine Aufforderung für neue Kunstformate. Der Medienkünstler Mischa Kuball etwa verspiegelte den 40 Meter langen Bau von außen und projiziert im Inneren blau flutende Wellen auf den Boden, unterlegt von Strömungsgeräuschen. Im Sommer werden die Türen zum Garten aufgeschoben und der Besucher kann eine Pause im Grünen einlegen. Die Passerelle schafft die Verbindung zu einem Wohngebäude aus den 1970er-Jahren, das unter Erhaltung eines Wohnanteils für Ausstellungszwecke umgebaut und erweitert wurde. Im westlichen angrenzenden Trakt der Museumspädagogik lenkt ein Panoramafenster den

Auch das Bild der ‚Scheune' selbst verändert sich zur Gartenseite. Mit raumhohen Glasfenstern öffnet sich das Foyer zum Bauerngarten. | The look of the "barn" itself also changes on the garden side, where the foyer's floor-to-ceiling windows give onto a farmer's garden.

Insgesamt sechs Museumsbauten und „Grethjens Gasthof" gruppieren sich um die Grünflächen mit den alten Linden. | A total of six museum buildings and "Grethjens Gasthof" restaurant are grouped around green areas with old lime trees.

Umgebaute Bestandsbauten sind in das Ensemble integriert und behalten einen Teil ihrer bisherigen Funktionen bei. Der gartenhausähnliche Bau wurde im Inneren von einer Bühnenbildnerin als „Blauraum" für die Museumspädagogik gestaltet und bietet zur Dorfseite hin mit dem größten Fenster der Insel einen weiten Blick über die Marsch. | Converted buildings are integrated into the ensemble, partially maintaining their previous functions. The garden-house-like building includes a "Blue Room" conceived by a stage designer for museum education and features on the village side the island's biggest window, offering a panoramic view across the marsh.

taken to be one of the typical barns in the area. Two floor-to-ceiling windows and a hidden museum entrance are all that hint at its actual use. Inside, the barn association is abstracted: the foyer opens onto the garden, and the exhibition gallery with open roof area is conceived as a classic white cube with floors, window elements and door elements of light-coloured oak. Daylight shines down through the glazed strip of the roof ridge. The rapid alternation of sun and clouds here, characteristic for these northern coastal climes, creates a play of light and shadow across the exhibition space. In a salon-style hanging, paintings from the collection of the founder and building client, Frederik Paulsen, are presented: Dutch, Scandinavian and German painters, including big names such as Max Beckmann, Johan Christian Clausen Dahl, Edvard Munch and Peder Severin Krøyer, along with regional Frisian artists.

From the main building, additional exhibition rooms proceed into and around the garden. Glazed passageways connect two further brick structures to the "barn", creating with their flat roofs – equipped with glazed skylights – an abstract ensemble of rectangular bodies. Inside these annexes, the historically oriented collection of painting is supplemented with special exhibitions of contemporary art – a film collage by artist Fiona Tan, for example, in which photographs of water run the gamut from idyllic impressions to the unleashed forces of nature.

An elongated glazed walkway – the garden room – borders the grounds to the south and appears with its unspecified and ambiguous function to challenge artists to come up with new formats. Media artist Mischa Kuball, for instance, chose to mirror the 40-metre-long building from outside, while inside he projected surging blue waves across the floor accompanied by the sound of rushing water. In summer, the doors to the garden can be slid open, allowing visitors to enjoy some fresh air.

The walkway creates a link with a residential building from the 1970s that has been converted and extended for exhibition purposes, while one section was preserved as living space. In the western tract,

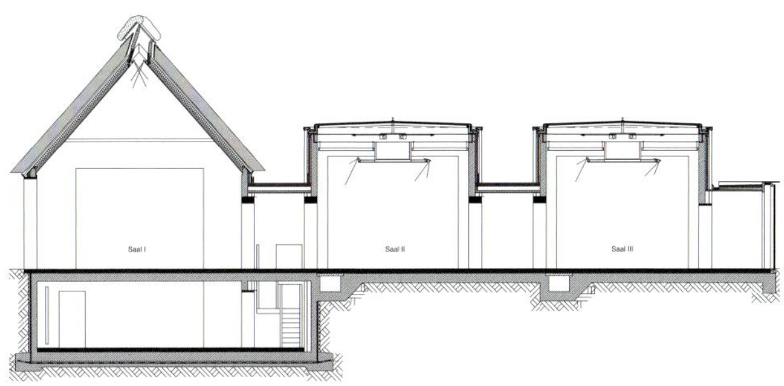

Schnitt durch die drei Ausstellungssäle
Section through the three exhibition galleries

Die beiden Ausstellungssäle mit den Flachdächern werden über Tageslicht-Glasdecken von oben natürlich belichtet. | The two flat-roofed exhibition halls receive daylight from above through glazed ceilings.

Verbindung von Kunst und Leben: Schülerinnen und Schüler aus dem Abiturjahrgang des Gymnasium Insel Föhr erarbeiten die Ausstellung „Zwischen Stille und Sturm". Die präsentierten Gemälde spiegeln in ihren Motiven Dasein und Lebensbedingungen der Bewohner Nordfrieslands im ausgehenden 19. Jahrhundert wider. | Symbiosis of art and life: pupils in their final year of secondary school on the Island of Föhr putting together the exhibition "Between Calm and Storm". The motifs in the exhibited paintings reflect the way of life of the people of North Frisia in the late 19th century.

Blick auf das grüne Marschland. Auch die Dorfbäckerei an der Hauptstraße ist integriert; und nach einem eingeschobenen Grundstück bildet „Grethjens Gasthof" das abschließende Glied des Museumsensembles. In dem zweigeschossigen Gebäude an der Stelle des früheren Dorfkrogs gleichen Namens, der schon um die Jahrhundertwende als Malertreffpunkt galt, tragen heute Museumsgastronomie, ein Festsaal für die Dorfgemeinde und Wechselausstellungsbereiche zur Verbindung von Kultur und Alltagsleben bei. Die weiß geschlemmten Ziegelfassaden, Gesimsbänder und durch Sprossen unterteilte Kastenfenster entsprechen dem Bild eines skandinavischen Herrenhauses aus dem 19. Jahrhundert, das als Genrestück in die Museumssammlung eingehen könnte; es mag als bildhafte Reminiszenz an jene Zeit gesehen werden, als die ersten Maler hier Quartier fanden.

Gasthof und ‚Ausstellungsscheune' als motivische Zitate aus Historie und Tradition bestimmen den ersten Blick auf das Museum. Doch die heterogene Struktur des Gesamtensembles bricht das opportun historisierende Bild des Gasthofs und bildet eine Collage mit vielschichtigen Bezügen. Die Bestandsgebäude und -nutzungen werden ebenso selbstverständlich in das Areal integriert, wie der Seemannschor zu einer Ausstellungseröffnung singt, Dorfbewohner in Gummistiefeln willkommen sind und Föhrer Schüler eine eigene Bilderschau kuratieren.

In drei Bauabschnitten, während derer sich Raumprogramm und -struktur immer wieder verändert haben, entstand eine prozessuale und beziehungsoffene Architektur, die friesische Tradition mit zeitgenössischer Kontingenz vereint und den Dialog von Kunst und Lebenswelt stimuliert.

dedicated to museum education, a panoramic window looks out onto green marshland. Even the village bakery on the main street is integrated; and after an intervening plot, the Grethjens Gasthof restaurant then forms the final link in the chain of museum buildings. In this two-storey structure, erected on the site of an old village inn of the same name that was already frequented by painters around the beginning of the last century, the museum café, a large hall for the use of the community and spaces for changing exhibitions contribute to bringing together culture and everyday life in the village. The whitewashed brick façade, white cornice bands and small-paned casement windows echo the style of a 19th-century Scandinavian manor house as in a genre piece in the museum's collection; this can be regarded as a pictorial reminiscence of the era when the first painters made their homes here on the island.

Restaurant and "exhibition barn", as quotes of historical and traditional motifs, dominate the visitor's first impression of the museum. And yet the heterogeneous structure of the complete ensemble then breaks with the opportunely historicising image of the village inn and forms a collage of multi-layered references. The existing building stock is incorporated into the complex in a matter-of-fact way, just as a sailors' choir is asked to sing for an exhibition opening, village inhabitants are welcome to view the art in their rubber boots and Föhr schoolchildren are invited to create their own picture show.

In three building phases, during which the spatial programme and structure continually evolved, a process-based and associative architecture has emerged here that unites Frisian tradition with contemporary contingencies and thus stimulates the dialogue between art and local lifestyles.

Auch die Übereinkunft von Museumsarchitektur und Lebenswelt erscheint hier nur folgerichtig. Das Museumsensemble wurde in die kleinteilige Struktur des Föhrer Dorfes Alkersum eingewoben und den Haupt-Ausstellungssaal könnte man zunächst für eine traditionelle Scheune halten. | The harmony between museum architecture and way of life seems only logical here. The museum ensemble was woven into the intricate structure of the Föhr village of Alkersum – at first glance, the main gallery building might be taken for a traditional barn.

ARCHITEKT | ARCHITECT

SYRA – SCHOYERER ARCHITEKTEN

GEBÄUDE | BUILDING

HOCHWASSERPUMPWERK
MIT HUBWEHRANLAGE UND AUSLASSBAUWERK

TEXT CHRISTOF BODENBACH

19

ARCHITEKTEN | ARCHITECTS

SYRA – SCHOYERER ARCHITEKTEN BDA, Mainz
Hauptstraße 17–19
55120 Mainz

SYRA – SCHOYERER ARCHITEKTEN BDA, Frankfurt am Main
Siolistraße 10
60323 Frankfurt am Main
www.schoyerer.de

WETTBEWERB UND ENTWURF COMPETITION AND SCHEMATIC DESIGN

Julian Andreas Schoyerer

MITARBEITER | TEAM

Jörg Artmann, Florian Thein, Mareike Hecker

BAUHERR | CLIENT

Stadt Mainz, Wirtschaftsbeterieb Betriebszweig Entwässerung, Mainz

TRAGWERK | STRUCTURE

Büro Strehl, Stockach

PUMP UND WEHRTECHNIK PUMPING AND WEIR TECHNOLOGY

UHRIG Straßen-Tiefbau GmbH, Geisingen

FERTIGSTELLUNG | COMPLETION

2009

STANDORT | LOCATION

Mainz Gassnerallee / Rheinuferpromenade
55120 Mainz-Mombach

FOTOS | PHOTOS

SYRA – SCHOYERER ARCHITEKTEN BDA, Mainz

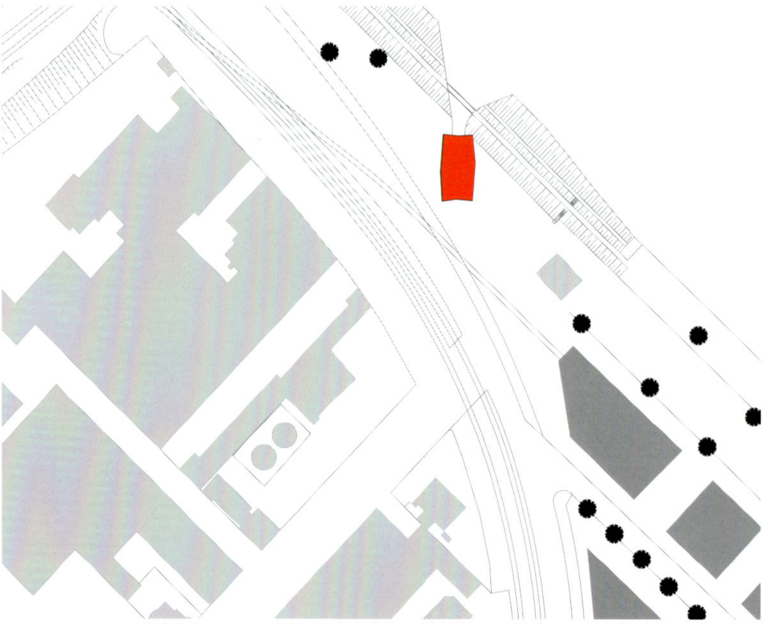

Lageplan | Site plan

Blick auf den Mainzer Zoll- und Binnenhafen mit dem Hochwasserpumpwerk.
View of Mainz's inland port with floodwater pumping station

Wer mit der S-Bahn von Wiesbaden nach Mainz unterwegs ist und aufmerksam aus dem Fenster schaut, der entdeckt kurz nach dem Überqueren des Rheins, überragt von Fabrikschornsteinen, eingezwängt zwischen Portalkränen und Lagerhallen, einen dunkelgrauen Block direkt am Ufer. Seine Bestimmung erschließt sich nicht auf den ersten Blick; beinah so geheimnisvoll wie der schwarze Monolith in der Anfangsszene von Stanley Kubricks Film „2001: Odyssee im Weltraum" liegt er da. Nur die mit fassadenbündigen Stahlgitterrosten verschlossenen Öffnungen verraten, dass der fugen- und fensterlose Körper wohl doch nicht vom Himmel gefallen ist, sondern einen Zweck erfüllen und innen hohl sein muss.
Das, was da am nordwestlichen Rand des Mainzer Zoll- und Binnenhafens steht, ist ein Hochwasserpumpwerk. Genauer gesagt: ein Pumpwerk mit Entlastungskanal, Hochwasser-Hubwehr und ‚Auslassbauwerk'. Es bewahrt die Mainzer Innenstadt im Fall von gleichzeitigem Hochwasser und Starkregen vor einer Überflutung durch einen Rückstau im Kanalnetz. Die enormen Wassermengen, die im Ernstfall in den Fluss gepumpt würden, geboten die Ausrichtung der Anlage schräg zur

If you take the commuter train from Wiesbaden to Mainz and pay attention to the sights passing by, you will discover, shortly after the train crosses the Rhine, a dark grey block set directly on its banks, squeezed in amongst the gantry cranes and warehouses, with factory smokestacks towering above it. At first glance, it's not clear just what this structure is that rises almost as mysteriously as the black monolith in the opening scene of Stanley Kubrick's film "2001: A Space Odyssey". Only the openings covered by steel grates flush with its surface reveal that the seamless, windowless structure apparently hasn't fallen from the sky and that it must serve some sort of purpose and be hollow inside.
In fact, this curious object on the north-western edge of Mainz's harbour is a floodwater pumping station. To put it more precisely: a pumping station with overflow channel, floodwater weir and spillway. It protects the city centre from flooding

Der Baukörper ist als schwerer Monolith, der auf einer Wasserader lagert, entworfen.
The body of the building is designed as a heavy monolith resting atop the waterway.

Uferlinie, in Fließrichtung. So wird verhindert, dass die rettende Operation zu stark in die Strömungsverhältnisse des Oberrheins eingreift. Dass dieses Pumpwerk nicht, wie so viele technische Betriebsgebäude in unseren Städten, ohne jeglichen Gestaltungsanspruch gebaut wurde, ist der geplanten Umwandlung des knapp 30 Hektar großen Zoll- und Binnenhafens in ein neues Stadtquartier zu verdanken. 1400 Wohnungen und 4 000 Arbeitsplätzen sollen hier neben sanierten Industriedenkmälern entstehen, ‚Hafeninseln' mit Grachten, eine Marina und natürlich eine Uferpromenade. An deren künftig westlichem Ende, unmittelbar vor der Kaiserbrücke, die den neuen Stadtteil von der industriell genutzten ‚Ingelheimer Aue' trennt, steht das Hochwasserpumpwerk.
Doch wie soll so ein Pumpwerk aussehen? Vorbilder gibt es so gut wie keine, von einer Typologie ganz zu schweigen. Die Architekten erinnerten sich an die ‚sprechende Architektur' von Étienne-Louis Boullée und Claude-Nicolas Ledoux und entwarfen den Baukörper als schweren Monolith, der auf einer Wasserader lagert und sie so reguliert. Die Technikhülle mit ihren gekanteten Seitenflächen und Traufkanten wurde komplett in Ortbeton errichtet und erhielt ihre unregelmäßige Oberflächenstruktur durch eine spezielle Steinmetztechnik. Bis zu 30 Millimeter tief ‚gespitzt' behauen, wirkt der Block eher

when high water in the river coincides with heavy rain by preventing the sewer system from backing up. The enormous amounts of water that must be pumped into the river in such an emergency mean that the station had to be laid out diagonally to the shoreline, in the direction of flow. This prevents the rescue operation from intervening too strongly in the flow of the Upper Rhine. The fact that attention was paid to the design of this pump station, something that happens rarely in technical services buildings in our cities, is owing to the current plans to convert the nearly 30-hectare harbour into a new and attractive city quarter for Mainz. 1,400 apartments and 4,000 jobs are to be created here amongst refurbished industrial monuments, along with "harbour islands" separated by canals, a marina and of course a waterfront promenade. At its future western end, right before the Kaiserbrücke bridge that separates the new district from the industrial "Ingelheimer Aue" area, stands the floodwater pumping station.
But what is a pumping station like this supposed to look like? There are almost no models available, let

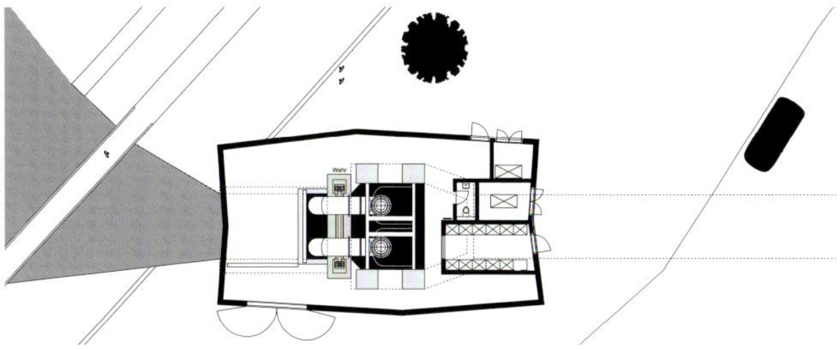

Grundriss Erdgeschoss | Floor plan of ground floor

geformt als gebaut; auf seinen Wänden entsteht ein lebhaftes Spiel von Licht und Schatten. Das Flachdach wird einfach über die raue Fassade entwässert, peu à peu soll der Block so partiell vermoosen. Das Altern der Oberflächen gehört zum Entwurfskonzept. Die Architekten wünschen sich, dass Entstehungszeit und Herstellungsprozess auf diese Weise mit der Zeit verwischen.

Der Weg der geplanten Uferpromenade ist durch eine Fußgängerbrücke unterhalb des Pumpwerks schon vorgezeichnet. Wir sind gespannt, ob künftige Flaneure die Architektur des konzeptionell etwas zu ambitionierten Pumpwerks bei ihren Spaziergängen dann im Sinne Walter Benjamins „weniger in einem gespannten Aufmerken als in einem beiläufigen Bemerken" wahrnehmen.

alone a typology. The architects therefore recalled the "speaking architecture" of Étienne-Louis Boullée and Claude-Nicolas Ledoux and designed the building as a ponderous monolith that rests atop a waterway and, in doing so, regulates it. The technical envelope with its canted side planes and eaves was constructed completely of cast-in-place concrete and then furnished with an irregular surface texture using a special stonemason's technique. Pointed chisels were used to chip the surface up to 30 millimetres deep, making the block look more moulded than poured and creating a lively play of light and shadow across its walls. The flat roof simply drains down across this rough façade, which can be expected to become gradually covered in moss. The ageing of the surfaces is all part of the plan. The architects hope that time will in this way eventually obliterate the construction process, making the station seem a natural part of the scene.

The course of the planned waterfront promenade is already predetermined by a pedestrian bridge below the pumping station. We will be interested to see whether future strollers will one day perceive the architecture of the conceptually slightly over-ambitious pumping station as Walter Benjamin once predicted for other architectural works: "much less through rapt attention than by noticing the object in incidental fashion".

Beinahe so geheimnisvoll wie der schwarze Monolith in der Anfangszene von Stanley Kubricks Film „2001: Odyssee im Weltraum" | Almost as mysterious as the black monolith in the opening scene of Stanley Kubrick's film "2001: A Space Odyssey"

Die Oberfläche ist bis zu 30 Millimeter tief ‚gespitzt' behauen. | The surface has been texturised with dents up to 30 millimetres deep created by pointed chisels.

GEDANKENSPIELE ZU LINGANG NEW CITY (SHANGHAI)

FOOD FOR THOUGHT ABOUT LINGANG NEW CITY (SHANGHAI)

NACHHALTIGER TROPFEN

A SUSTAINABLE DROP

DIRK MEYHÖFER

E2

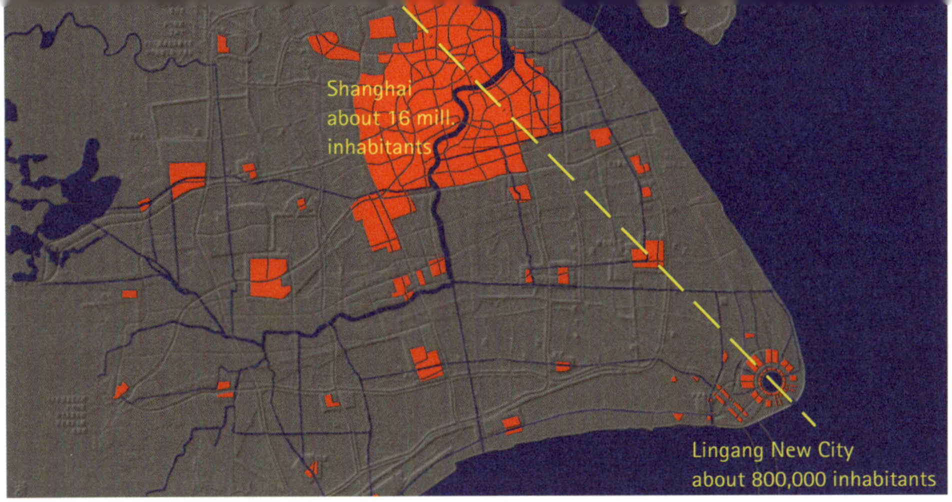

Um das enorme Bevölkerungswachstum von Shanghai aufzunehmen wurde ein internationaler Wettbewerb zur Planung einer neuen Hafenstadt ausgelobt. | Due to the need to house Shanghai's rapidly growing population, an international competition was held for a new harbour city.

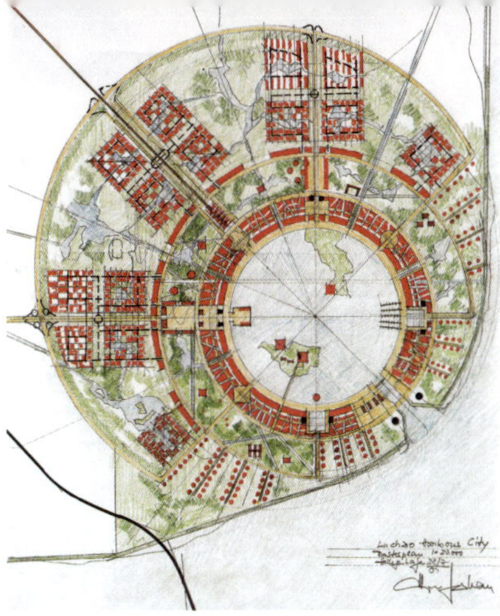

Skizze von Meinhard von Gerkan für Lingang New City | Sketch by Meinhard von Gerkan for Lingang New City

WARUM UTOPIEN SO GAR NICHT FÜR DEN ALLTAG TAUGLICH SIND

Als sich vor gut zehn Jahren abzeichnete, dass es das deutsche Architekturbüro von Gerkan, Marg und Partner (gmp) sein könnte, das für die damalige Retorten- und Hafenversorgungsstadt Luchao mit 300 000 Einwohnern planen sollte, wurde sofort das gute alte Stadtbau-Gen der europäischen Architekten des 20. Jahrhunderts spürbar. Südlich von Shanghai am Zugang zur 32,5 Kilometer langen Donghai-Brücke, die zum weltgrößten Tiefwasserhafen Yangsham führt, sollte eine Art Idealstadt der europäischen Stadtbaukunst entstehen. Möglicherweise beflügelt durch den innerstädtischen See, der Außenalster seiner Heimatstadt Hamburg, aber noch eindeutiger getragen durch eine jahrhunderte-alte ‚Ideal-Stadt-Philosophie' hatte Chefplaner Meinhard von Gerkan einen kreisrunden See als kosmisches Zentrum seiner neuen Stadt entworfen, nannte es prosaisch „aus einem Tropfen geboren"[1] und hatte die Chinesen und das gesamte internationale Feuilleton auf seiner Seite. Es sei die Wiederbelebung vergangener Stadtutopien, schrieb Niklas Maak in der „FAZ"[2], der sich immer gern der Aufbruchssymbolik der Moderne in seinen Artikeln widmet, sie erinnere an Vitruvs kreisförmige Idealsstadt und so weiter. Was war es wirklich? Ein sich stark geometrisch orientierender Stadtaufriss rund um den See, mit einem darauf zuführenden radialen Straßensystem, zwischen dem in entsprechenden Kreissegmenten gesiedelt werden konnte. Eine Stadt, die Orientierung und Ordnung versprach – eine Alternative zu den wild wuchernden Stadtwüsten des chinesischen Ostens?

Anlässlich der ersten großen Ausstellung zu Luchao wartete dann pflichtgemäß der damalige gmp-Kommunikationschef Bernd Pastuschka mit einem flankierenden Essay zur „Idealstadt im Spiegel der Zeit"[3] auf. Sehr richtig und ein bisschen forsch schrieb er gleich zu Anfang der Idealstadt auf den Leib, dass „sie ob Civitas oder Polis, Idee oder Utopie, allen gemeinsamen Ideen der Stadt eines gemeinsam ist: Ihr Ausgangspunkt ist immer ein Herrschaftsverhältnis. Ob es das Reich Gottes hat, der platonische Stadtstaat, die Kaiserstadt, ob es die faschistische, soziale oder demokratische Stadt ist, ohne Herrschaft und damit Macht scheint es keine Stadt zu geben". Das stimmt. Man möge dann nur noch als weitere Machthalter Kapital und Auto hinzufügen. Damit war schon einmal deutlich geworden, dass Durchführung und Fortführung eines

WHY UTOPIAS ARE NOT SUITABLE FOR EVERYDAY LIFE

As soon as it became clear ten years ago that the German architecture office of von Gerkan, Marg and Partners (gmp) might be chosen to plan the new Chinese port city of Luchao (population: 300,000), the good old town planning gene of 20th-century European architects was immediately apparent. The task: to create a kind of ideal city modelled on European urban development, located south of Shanghai at the entry to the 32.5- kilometre-long Donghai Bridge, which leads to the world's largest deep-water harbour, Yangsham. Perhaps inspired by the intra-urban Aussenalster lake in his home city of Hamburg, but even more clearly rooted in a centuries-old "ideal city philosophy", chief designer Meinhard von Gerkan created a circular lake as the cosmic centre of his new city and called it prosaically "born from a drop"[1], winning over the Chinese, as well as the entire international arts and culture press. It was a revival of past utopias, wrote Niklas Maak in the Frankfurter Allgemeine Zeitung newspaper.[2] Maak frequently praises in his reviews the spirit of departure symbolised by Modernism, and here pointed out how Luchao is reminiscent of Vitruvius's circular ideal city. But what was it really? An extremely geometrical urban layout situated around a lake, with an integrated radial network of streets and residential areas in the segments of the circle between them. It was a city promising clear orientation and order – perhaps an alternative to the rampantly growing urban wastelands of eastern China?

On the occasion of the first large-scale exhibition on Luchao, the then head of communication for gmp, Bernd Pastuschka, dutifully prepared an accompanying essay about "The Ideal City as a Reflection of the Times."[3] He starts off by describing the ideal city, perfectly correctly and a bit brashly: "Be it civitas or polis, idea or utopia, all shared ideas about cities have one thing in common: the point of departure is always a power relationship. Whether it is the kingdom of God, the Platonic city-state, the imperial city, or a fascist, socia-list or democratic city, there appears to be no city without a ruler who possesses power." That's right. And, we might add capital and cars, as

Claude-Nicolas Ledoux: Ville de Chaux / Arc-et-Senans
Claude-Nicolas Ledoux: Ville de Chaux / Arc-et-Senans

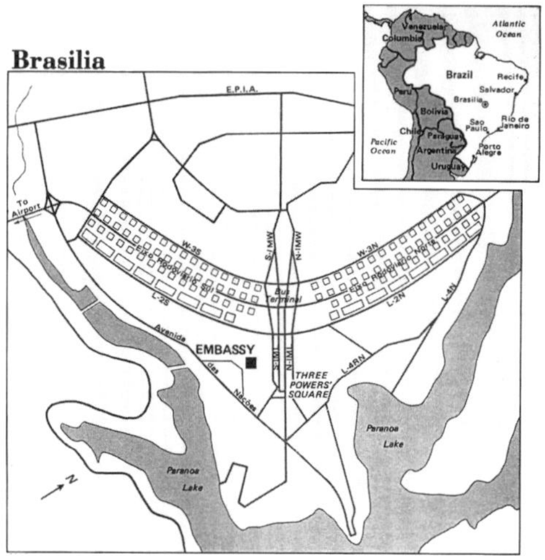

Plan von Brasilia | Plan for Brasilia

Idealstadtkonzepts niemals allein eine Sache der philosophischen und theoretischen Erkenntnis sein kann. Schaut man weiterhin auf Veröffentlichungen zur Idealstadt, dann sind sie geprägt von geometrischen Zeichen, von Kreisen, Dreiecken und Quadraten entsprechender semantischer Bedeutung wie Harmonie oder Gleichberechtigung. Idealstadtideen reichen von der Antike bis heute und über die Sollbruchstücke der Geschichte im 18. Jahrhundert, die man gern revolutionär nennt und beispielsweise durch Idealstadtentwürfe des Revolutionsarchitekten Claude-Nicolas Ledoux wie Arc-et-Senans sozialistisch-utopisch geprägt waren.

Die Rolle der Utopie für die real existierende Stadt darf aber durchaus infrage gestellt werden oder wie der französische Philosoph Frédéric Rouvillois sagte[4]: „Die Utopie existiert nicht, denn sie ist ein Nichtort – das zumindest bedeutet das Wort im Griechischen –, der sich im Spannungsfeld von Traum und Hoffnung bewegt. Die Umsetzung der Hoffnung ist allerdings zugleich ihre Überwindung – paradoxerweise bedeutet demnach die Realisierung einer Utopie ihr Ende." Konkreter bezogen auf Idealstaaten und -städte moniert Rouvillois deren geradezu geometrische Ordnung, die geplant und nicht organisch gewachsen war. Der Wunsch nach Perfektion drücke sich darin aus, dass das Leben der Menschen bis ins kleinste Detail geregelt sei. Ein anderes Wort für Utopie ist Ordnung – und widerspricht das nicht den humanphilosophischen Ansprüchen an die Stadt ein wenig?

Die durchgehende Ballade von geometrischen Zeichnungen für Form als Symbol[5] entpuppt sich möglicherweise als schöner Schein. Sei es wie es sei, im 20. Jahrhundert machen die Idealstadtideen noch einmal einen kapriziösen Quantensprung und lösen viel zu spät das Versprechen ein, Inhalte der industriellen Revolution für die ideale Stadt umzusetzen. Die Helden und Protagonisten sind bekannt, heißen Costa, Niemeyer und eben auch Le Corbusier. Sie arbeiten immer auch mit symbolischen Mitteln: für Chandigarh, die neue Hauptstadt des Punjab mit der „offenen Hand", für Brasilia, der Hauptstadt Brasiliens, mit den Gesten eines Supervogels oder eines von Flügel beseelten Wesens; ‚Flugzeug' wäre zu wenig als Kommentar für die Superfigur des gebauten Weichbildes der Stadt Brasilia.

other possessors of power ... This clarifies the fact that the realisation and perpetuation of an ideal city concept is never solely a matter of philosophical and theoretical perceptions. If one looks at publications about ideal cities, they are full of geometric figures, e.g. circles, triangles and squares, with their respective semantic meaning (harmony, equality). Concepts of ideal cities have been around since antiquity and include historical fragments of the 18th century, which we like to call revolutionary, and were marked by ideal city designs influenced by socialist, utopian ideals, for example the plans for Arc-et-Senans devised by revolutionary architect Claude-Nicolas Ledoux.

It is, however, legitimate to challenge the role of a utopia in relation to a real, viable city. In the words of the French philosopher Frédéric Rouvillois[4]: "Utopia does not exist, for it is a non-place – which is what the word means in Greek – and hovers in the area of conflict between hopes and dreams. Transforming hope into reality leads itself, however, to its own demise, as the realisation of a utopia paradoxically signifies its end." Rouvillois more specifically questions the geometric order of ideal states and cities, which are planned and do not arise organically. The desire for perfection is expressed in the regulation of every single aspect of people's lives. Another word for utopia is order – does this not slightly contradict humanist philosophical ideas about what makes a city great?

The consistent story of geometric figures as a symbol[5] for ideal forms may turn out to be a beautiful illusion. Whatever the case, in the 20th century ideas about ideal cities once again took a capricious quantum leap and made good much too late on the promise of implementing aspects of the industrial revolution in such cities. The heroes and protagonists are well known, and have names like Costa, Niemeyer and even Le Corbusier. They always work with symbolic imagery: for Chandigarh, the new capital city of the Punjab, it's an "open hand"; for Brazil's capital, Brasilia, it's the gesture of a super-bird or a creature with a winged soul; an airplane would not have been expressive enough as super-figure conveying Brasilia's soft-contoured image.

Brasilia, Esplanada dos Ministérios | Brasilia, Esplanada dos Ministérios

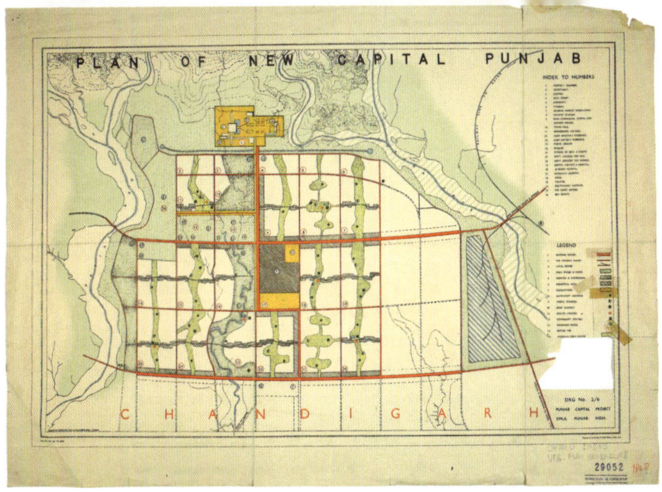

Le Corbusier: Masterplan Chandigarh | Le Corbusier: Masterplan for Chandigarh

EIN BESUCH IM NOVEMBER I: BRASILIA – WENN DIE IDEALSTADT IN DIE JAHRE KOMMT

Brasilia wird in diesem Jahr 50. Wer als ‚Fachbesucher' die Stadt zum Jubiläum wiedersieht, trägt die schwere Last aller theoretisch-idealtypischen Verankerungen, aller Bezüge auf Architekturgeschichte und -theorie und auf die CIAM-Moderne der Vorkriegszeit mit sich. Oscar Niemeyers Kathedrale oder Regierungspaläste spuken im Kopf der Architekten und Architekturtheoretiker herum wie Spolien eines Arkadiens des 20. Jahrhunderts – unlöschbar, aber auch weiter verwendbar?

Längst hat sich auch die optimistische Metapher des weit schwingenden Fluggeräts im Stadtgrundriss verflüchtigt, weil sie umwuchert worden ist. Die Seenlandschaft am Motorblock besteht, aber sie wird zur Basis von Quartieren der Superreichen, ein bisschen Südkalifornien grüßt herüber. Die Stadt ist irgendwann nicht mehr in der Vorgabe ihrer Architekten weitergebaut worden, stattdessen ist rundum eine typische Planktonlandschaft mit Strips, Großsiedlungen, andererseits sind auch ‚gated communities' entstanden, die flankiert von wachsenden ‚Favelas' wiederum bedroht werden – ganz normaler brasilianischer Stadtwahnsinn eben.[6]

Aber Brasilia bleibt 50 Jahre nach seiner metaphysischen Geburtsstunde in einigen Punkten weiter vorbildlich. Es zeigt sich, dass die architektonische Kleinarbeit eines radikal artistischen Oscar Niemeyer in den Biotopen der Stadt, die hier Superquadras heißen und rechteckig gerasterte Heimaten geworden sind, ein erstaunliches Kleinklima von Lebensqualität geliefert hat. Nicht höher als sechs Geschosse sollten sie sein; dafür nach Le Corbusierschen Vorbild auf ‚Pilotis' schwebend, eng verbunden jeweils mit Läden und Schulen. Das ist heute sichtbar, erlebbar und lobenswert. Was man nicht sieht, ist der ursprüngliche Ansatz in den Quadras, arm und reich zu mischen. Brasilia ist im Kern natürlich das Quartier der Regierungsbeamten, deswegen auch überdurchschnittlich sicher und möglicherweise deswegen auch gepflegt und irgendwie schön. Die Immobilienpreise bestätigen es. Brasilias weiteres soziales Schicksal war trotz seiner fast autistischen und somit stark steuerbaren Lage nicht wirklich planbar. Aber die Spolien leben weiter.

A VISIT IN NOVEMBER I: BRASILIA – WHEN AN IDEAL CITY GETS ON IN YEARS

Brasilia is turning 50 this year. Those who revisit the city for the jubilee as "experts" carry the heavy burden of all theoretical, ideal-typical roots, all references to architectural history and theory and to the CIAM pre-war Modernists. Oscar Niemeyer's cathedral and government palaces haunt the minds of architects and architectural theorists like the spoils of a 20th-century Arcadia – indelible, but still useful?

The optimistic metaphor of the swooping flying machine inscribed in the city's layout has long since evaporated, overgrown as it is today with the proliferation of subsequent building. The lakeland set at the engine block still exists, but is used to accommodate the super-rich, southern-California style. The specifications prescribed by the architects were abandoned somewhere along the way, resulting in a typical plankton landscape with strips and large suburban housing estates, along with gated communities which are, however, being threatened by the spread of favelas – all part of the usual Brazilian urban madness.[6]

But 50 years after its metaphysical birth, Brasilia nonetheless remains a model city in some respects. The architectural detail work carried out by the radically artistic Oscar Niemeyer in the city's biotopes, here called superquadras, which have become rectangular-grid residential areas, has provided an incredible microclimate for quality of life. Buildings were limited to six storeys but float atop Le Corbusier's pilotis and are closely connected to shops and schools. Today, this ideal is still visible, tangible and commendable. What you do not see is the original approach of mixing the classes within the quadras. Brasilia is at heart naturally a district for government officials and consequently has a below-average crime rate. Perhaps for this reason, the city is also well-maintained and quite beautiful. Real estate prices confirm its status. Brasilia's further social destiny was not really foreseeable, despite its almost autistic and hence manageable situation. But the spoils live on.

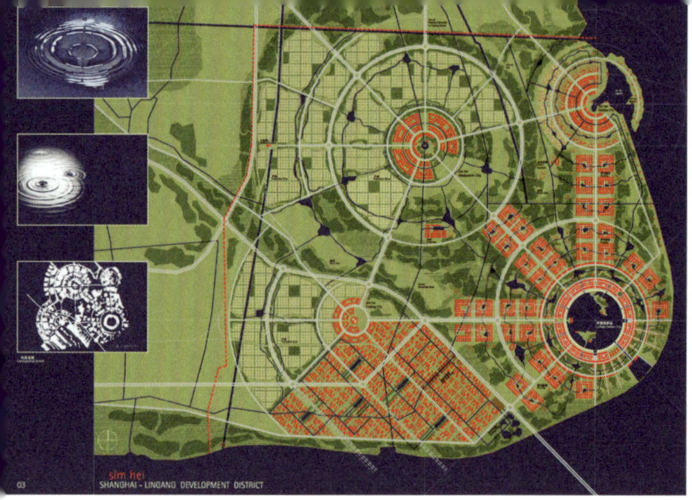

Masterplan von Lingang New City | Masterplan for Lingang New City

Modell | Model

BESUCH IM NOVEMBER II: LINGANG IM AUFBAU

Eine Generation später sind es andere Länder, die zu urbanistischen Großtaten aufrufen. China will und muss dabei nicht demokratische Ideale spiegeln, aber westliche Stadtmuster imponieren dort schon. Mit dem derzeitigen Motto der Expo „Better City, Better Life" soll ein Bekenntnis um die Welt gehen, dass die Zukunft der Menschheit und damit Chinas (oder anders herum?) nur in besser gemachten Städten liegen kann. Die Entwicklung der Megacity Shanghai erfüllt dies so ganz und gar nicht – wie man gerade in Pudong erleben darf, wo historische, menschliche Wohnquartiere gegen ein endloses Hochhausmeer internationaler Machart getauscht werden. Die Chinesen fragten ob des Chaos dann schon einmal die Deutschen um Rat, deren altväterlicher Kolonialstil in Tsingtau hatte sie begeistert. Zu einem Anting als New German Town war es ursprünglich gekommen, wie Albert Speer jun. gern überliefert, weil Chinesen Fachwerk so gern mögen. Zumindest haben sie dort menschlichere Strukturen als gewohnt bekommen. Auch Luchao war trotz aller strenger Geometrie von deutscher Emotion und Wärme geprägt, denn so kann man den Hauptgedanken vom Wohnen am Wasser durchaus bezeichnen.

Ein zweiter Novemberspaziergang nur wenige Tage später, aber meilenweit entfernt, auch nicht auf der südlichen, sondern der nördlichen Halbkugel, führt nach Lingang, wie Luchao jetzt heißt. Es liegt nach einer einstündigen Autofahrt von Pudong in Richtung Süden in besserem Licht und unter klarerem Himmel als Shanghai selbst. Ein gewaltiges Stadtfragment, der See ist fertiggestellt, gar eingewachsen schon ein wenig. Der geistige Stadtmittelpunkt mit Rathaus und Maritim Museum zeugt von geometrisch strenger Baukunst von gmp. Man sieht viele Straßen mit absurder Spurenvielfalt, aber ohne Verkehr. Doch selbst von der Aussichtsplattform oben am Rathaus ist die geometrische Großform noch nicht oder nicht mehr zu registrieren, stattdessen unendliche Landschaft ähnlich einem brachliegenden Stück Ostfriesland im Wind. Der Tropfen ist zum Meer geworden, zum Binnenmeer. Ein wichtiger Vorwurf aus dem weit entfernten Europa, warum man denn bitte direkt am Strand des Gelben Meeres einen künstlichen See bauen muss, entkräftigt sich bei der Besichtigung des groben Strandes und seinen asphaltierten Deichen von selbst. Auch die ersten chinesischen Freizeiteinrichtungen und Honeymoon Hotels können nicht davon ablenken, Sylt liegt woanders, nämlich am „Tropfen", und der ist schon heute

A VISIT IN NOVEMBER II: LINGANG UNDER CONSTRUCTION

A generation later, other countries call for mighty urban deeds. China does not have any desire, nor is it obliged, to reflect democratic ideals, but Western city models nevertheless impress. The theme of the current EXPO, "Better City, Better Life", aims at communicating a commitment around the world that the future of humankind, including China (or the other way round?) lies in making better cities. The development of the megacity of Shanghai does not fulfil this idea at all – as one can see particularly in Pudong, where historic, humane living areas are being replaced by an endless sea of skyscrapers based on the international model. The Chinese once sought counselling for this chaos from the Germans, whose patriarchal colonial style they so admired in Tsingtau. And Albert Speer Jr. originally conceived Anting as a New German Town because, as he likes to recount, the Chinese just love half-timbered buildings. There, at least, they were provided with more liveable structures than usual. Luchao, too, was hallmarked by German emotion and warmth despite strict adherence to geometry, as evidenced by the main theme of living on the waterfront.

A second November walk, just a few days later but miles away, and not in the southern but in the northern hemisphere, leads to Lingang, as Luchao is now named. It is an hour's drive south from Pudong, and the light is better and the sky clearer than in Shanghai. It is a huge city fragment where the lake is finished and has even integrated itself into the landscape a bit. The spiritual city centre with a city hall and the Maritime Museum bears witness to gmp's strictly geometric architecture. There are many streets with an absurd number of lanes, but no traffic. And yet even from the observation deck at the top of city hall, the geometric master plan is not yet, or no longer, visible. One sees instead an endless landscape looking like a fallow piece of East Frisia in the wind. The "drop" has become a sea, an inland lake. A key criticism from distant Europe as to why one would construct a man-made lake right on the coast of the Yellow Sea is defused upon seeing its rough beach and asphalt embankment. The first Chinese recreational facilities and honeymoon hotels at this sea cannot distract from the

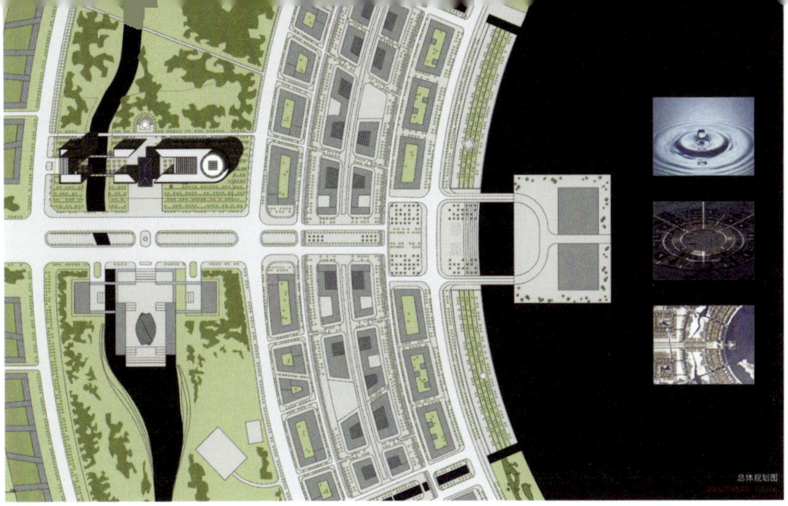

Masterplan des Verwaltungszentrums des Shanghai Nanhui Districts und Maritim Museum im ersten Grüngürtel von Lingang | Masterplan of the Administrative Centre for Shanghai's Nanhui District and the Maritime Museum, located in Lingang's first green belt

Das Maritim Museum | Maritime Museum

eine Wochenendsensation für die chinesische motorisierte Upperclass – das ist neu im Reich der Mitte: künstliche, blühende Landschaften, wo sonst nur verseuchte Steppen oder übersiedelte Großmanhattans existieren. Allein dafür muss China den deutschen Architekten dankbar sein.
Auch die architektonischen Ansätze sind gut, nicht so sensationell wie bei Oscar Niemeyer, aber das neue Hotel auf einer Halbinsel im See der britischen Architektenfirma Atkins und auch das Maritim Museum von gmp schenken der neuen Stadt erste Landmarken. Die städtische Kante an der Promenade des Sees entsteht, vom Meer her, aus dem Niemandsland betrachtet, winzig. Städte-Bau kann man das (noch) nicht nennen. Da hätten sich die Europäer mehr trauen dürfen. Die ersten Wohncluster zwischen den radial verlaufenden Straßen sind gebaut – ohne gmp –, chinesisch finanziert und organisiert, aus der Höhe betrachtet eng bebaute Investorendurchschnittsware. Aus der Nähe gesehen jedoch erheblich besser als in den Silos von Pudong.
Doch ausgerechnet Pudong könnte das Schicksal werden von Lingang und deren deutschen Chefarchitekten von gmp. Die alte Landkreisstruktur und damit die Bauherrenschaft wurden ausgetauscht. Pudong verwaltet jetzt Lingang New City und Pudong ist das chinesische Dubai von Shanghai, gemessen an seinem rasenden Wachstum, das sich mit all dem Größenwahn – von höchsten Skyscrapern, längsten Achsen, breitesten Autobahnen und schnellstem Transrapid – als chinesische ‚Idealstadt' ausdrückt. Die chinaerfahrenen Architekten von gmp lernen wieder einmal, wie schwierig es ist, die chinesische Karte zu spielen, denn das Spiel wird immer schneller. Gezinkte Karten tauchen auch schon auf. Es entsteht hier keine Hamburger HafenCity, sondern gleich ein ganzes Hamburg. Von 1,2 Millionen Einwohnern ist inzwischen die Rede. Die zweite Brücke zum Tiefseehafen kommt. Zwei Universitäten, eine davon eine maritime, sind in kürzester Zeit als gepflegte ‚gated' Campus-Universitäten entstanden. In Hamburg diskutiert man darüber Jahrzehnte. Trotz der stoischen Ost-West-Ausrichtung der vielen Wohnbauten und Wohnheime – wie es in China fast ein Naturgesetz ist – entstehen gediegene Stadtbezirke mit Wasser und Grün. Ein Stück Amerika am Gelben Meer, das hier wirklich so aussieht, und ohne Mitwirkung von gmp. Eine neue U-Bahnlinie, Shanghais längste, integriert Lingang in die Megacity und macht es vielleicht einmal zum beliebtesten Stadtteil.
Die noch günstigen Immobilienpreise ziehen an, weil Lingang ein lebenswerter Ort für junge erfolgreiche chinesische Familien werden kann.

fact that the high-class resort is elsewhere, namely at the "drop". Today, the new lake area is already a weekend getaway for the motorised Chinese upper class. This is a new development for the Middle Kingdom: artificial, flourishing landscapes, where otherwise only contaminated steppe or overpopulated Manhattan-style settlements exist. If only for this, China owes a debt of gratitude to the German architects.
The architectural approach is sound – not as sensational as Oscar Niemeyer, but the new hotel on a peninsula in the lake by the British architecture firm Atkins and the Maritime Museum by gmp have given the new city its first landmarks. The city's edge along the lake promenade, when viewed from the no-man's-land of the lake, is tiny. One cannot (yet) call it urban planning. The Europeans could have tried something bolder. The first residential clusters between the radial streets have been built without gmp, financed and organised by the Chinese. When viewed from above, they look like your average cramped investor-planned structures. But up close they are still significantly better than the concrete tower blocks of Pudong.
Pudong of all things could however be Lingang's fate and that of its German chief architects at gmp. The old county system and hence also the client has been replaced. Pudong now administers Lingang New City, and Pudong is the Chinese Dubai of Shanghai, as measured by its rapid growth, expressed by all the megalomania of a Chinese "ideal city" – the highest skyscrapers, longest axes, widest motorways and fastest Transrapid train. Those architects at gmp who have experience in China are once again learning how difficult it is to deal cards to the Chinese, as the game continually picks up speed. And some of the cards are marked. This is not HafenCity in Hamburg, but rather the whole city of Hamburg. Now there is talk of 1.2 million inhabitants for Lingang. The second bridge to the deep-sea port is being planned. Two universities, one of them with a maritime focus, have sprung up practically overnight as groomed, gated campuses. In Hamburg, the idea would first have been discussed for decades. Despite the stoic East-West alignment of the many houses and residential buildings – which is almost a natural law in China – there are high-class boroughs

Straßenansicht Maritim Museum | Maritime Museum from the street

Rendering des Dishui Lake Hotel von Atkins | Rendering of Dishui Lake Hotel by Atkins

Die einstigen Masterplaner sind erst einmal Randfiguren, was den weiteren Städtebau und das Wachstum betrifft. Ob gmp dabei städtebaulich und stadtpflegerisch jemals die Aufgabe wie einst Niemeyer bekommen werden, einen „Quadra" zu gestalten, das ist mehr als fraglich. Inwieweit sie als Architekten weiter wirken können, mag man an einer kleinen Randepisode ablesen: Ihr hanseatisch-modern korrekter, präziser Verwaltungsbau hat ohne ihr Zutun seine neutrale moderne Aura verloren. Ein Gitterzaum, drei Fahnenmasten und ein Hoheitszeichen machten die hanseatische Moderne zum chinesischen Regierungsgebäude. So leicht geht das mit deutscher, symmetrischer Architektur.

DER TROPFEN-MYTHOS UND UND SEINE ZUKUNFT

Ist Stadt planbar? Nein, nicht in der Konsequenz, mit der Städtebauer des 20. Jahrhunderts an die Arbeit gegangen sind, nicht mit dem möglicherweise für die Ewigkeit gesetzten technokratischen Verständnis, nicht mit der ausgesprochenen Doktrin, nur so und bitte nicht anders. Schon gar nicht mit den inzwischen obsolet gewordenen Lehren einer entmischten und verkehrsgerechten Stadt. Oder einer Lehre, die den Gesetzen des Immobilienmarkts gehorcht. Einer, die aus der üblichen Überfliegerpose des klötzchenschiebenden Städtebauers entsteht.
Wer ist schuld? Als spätestens in den 1970er- und 1980er-Jahren die Utopisten der Moderne mit ihrer chaotisch autogerechten Stadt Bankrott anmeldeten, als die Städte gemordet und gestorben waren, hielten sich Stadtforscher und -theoretiker zurück, wie der Soziologe Angelius Eisinger und Professor für die „Kultur der Metropolen" an der HafenCity-Universität Hamburg sagt. In die Lücke stießen Stilistiker, Schönlinge, Architekten mit eindringlicher Signatur der Marke Gehry, Hadid und Libeskind. Und die Folge war eine Eventisierung und Disneylandisierung der Planung. Rem Koolhaas kürzte den Leidensweg verbal einmal so ab: „Jedes Beharren auf dem Urzustand der Stadt führt über Nostalgie in die Belanglosigkeit. Die Stadt gibt es nicht mehr!"[7] Es ist ausgerechnet fünf vor zwölf, zu einem Zeitpunkt, wenn über die Hälfte der Menschheit in Städten lebt, 30 Prozent davon wiederum in Slums. „Welche Konzepte haben wir für die Zukunft der Städte?", fragte der deutsche Beitrag

with water and green areas. It is a piece of America on the Yellow Sea, which is what it really looks like here, without advice from gmp. A new subway line, Shanghai's longest, integrates Lingang into the megacity and may one day make it the most popular city district. The still-affordable real estate prices are rising, because Lingang could become a popular place to settle for young, successful Chinese families.
The former master planners are now standing on the sidelines with regard to further town planning and growth. It is uncertain whether or not gmp will ever receive a commission for urban planning and development, to design a quadra, as Niemeyer once did in Brasilia. To what extent gmp will continue to play a role as architects at all may be gauged by looking at a minor, fringe incident. Through no fault of their own, their correctly modern, Hanseatic, precise office building has lost its neutral modern aura; a fence, three flagpoles and a national emblem have transformed this paragon of Hanseatic modernism into a Chinese government building. That's easy to do with German, symmetric architecture.

THE MYTH OF THE DROP AND ITS FUTURE

Can a city be planned? No, at least not with the consistency that 20th-century architects have tended to bring to the task: not with perpetual technocratic understanding, not with the pronounced doctrine "this is the only way", and not at all with the now obsolete thesis of a desegregated city catering to future traffic patterns. Or based on a model that obeys the laws of the real estate market – one that arises from the customary high-flyer posing of a block-pushing city planner.
Who is to blame? According to the sociologist and professor for "Metropolis Culture" at Hamburg's HafenCity University, Angelius Eisinger, things began to change when the modern utopians declared the bankruptcy of their chaotic, car-friendly city in the 1970s and 80s, at a time when cities were murdered and dead. Back then, the city experts and theorists refrained from comment. In their place sprang up stylists, pretty boys, architects with vivid signature brands such as Gehry, Hadid and Libeskind. The result was to make planning

Verwaltungszentrum des Shanghai Nanhui Districts
Administrative Centre for Shanghai's Nanhui District

Verwaltungszentrum, Blick vom Hochhaus auf den Dishui See
Administrative Centre, view from high-rise toward Dishui Lake

auf der 8. Architekturbiennale 2009 in São Paulo in seiner Präambel. „Wie erhalten alle Menschen Zugang zu den Segnungen der Städte? Wie machen wir die Hinterhöfe unserer Städte zu lebenswerten Orten? Wie werden wir alle würdig wohnen können? Wie können aufgegebene und wertlose Flächen zur Metamorphose erweckt und zurück ins urbane Leben geholt werden? Wie wird Stadt als ‚ecoscape' – zur Stadtlandschaft, die endlich mehr Energie erzeugt als sie verbraucht?"[8] Eine Menge unbeantworteter Fragen. Erst wenn wir sie beantwortet haben, könnte Stadt wieder planbar sein.

Für Lingang kann man die Frage nach der Zukunft in einem Punkt sehr, sehr positiv beantworten. Die Grundidee war einzigartig gut und mehr als ein geometrisches Schattenspiel ideeller Werte: Der Tropfen steht für Wasser und Wasser für Leben. Der Stein ist gesetzt, für eine Stadt, wie China sie nur in der Geschichte und nicht in der Moderne kennt. Das allein reicht aus für Ruhm und Ehre und das Bundesverdienstkreuz dafür, dass man deutsche Planungsideen nach China exportiert hat. Mit Klötzchen spielen kann man getrost anderen überlassen.

1 Luchao – Aus einem Tropfen geboren: architecture for China von Gerkan, Marg und Partner (Ausst.-Kat.), Altenburg 2003.

2 Niklas Maak, „Wiedergeburt der Idealstadt", in: Frankfurter Allgemeine Zeitung vom 7. 10. 2002.

3 Bernd Pastuschka, in: Luchao – Aus einem Tropfen geboren, a.a.O., S. 28ff.

4 In der bemerkenswerte Sendereihe zur Philosophie auf Arte: www.arte.tv/de/Die-Welt-verstehen/philosophie/3012272.html.

5 Luchao – Aus einem Tropfen geboren, a.a.O., S. 28ff.

6 Dirk Meyhöfer „Der deutsche Koffer", in: Süddeutsche Zeitung vom 03. 12. 2007.

7 Rem Koolhaas, Gespräche mit Studenten, Rice University, 1996.

8 „Cidade para Todos" – Deutscher Beitrag auf der 8. Architekturbiennale 2009 in São Paulo.

an event in the grandstanding Disneyland manner. Rem Koolhaas once concisely summarised the ordeal: "Any insistence on maintaining the original form of the city is an exercise in nostalgia which leads to irrelevance. The city no longer exists!"[7] Time is now running out in an era when over half of humanity lives in cities, 30 per cent in slums. "What concepts do we have for the future of cities?" asked the German contribution to the 8th Architecture Biennial in São Paulo in 2009 in its preamble: "How do we grant all people access to the blessings of cities? How can we make liveable spaces out of the backyards of our cities? How will we all be able to live in dignity? How can we turn abandoned, worthless spaces back into urban living areas? How can we turn cities into "ecoscapes" – urban areas that at last generate more energy than they use?"[8] Plenty of unanswered questions. Only when we have found answers can we again begin to plan cities.

For Lingang, questions about at least one aspect of the future have very positive answers. The basic idea was uniquely good and more than a geometric shadow-play of ideal values: the drop stands for water and water for life. The foundation has been laid for the kind of city that China knew in its past, but not in modern times. This alone is deserving of fame and glory, and of the Federal Cross of Merit for exporting German planning concepts to China. We will happily leave playing with blocks to the others.

1 Luchao – Aus einem Tropfen geboren: architecture for China von Gerkan, Marg und Partner (exh. cat.), Altenburg 2003.

2 Niklas Maak, "Wiedergeburt der Idealstadt", in: Frankfurter Allgemeine Zeitung, 7 October 2002.

3 Bernd Pastuschka, in: Luchao – Aus einem Tropfen geboren, op. cit., p. 28ff.

4 In the noteworthy philosophy series featured by television station Arte: www.arte.tv/de/Die-Welt-verstehen/philosophie/3012272.html.

5 Luchao – Aus einem Tropfen geboren, op.cit., p. 28ff.

6 Dirk Meyhöfer, "Der deutsche Koffer", in: Süddeutsche Zeitung, 3 December 2007.

7 Rem Koolhaas, Gespräche mit Studenten, Rice University, 1996.

8 "Cidade para Todos" – German contribution to the 8th Architecture Biennial in São Paulo, 2009.

DEUTSCHER ARCHITEKTUR EXPORT

GERMAN ARCHITECTURE EXPORT

20–23

INTERNATIONAL
INTERNATIONAL

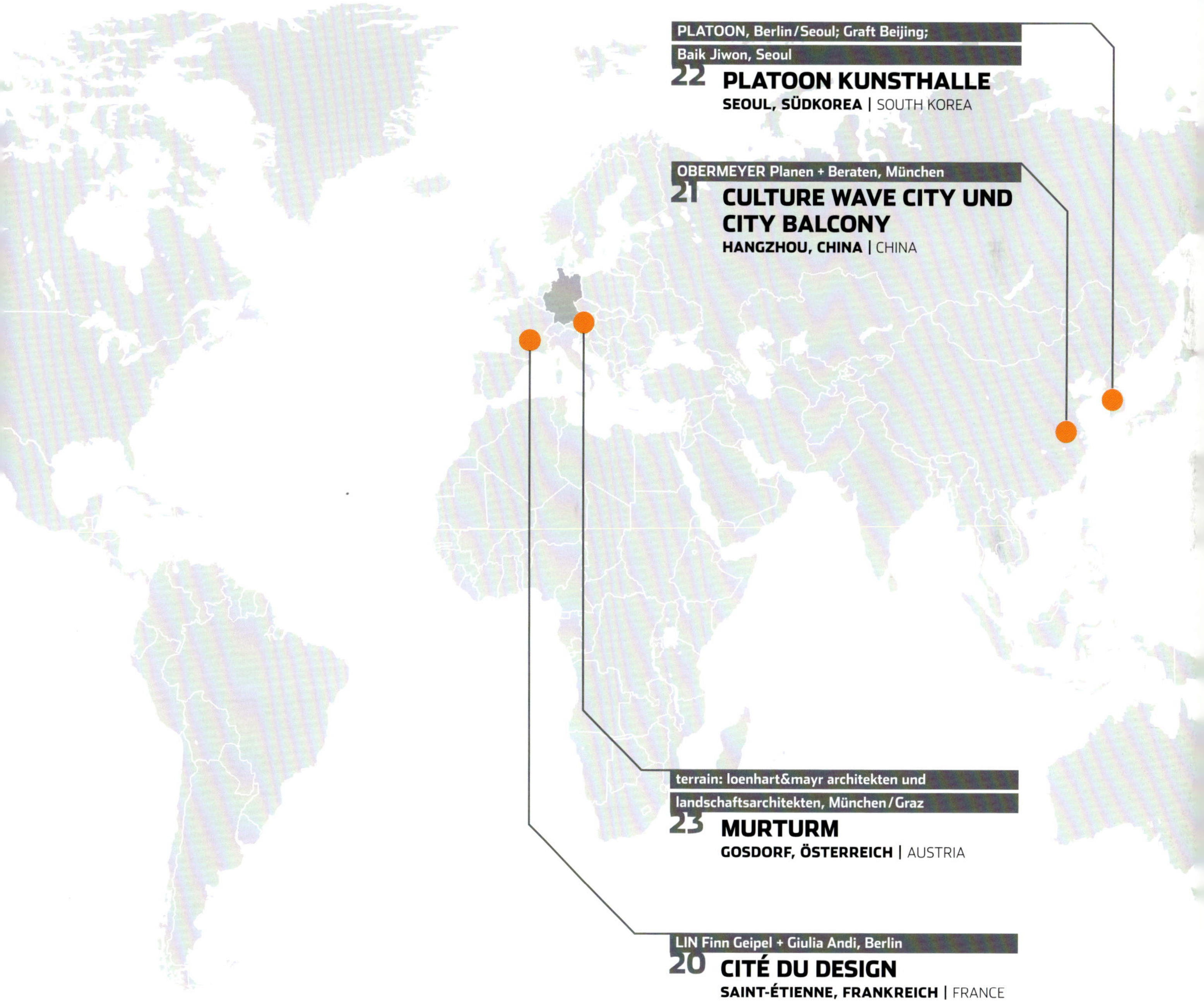

ARCHITEKT | ARCHITECT

LIN FINN GEIPEL + GIULIA ANDI

GEBÄUDE | BUILDING

CITÉ DU DESIGN

SAINT-ÉTIENNE, FRANKREICH | FRANCE

TEXT ANNE KOCKELKORN

20

Die 193 Meter lange „Platine", daneben die ehemalige Manufaktur
The 193-metre-long "Platine", next to it the former factory

ARCHITEKTEN | ARCHITECTS

LIN Finn Geipel + Giulia Andi Architects Urbanists Helmholtzstraße 2–9 10587 Berlin www.lin-a.com

STÄDTEBAULICHER RAHMENPLAN, BAUANTRAG GESAMTENSEMBLE
URBAN MASTER PLAN, BUILDING APPLICATION FOR COMPLETE ENSEMBLE

LIN Finn Geipel + Giulia Andi, Berlin / Paris

WETTBEWERB UND ENTWURF
COMPETITION AND SCHEMATIC DESIGN

LIN Finn Geipel + Giulia Andi, Berlin / Paris

MITARBEITER | TEAM

Stefan Jeske, Philip König (Projektleiter | project manager**) Jacques Cadilhac, Jan-Oliver Kunze, Judith Stichtenoth, François Maisonnasse, Muriel Poncet, Marielle Gilibert, Heiko Walth**

BAUHERR | CLIENT

Saint-Étienne Métropole

AUSFÜHRUNGSPLANUNG
EXECUTION PLANNING

LIN Finn Geipel + Giulia Andi, Berlin / Paris

BAULEITUNG / PROJEKTSTEUERUNG
SITE MANAGEMENT / PROJECT GUIDANCE

LIN Finn Geipel + Giulia Andi, Berlin / Paris Benjamin Wallerand, Lyon Maurice Guitton, Lyon

TRAGWERK | STRUCTURE

Werner Sobek + Thomas Winterstetter, WSI, Stuttgart / New York

AUSSTELLUNGSARCHITEKTUR
EXHIBITION ARCHITECTURE

LIN Finn Geipel + Giulia Andi, Berlin / Paris (Ausbau und Mobiliar interior fittings and furniture**)**

ENERGIEKONZEPT
ENERGY CONCEPT

Matthias Schuler + Arnaud Billard, Transsolar, Stuttgart / New York

LANDSCHAFTSARCHITEKTEN
LANDSCAPE ARCHITECTS

Clément Willemin + Frank Poirier, BASE, Paris

HAUSTECHNIK | M & E ENGINEERS

Fréderique Binvignat + Christian Desquiens, BETOM Ingénierie, Corbas, Frankreich | France

FERTIGSTELLUNG | COMPLETION

Oktober 2009 | October 2009

STANDORT | LOCATION

Cité du design 3, rue Javelin Pagnon 42000 Saint-Étienne, Frankreich | France
http://www.citedudesign.com

FOTOS | PHOTOS

LIN Finn Geipel + Giulia Andi Fotograf | Photographer **Christian Richters Jan-Oliver Kunze, LIN François Maisonnasse, LIN**

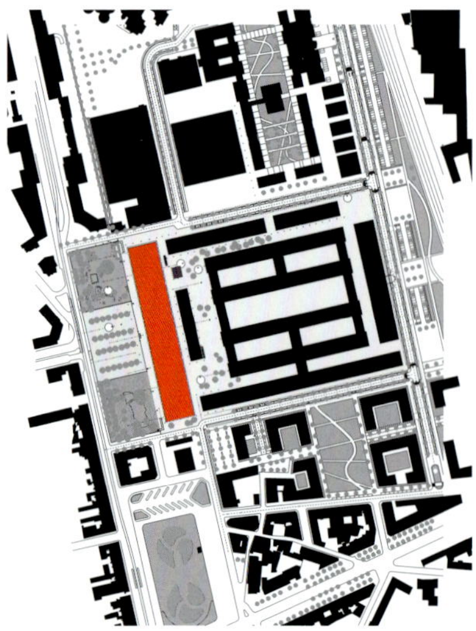

Lageplan | Site plan

Blick aus dem Garten im Süden auf die „Platine“. | View from the garden to the south of the “Platine”.

Von der Tramstation „Cité du Design“ blickt man über leeres Kopfsteinpflaster und in Perspektive gestutzte Platanen auf ein schmiedeeisernes Gittertor. Dahinter thront ein Mansardendach im kolossalen Stil des Second Empire; zwischen Gitter und Sandsteinfassade schimmert eine eingeschossige Wand aus Dreiecken, Glas und Aluminium hindurch. Beim nächsten Blick bemerkt man einen zweiten Fremdkörper links dahinter – ein 31 Meter hohes Metallgerüst als Aussichtsturm – und steht kurz darauf im Foyer zwischen runden Kiosken für Shop, Cafeteria oder Informationsdisplay. Hier herrscht Betrieb. Ältere Ausstellungsbesucher mischen sich mit Schulklassen und begegnen Kunststudenten, die als Kartenabreißer engagiert sind. Dass sich die französische Mittelstadt Saint-Étienne mit diesem Neubau als internationale Plattform des Industriedesigns zu etablieren sucht, hat historische Gründe: Im 19. Jahrhundert

From the Cité du Design tram station one looks across empty cobblestone streets and a row of pruned plane trees receding into the distance to a wrought-iron gate. Behind it looms a mansard roof in the colossal style of the Second Empire, and between gate and sandstone façade a one-storey wall of triangles of glass and aluminium glints in the sun. Another glance reveals a second foreign body set back to the left, 31-metre-high metal scaffolding as an observation tower, and soon one is standing in a foyer between round kiosks for shop, cafeteria and information display. Things are bustling here. Older exhibition visitors rub elbows with school classes and encounter art students taking the admission tickets.

war die Stadt Zentrum der französischen Waffen- und Montanindustrie, 1870 wurde nördlich der Stadtmauer ihre größte Waffenmanufaktur in Betrieb genommen, entsprechend waren die 12 Hektar des Areals durch Mauer und Gittertor von der Stadt abgeschottet. Erst in den 1980er-Jahren wurde die Produktion eingestellt und das Gelände für die Stadtentwicklung frei – jetzt strategisch günstig in Nähe von Bahnhof und Stadtzentrum gelegen. 1991 wurde das Fachgebiet Design an der Kunsthochschule Saint-Étienne gegründet und 1998 die Design-Biennale der Stadt ins Leben gerufen; 2003 taten sich dann Stadt und Agglomeration zusammen, um eine Institution zu etablieren, die Kunsthochschule, Biennale und Industrieunternehmen zusammenführen sollte. Das Wettbewerbsverfahren für das Gebäude konnte Ende 2004 das Büro LIN (Finn Geipel und Giulia Andi) aus Berlin für sich entscheiden.

Städtebaulich scheint das Angebot der „Platine" – wie die Architekten ihre Halle zärtlich genannt haben – so einfach wie möglich: 193 x 31 Meter aufgeständerter Fußboden vermitteln zwischen Stadt und ehemaliger Manufaktur; darunter ein Infrastrukturkeller für die Haustechnik. Für diese Art der flexiblen Strukturangebote gibt es einige berühmte Vorläufer, vom Christal Palace über den Fun Palace bis zu den Multifunktionsbauten des holländischen Strukturalismus: Immer soll ein freiliegendes Metalltragwerk unter der Prämisse der Flexibilität

Historisches Tor und „Platine" | Historical gate and "Platine"

There are historical reasons behind the efforts being made by the mid-sized French city of Saint-Étienne to establish itself with this new complex as an international platform for industrial design. In the 19th century the city was the centre of French arms manufacture and of the coal, iron and steel industries, and in 1870 the country's biggest weapons factory went into operation north of the city walls, its 12 hectares of grounds blocked off from the rest of the city behind walls and iron gates. It was not until the 1980s that the plant ceased production and the land was opened up for urban development – strategically located near the railway station and city centre. In 1991 a Department of Design was established at the Saint-Étienne Academy of Art, and in 1998 a Design Biennial was inaugurated in the city; in 2003 the city and agglomeration then came together to establish an institution uniting what was now the School of Art and Design, the Biennial and various industrial enterprises. The architecture firm of LIN (Finn Geipel and Giulia Andi) from Berlin emerged triumphant from a competition for the building held in late 2004.

In terms of urban planning, what is offered by the "Platine" – as the architects affectionately dubbed their hall – is as straightforward as possible: 193 x 31 metres of elevated floor space mediate between the city and the former factory, with an infrastructure cellar underneath for the building services. There are a few famous forerunners for this flexible type of structure, from the Crystal Palace to the Fun Palace to the multifunctional buildings of Dutch Structuralism: in each case an exposed metal support framework allows for performative uses under the premise of flexibility. This conceptual basis also prompted the competition decision in this case, because the space designed by LIN seemed open enough to react to the as yet undetermined competition programme.

Now, however, the actual architectural execution paints a different picture: the finished building asserts itself as both embedded infrastructure and autonomous design object. The "mono-espace" of the hall is divided according to function into different acoustic and climatic areas, so that a later conversion would seem to be structurally possible, but hardly practicable; the detailing is so precise that

Fassadendetail. Die Hülle der „Platine" besteht aus 14 000 gleichseitigen Dreiecken. | Façade detail. The shell of the "Platine" is made up of 14,000 equilateral triangles.

Die „Platine" | The "Platine"

performative Nutzungsweisen ermöglichen. Diese Konzeptgrundlage war in diesem Fall auch Anlass für den Wettbewerbsentscheid, denn der Raum schien offen genug, um auf das noch unbestimmte Wettbewerbsprogramm reagieren zu können. Die architektonische Ausführung zeichnet jetzt ein anderes Bild: Hier behauptet sich der Bau gleichermaßen als eingebettete Infrastruktur und autonomes Designobjekt. Der ‚Mono-Espace' der Halle ist nach Funktionen in akustische und klimatische Bereiche eingeteilt, sodass eine spätere Umnutzung zwar konstruktiv möglich, aber kaum praktikabel scheint; die Detaillierung ist so genau, dass sie eher dem millimetergenauen Zuschnitt industrieller Prototypen entspricht als dem Großmaßstab der Infrastruktur. Der stufenlose Betonboden folgt in Längs- und Breitseite dem doppelten Geländegefälle, liegt an der Nordseite eineinhalb Meter tiefer als an der Südseite, und im Westen 40 Zentimeter tiefer als im Osten. Das Dach ist an den Nord- und Südkanten flach, aber in der 100 Meter entfernten Gebäudemitte um einen Meter gewölbt, sodass jeder Querträger der Dachkonstruktion einem anderen Wölbungsgrad folgt und individuell zugeschnitten ist. Die 14 000 Fassadenpaneele sind nach Farbe und Material in zehn Typen untergliedert: Aluminium, Einfachverglasung, Sonnenschutzglas oder Photovoltaikpaneele erlauben Belüftungs- und Belichtungsvarianten

it corresponds more to the millimetre-by-millimetre customisation of industrial prototypes than the grand scale of infrastructure. The stepless concrete floor follows the double slope of the land in both axes, lying on the northern side one-and-a-half metres lower than on the south side, and in the west 40 centimetres lower than in the east. The roof is flat at the northern and southern edges, but bulges one metre higher in the middle of the building, 100 metres away, so that each cross-beam of the roof structure follows a different curvature and had to be individually adapted. The 14,000 façade panels are divided according to

Blick aus dem Ausstellungsbereich auf die „Agora" im Zentrum der „Platine". | View from the exhibition area of the "Agora" at the centre of the "Platine".

Fassadendetail mit Photovoltaik-Paneelen
Detail of the skin – modular (photovoltaic) panels

für Seminarraum oder Gewächshaus, Restaurant oder Auditorium. Mit den dreieckigen Windschutzblechen für den Rauchabzug erinnert diese Fassade an einen Gürteltierpanzer, dessen eingeschriebener Nutzungscode nur vom Dach aus lesbar ist.

Die Unterteilung in Funktionsabschnitte zerstört zwar einerseits den Raumeindruck der offenen Halle, andererseits steht genau diese stille Anpassung für einen wesentlichen Aspekt des Industriedesigns: im Hintergrund unaufdringlich zu funktionieren und als Alltagsgegenstand beiläufig als ‚angenehm' bemerkt zu werden. Schade jedoch, dass die beiden markantesten Orte der Neubauten nicht öffentlich zugänglich sind. Die Dachaufsicht bleibt unsichtbar, da das obligatorische Aufsichtspersonal für Fahrstuhl und Aussichtsplattform nur einen Tag im Monat bezahlt wird. Auch der Keller der „Platine" kann bisher nur von Haustechnikern betreten werden: Hier sind die 200 Meter Gebäudestrecke unter dem Grollen der Klimaanlage bei 10° Celsius kälteren Temperaturen körperlich erfahrbar. Bleibt zu hoffen, dass sich Kunststudenten und Publikum langfristig beide Orte aneignen können.

colour and material into ten types: here, aluminium, simple glazing, sun-protective glass and photovoltaic panels allow variations in ventilation and lighting individually tailored to seminar room or greenhouse, restaurant or auditorium. With its triangular metal wind-protection flaps for the flues, the façade resembles the armour of an armadillo, with an inscribed usage code that can only be read from the roof.

Although the division of the building into functional sections destroys the spatial impression of the open hall, it is precisely this silent adaptation that stands for an essential aspect of industrial design: i.e. to function inconspicuously in the background and be noticed in passing as a "pleasant" everyday object. It is nevertheless a shame that the two most striking spots in the new buildings are not open to the public. The rooftop view remains a well-kept secret, since the obligatory guards for the elevator and outlook platform are only paid to work one day a month. The cellar of the "Platine" can likewise be entered only by in-house technical staff. Here, the 200 metres spanned by the building can be physically experienced at 10° Celsius to the rumbling of the air conditioner. We can only hope that art students and the public will eventually be able to claim both these places as their own.

Ansicht von Norden | View from the north

Ausstellungsbereich B der „Platine“ | The "Platine" exhibition space B

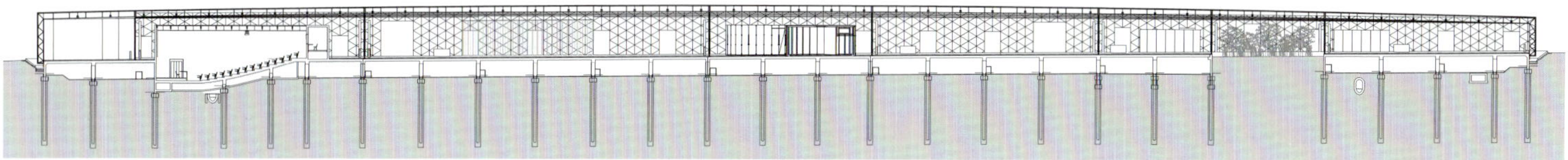

Längsschnitt der „Platine“ | Longitudinal section of the "Platine"

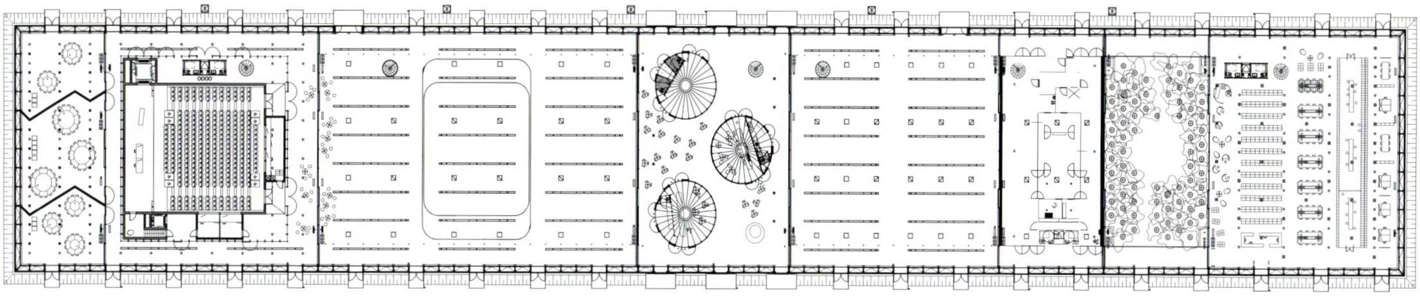

Grundriss „Platine“ | Floor plan of the "Platine"

ARCHITEKT | ARCHITECT

OBERMEYER PLANEN + BERATEN

GEBÄUDE | BUILDING

CULTURE WAVE CITY / CITY BALCONY

HANGZHOU, CHINA

TEXT HAORU CHEN, JIANG SHI YU

21

ARCHITEKTEN | ARCHITECTS

OBERMEYER
Planen + Beraten GmbH
Hansastraße 40
80686 München | Munich
www.opb.de

STÄDTEBAULICHER RAHMENPLAN, BAUANTRAG GESAMTENSEMBLE
URBAN MASTER PLAN, BUILDING APPLICATION FOR COMPLETE ENSEMBLE

OBERMEYER Planen + Beraten GmbH

WETTBEWERB UND ENTWURF
COMPETITION AND SCHEMATIC DESIGN

OBERMEYER Planen + Beraten GmbH

MITARBEITER | TEAM

Projektleitung | project management
Alexander Jeckel
Projektteam | project team
Sabine Wutzlhofer, Bing Chen, Richard Vollmar, Jin Wang

BAUHERR | CLIENT

Hangzhou CBD Construction & Management Committee New CBD Construction Headquarters, Hangzhou, China

AUSFÜHRUNGSPLANUNG
EXECUTION PLANNING

ECADI, Shanghai, China; OBERMEYER Planen + Beraten GmbH

BAULEITUNG / PROJEKTSTEUERUNG
SITE MANAGEMENT / PROJECT GUIDANCE

ECADI, Shanghai, China; OBERMEYER Planen + Beraten GmbH

TRAGWERK | STRUCTURE

OBERMEYER Planen + Beraten GmbH (Projektleitung | project manager **Markus Sailer)**
ECADI, Shanghai, China

LANDSCHAFTSARCHITEKTEN
LANDSCAPE ARCHITECTS

Prof. Rainer Schmidt Landschaftsarchitekten, München (Projektleitung | project manager **Jörg Michel)**
ECADI, Shanghai, China

HAUSTECHNIK | M & E ENGINEERS

OBERMEYER
Planen + Beraten GmbH
ECADI, Shanghai, China

FERTIGSTELLUNG | COMPLETION

Juni 2009 | June 2009

STANDORT | LOCATION

Hangzhou Central Business District
310016 Hangzhou, China

FOTOS | PHOTOS

LIU QIHUA, Shanghai, China

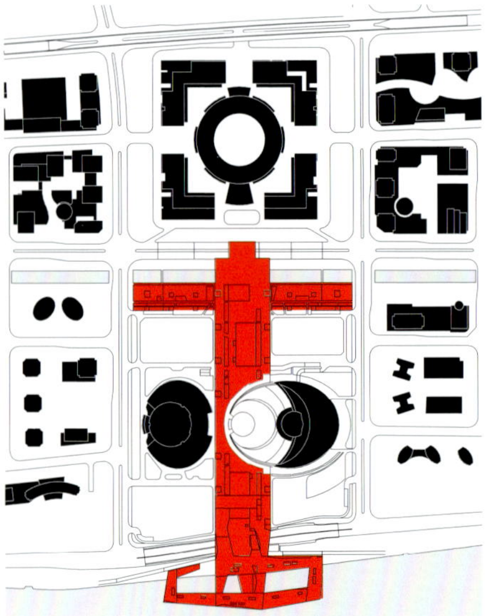

Lageplan Culture Wave City und City Balcony
Site plan of Culture Wave City and City Balcony

City Balcony als Aussichtsplattform | City Balcony as observation platform

Die Qianjiang-New City – ein vier Quadratkilometer großes Stadtentwicklungsgebiet am Qian Tang Fluss – entstand mit dem Ziel, das Verwaltungs- und Geschäftsviertel der Stadt Hangzhou auf das unbebaute Areal am Flussufer zu verlegen. Hier konnte, ohne viel Rücksicht auf Stadterneuerung und Denkmalschutz nehmen zu müssen, die Neustadt als Stadt der Zukunft ausgewiesen werden.

Der „City Balcony“ (Stadtbalkon) ist im Vordergrund angeordnet, dort, wo die neue Stadtachse auf den Fluss trifft. Hinter ihm liegt der „Sun and Moon“-Platz mit dem Konferenzzentrum in Form einer goldenen Kugel und dem Opernhaus in Gestalt einer Mondsichel. Der hintere Abschluss ergibt sich durch fünf kreisförmig angeordnete Glastürme; sie bilden den größten Stadtverwaltungskomplex in ganz China. Diese Achse wird von großmaßstäblichen Bauten und ebenso dimensionierten öffentlichen Plätzen flankiert. Architekten aus aller Welt kamen nach Qianjiang, um an dieser großen Bauaufgabe teilzuhaben, darunter das deutsche Büro OBERMEYER Planen + Beraten, das den „City Balcony“ entworfen hat.

Für die Stadt signalisieren diese Projekte die ehrgeizige Ambition, Hangzhou als eine der dynamischsten Städte des Landes darzustellen. Für die Bewohner ist die Pracht des neuen Stadtteils eine Geste der Offenheit gegenüber Gästen aus aller Welt.

The new city of Qian-jiang is a four-square-kilometre CBD development along the Qian Tang River, aimed to shift Hangzhou city's administration and business functions out of its old town and onto the unoccupied mud shore. Without much concern for urban renewal and historical preservation, the new city was designated as the city of the future.

The City Balcony is at the forefront, where the new city axis meets the river. Behind it is the Sun and Moon public square, with a conference centre resembling a golden globe and an opera house shaped like the crescent moon. In the centre background, five glass towers stand in a circle to form the largest civic municipal building in China. This axis is lined with grand structures and super-scale plazas. International architects have flown in from everywhere to join this great party of construction. Amongst them, the German firm OBERMEYER Planen + Beraten is designing the City Balcony.

For the city, these projects reveal a new ambition to put Hangzhou on the map of the nation's powerhouses. For its people, the magnificence of the new city represents an open gesture to people everywhere.

Überdachte Struktur der Culture Wave City | Roofed structure of Culture Wave City

Culture Wave City: Unterstadt mit Geschäftszone | Culture Wave City: lower city with business zone

In Hinblick auf die Planer und Architekten scheint deren bester Beitrag darin zu bestehen zu bauen und weniger darin, sich um die Repräsentation von Macht und Reichtum zu kümmern. Dank der explosionsartigen Ausweitung des privaten und öffentlichen Verkehrs, sind der neue Stadtteil und seine Einrichtungen problemlos für die Bewohner aus dem Umland erreichbar. An den wichtigsten Feiertagen und zu zahlreichen öffentlichen Veranstaltungen strömen große Menschenmengen durch die Abfolge von öffentlichen Plätzen, die durch die neue Achse verbunden sind, bis sie schließlich an das eigentlichen Ziel gelangen – den „City Balcony". Es ist die zentral gelegene Aussichtsplattform, von der sich die diversen Feuerwerksspektakel über dem Fluss ideal genießen lassen. Wendet man den Blick zurück, dann zeugt die hoch aufragende Stadtsilhouette vom Fortschritt der neuen Stadt und dem neu erworbenem Wohlstand. Die vielen offenen Plattformen dieses Stadtbalkons sorgen für großartige Ausblicke und bieten einen ununterbrochenen Rundgang. Dank dieser Strategie lassen sich zwei Fliegen mit einer Klappe schlagen: Alle Stadtbewohner sind eingeladen an dem großen Auftritt der neuen Stadt teilzuhaben und werden so zugleich Zeugen ihres unglaublichen Fortschritts.

Der riesige Baukörper des „City Balcony"-Projekts besteht aus einem künstlichen Hügel, der von allen Richtungen her erreichbar ist. Der Hauptzugang erfolgt über die Erweiterung der „Citizens Plaza" im Norden. Von einer Freifläche gelangt man langsam über ein Netz von Treppen, Rampen, Aufzügen, Rolltreppen und Amphitheatern auf unterschiedliche Niveaus. Die steinernen Stufen und Glasbrüstungen wurden in einem ‚übermenschlichen' Maßstab entworfen. Große Menschenmengen werden durch eine Reihe von abgesenkten Höfen zu dem erhöhten offenen Platz über der Hochuferstraße geleitet. Wenn man auf einem der an Piranesi erinnernden Plätze steht, ziehen die Objekte weiter unten mit scheinbar unglaublicher Geschwindigkeit vorbei, und weiter oben befördert das an einen Irrgarten erinnernde Netz von Rampen aus Edelstahl und Glas Massen von Besuchern an ihr Ziel.

Das letztliche Ziel aller Besucher ist das teils hügel-, teils pierähnliche Objekt, das hoch über dem Fluss schwebt und von aus dem Wasser ragenden Betonpfählen getragen wird. Von der Plattform aus hat man einen unvergleichlichen Blick auf den Fluss und die Stadtsilhouette. Der innere Kern der Struktur ist

For the planners and architects, it seems that the best contribution to make here is more to build, and less to worry about the unity of power and wealth. Thank to the explosion of automobiles and public transport, the new city and its facilities can be reached easily by citizens living elsewhere. In the frequent celebrations of holidays and events, people are drawn through an series of open public spaces linked by the new axis, and eventually arrive at the final destination – the City Balcony, a central stage for viewing the spectacular firework show on the river. When one turns around, the soaring height of the skyline shows the new city's progress and newly gained wealth. The multiple open platforms on the urban balcony provide grand views and allow an uninterrupted processional way. It is a strategy of killing two birds with one stone: all citizens are invited to the new city's show, and they bear witness to its incredible progress.

The giant City Balcony project is an artificially constructed hill approachable from all directions. The main access is from the extension of the citizens' plaza from the north. From a public courtyard, we ascend slowly via a web of steps, ramps, elevators, escalators and amphitheatres. The stone-paved steps and glass rails are designed on a super-human scale. Large crowds are drawn through a series of sunken courtyards to the elevated outdoor space above the riverside motorway. When you stand in one of the Piranesi-like spaces, objects pass below you with the velocity of the motorcars. Above you, the maze-like web of stainless-steel-and-glass conveyors carries crowds of people to their destinations.

The final destination for all visitors is the partly hill-like and partly dock-like object hovering above the river, supported by circular concrete pillars that rise from the water. The internal centre is the exhibition hall below the observation deck with another sweeping river view.

Stairways enclosed by translucent glass boxes project up onto the terrace, suggesting numerous

City Balcony: Passage über dem Qian Tang River
City Balcony: passage over the Qian Tang River

Culture Wave City mit Blick auf den City Balcony
Culture Wave City with view of the City Balcony

die Ausstellungshalle unter der Panoramaplattform, die eine weitere dramatischen Aussicht auf den Fluss bietet.
Von transparenten Glaskuben eingefasste Treppen leiten nach oben auf die Terrasse und bieten zahlreiche Wege in Richtung Ausgang. Der Besucher soll in einem dauernden Zustand der Bewegung bleiben. Ähnlich wie bei anderen monumentalen Bauten, wird man sich der übermenschlichen Dimension des Umgebenden erst in jenem Moment bewusst, wenn die Bewegung zum Stillstand kommt.
Bleiben wir also in Bewegung und nehmen den nächsten Ausgang von der Terrasse. Die abgesenkten Höfe wurden nicht möbliert, alle Räume sind miteinander verbunden und suggerieren ein vieldeutiges Programm. In den meisten Gebäuden dieses neuen Stadtteils sollen die Nutzungsprogramme dem Raum gemäß erfunden werden. Was bislang steht ist eine unfertige Schale endloser Möglichkeiten, die für die Zukunft offen sind. „Das Einzige was sicher ist, ist die Veränderung." An sich ein Klischee, aber in China vielleicht unvermeidliche Realität.

alternative routes out. Indeed, movement should be the constant state for all visitors. As in other large structures, when the movement stops, the super-human scale reappears.
Keep moving; take any exit from the terrace. The sunken courtyards have not been furnished, and all spaces are actively connected with each other, hinting at an ambiguous programme. In most buildings here, programmes are to be invented in accordance with the space. Here is an incomplete shell of infinite possibilities, left for the future. Is it a cliché to say "the only thing that doesn't change is change itself", or is it an inevitable reality in China?

Culture Wave City: Blick in den begrünten Lichthof | Culture Wave City: view into green atrium

Rampenanlage in Richtung des Qian Tang River | Ramp, looking toward Qian Tang River

KONZEPTENTWURF | CONCEPT DESIGN

PLATOON

ARCHITEKTONISCHE BERATUNG | ARCHITECTURAL CONSULTANCY

GRAFT BEIJING, BAIK JIWON

GEBÄUDE | BUILDING

PLATOON KUNSTHALLE

SEOUL, SÜDKOREA | SOUTH KOREA

TEXT PETER CACHOLA SCHMAL

22

KONZEPTENTWURF
CONCEPT DESIGN

PLATOON. cultural development
Alte Schönhauser Straße 3
10119 Berlin
www.platoon.org

ARCHITEKTONISCHE BERATUNG
ARCHITECTURAL CONSULTANCY

Graft Beijing CO. LTD.
No. 77 Back Street of Art Museum
Dong Cheng District 100010
China
www.graftlab.com
&
Baik, Jiwon
www.urbantainer.com

BAUHERR | CLIENT

PLATOON.seoul

AUSFÜHRUNGSPLANUNG
EXECUTION PLANNING

U-il Architects & Engineers,
Südkorea | South Korea

TRAGWERK | STRUCTURE

MIDAS IT, Südkorea | South Korea

FERTIGELEMENTEPLANUNG
PREFAB ENGINEERING

Ace special container,
Südkorea | South Korea

INNENRAUMENTWURF
INTERIOR DESIGN

Urbantainer,
Südkorea | South Korea

FERTIGSTELLUNG | COMPLETION

April 2009

STANDORT | LOCATION

97-22, Nonhyeon-dong,
Gangnam-gu, Seoul,
Südkorea | South Korea
www.kunsthalle.com

FOTOS | PHOTOS

© PLATOON
Foto | Photo
MYOUNG-RAE PARK

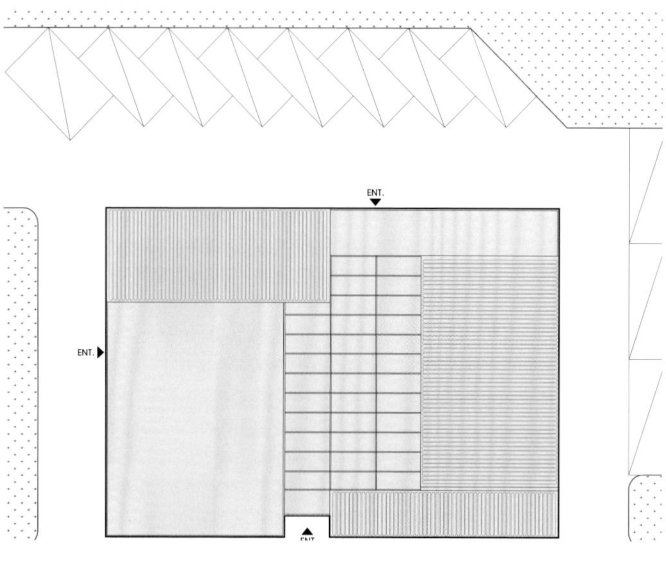

Lageplan | Site plan

Die PLATOON Kunsthalle besteht aus ISO-Frachtcontainern als Zeichen für eine flexible Architektur in einer globalisierten Kultur. | The PLATOON Kunsthalle is made of ISO freight containers as an emblem of a flexible mode of architecture in a globalised culture.

Sandwich, Wirsingsuppe, Currywurst, Boulette, Käspätzle, Schnitzel, Paprikagulasch und Flammkuchen – dazu Krombacher Bier vom Fass? Das Angebot in der Platoon Kunsthalle erstaunt, denn sie liegt im angesagten Cheongdam-Viertel auf der Südseite des großen Han Rivers im südkoreanischen Seoul, mit seinen internationalen Modeläden, teuren Clubs und Restaurants. Sie provoziert die koreanische Öffentlichkeit seit ihrer Eröffnung im April 2009 nicht nur mit ihren ungewohnten Köstlichkeiten. Auch von außen setzt der dreigeschossige, nato-oliv gestrichene Containerbau auf Konfrontation. Als eine nichtsubventionierte, der Clubszene nahen Alternative zum Goethe Institut könnte man diesen Ableger der Kommunikationsagentur Platoon verstehen, die in drei aufeinandergestapelten Seefrachtcontainern in Berlin-Mitte beheimatet ist.

In Seoul sind es sogar 28 Container, die so gruppiert wurden, dass sich ein überdachter Loungebereich von knapp 300 Quadratmetern in ihrer Mitte ergibt. Graft (Berlin und Beijing) haben hier ein spannendes, räumliches Gebilde aus fabrikneuen Containern realisiert, und nicht wie üblich aus abgenutzten, verschiedenfarbigen Kisten. Auf diese Weise konnten nicht nur Installationen besser integriert, sondern es

Sandwiches, cabbage soup, curry sausage, hamburgers, cheesy spaetzle noodles, schnitzel, goulash and tarte flambée – all washed down with Krombacher draught beer? The offerings on the menu at the Platoon Kunsthalle are quite astounding, because this art space is located not in Germany but in Seoul, South Korea, on the south side of the great Han River in the hip Cheongdam district with its international fashion boutiques and upscale clubs and restaurants. Since opening in April 2009, the exhibition venue has been offering the Korean public not only unusual culinary specialities, but plenty of food for thought as well. And the exterior of the three-storey container building painted in NATO olive-green is on a similar confrontation course with public sensibilities. This offshoot of the communication agency Platoon, whose headquarters in Berlin-Mitte are housed in three stacked sea freight containers, might be understood as a non-subsidised alternative to the Goethe Institute, closer in feeling to Seoul's club scene than to mainstream culture.

Seiteneingang | Side entrance

Rückseite der Kunsthalle | Back of the Kunsthalle

konnte auch richtig gebaut werden. Wände wurden ausgelassen, Glasflächen und Stahltreppen eingefügt, Glasoberlicht und Flachdach angeschweißt. Der Bau spielt mit dem Temporären, wurde aber über sechs Monate errichtet. So handelt es sich beim Straßenasphalt in der großen Halle, der nahtlos über große Garagentore nach außen führt, um eine gut gedämmte Bodenplatte mit integrierter Be-und Entwässerung, Bodentanks und Fußbodenheizung, die eine angenehme Temperierung der Halle und somit ein bodennahes Sitzen, wie in Korea üblich, ermöglicht.

Der militärische Habitus, der sich von der Namensgebung (Platoon ist eine militärische Untereinheit von etwa 25 Mann) über die faltbaren Sitzmöbel, die ausrangierten Bundeswehruniformen der Mitarbeiter mit ihren amerikanischen Hundemarken um den Hals bis hin zur Truppenküche im Café zieht, stammt von Platoon Berlin, und entspricht durchaus der Ausrichtung auf die bisher kaum existierende koreanische Subkultur: rau, industriell, subversiv. In Korea wirkt dies ziemlich exotisch.

Die ausgeklügelte räumliche Choreographie, die von Graft und Platoon gemeinsam entwickelt wurde, wird bei einem Rundgang sichtbar. Vom Eingang führt der Weg zur Bar vorbei an vier einzelnen, kleinen 10-Foot Containern (3,05 x 2,44 Meter) für Wechselausstellungen, eine Treppe hoch zu vier Standard 20-Foot Containern (6,09 Meter) für das „Artist in Residence" Programm und einem doppelt breiten Multifunktionsraum weiter ins zweite Obergeschoss, wo in vier langen 40-Foot Röhren (12,19 Meter) die Mitarbeiter arbeiten. Im Schnitt entsteht so eine umgekehrt abgetreppte Stapelung mit extremer Auskragung, die mit dem Containerbausystem problemlos machbar ist. Darüber erstreckt sich eine großzügige Dachterrasse mit Bar, die im Sommer zu Grillabenden inmitten der umgebenden Hochhausschluchten einlädt. Eine Brücke im obersten Geschoss führt zum gegenüberliegenden 100 Quadratmeter großen Konferenzraum aus drei Langcontainern, mit Blick

In Seoul, no less than 28 containers were used to build the Kunsthalle, grouped to create a roofed lounge area in the middle with nearly 300 square metres of floor space. Graft (Berlin and Beijing) have conceived an exciting spatial construct using shiny new containers rather than the usual worn-out boxes in various faded hues. This not only made it easier to integrate the necessary installations; it also enabled the building to be constructed properly. Walls were removed, glazing and steel stairways inserted, glass skylights and a flat roof welded on. The building flirts with temporariness, but was in fact erected over a period of six months. The floor of street asphalt in the huge hall, which seamlessly leads outside through large garage doors, is thus well insulated with an integrated water supply and drainage, floor tanks and heating, making for a pleasant ambient climate that allows visitors to sit close to the ground, as customary in Korea.

The military look, which pervades everything here from the name (a platoon is a military unit of about 25 men) to the folding seating furniture, the used German army uniforms and American dog tags worn by the staff, all the way to the troop kitchen in the café, originated with Platoon Berlin and reflects an orientation to the newly arising Korean subculture: raw, industrial, subversive. For Korea, this is all quite exotic.

The cleverly choreographed sequence of spaces, which was developed jointly by Graft and Platoon, unfolds during a tour of the premises. From the entrance the route leads past a bar to four small, separate 10-foot containers (3.05 x 2.44 metres) for changing exhibitions, then up the stairs to four standard 20-foot containers (6.09 metres) for the

Zentrale Lounge mit Bar | Central lounge with bar

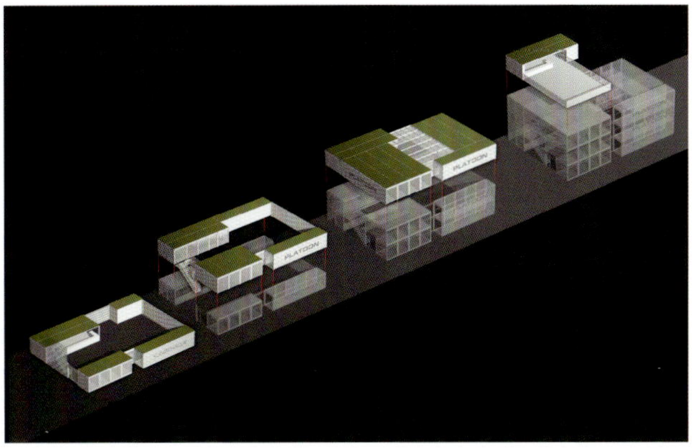

Schichtung der Containermodule | Layering of the container modules

Die Container wurden speziell für die Kunsthalle angefertigt. | The containers were made especially for the Kunsthalle.

Montage der Kunsthalle | Assembling the Kunsthalle

hinunter ins zentrale Geschehen. Über eine zweite Treppenanlage hinab wird der Rundweg geschlossen.

Mit diesem differenzierten Raumangebot aus kleinen, mittleren und großen Räumen, um eine zentrale Halle angeordnet, machte die ungewöhnliche Location schnell auf sich aufmerksam. Die resultierenden Vermietungen an Firmen aus dem Kreativbereich finanzieren fast das gesamte Programm mit seinen Gastkünstlern, Ausstellungen und vielfältigen Veranstaltungen, wie Nachtflohmärkten, Filmabenden oder Künstlergesprächen. Zusätzlich verdient Platoon an der Ausrichtung von Events, wie dem „Korean Music Award". Die Glaubwürdigkeit und gute Vernetzung garantiert dabei den Kunden eine starke Resonanz bei der gewünschten Zielgruppe.

Jüngst hat die koreanische Architektenkammer der Platoon Kunsthalle den Preis für das beste experimentelle Bauwerk Koreas verliehen. Für die Berliner hat sich ihr asiatisches Abenteuer bisher auf jeden Fall gelohnt. Ein Ableger, ein zweites Kulturzentrum aus 29 Containern, entsteht derzeit in der südkoreanischen Stadt Gwangju.

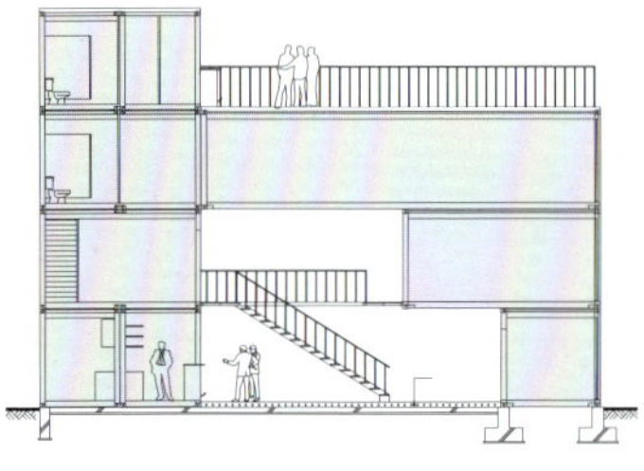

Schnitt | Section

artist-in-residence programme and a double-width multifunctional space, and then further upward to the second floor, where staff offices are housed in four 40-foot tubes (12.19 metres). The whole thus forms a stack with successively larger levels, meaning the upper storey is cantilevered out in the extreme, which is however unproblematic when building with containers. On top of it all is a spacious rooftop terrace with a bar, an inviting place for summer BBQ parties in the midst of the high-rises towering all around. A bridge leads from the uppermost storey to a 100-square-metre conference room opposite, composed of three long containers, from where there is a view down to the goings-on at the centre of the complex. Descending a second staircase ends the circuit.

With this varied array of small, medium-sized and larger spaces laid out around a central hall, this unusual venue soon attracted the attention of the locals. The resulting rentals to companies from various creative fields finance nearly the entire slate of guest artists, exhibitions and diverse events such as night-time flea markets, film evenings and artist talks. Platoon also earns money by hosting events like the Korean Music Awards. Its street credibility and good connections thereby guarantee clients of the Kunsthalle a resounding response from the target group.

Recently, the Korean Institute of Architects awarded the Platoon Kunsthalle the prize for the best experimental building in Korea. For the Berliners, this Asian adventure has certainly paid off. A further offshoot, a second cultural centre made of 29 containers, is already being built in the South Korean city of Gwangju.

Rooftop Bar | Rooftop Bar

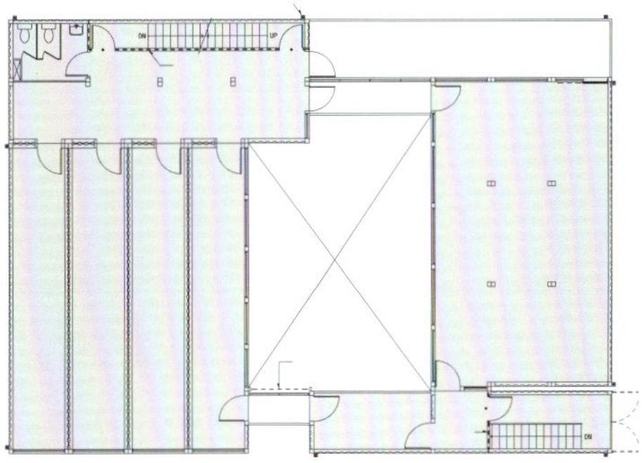

2. Obergeschoss | 2nd floor

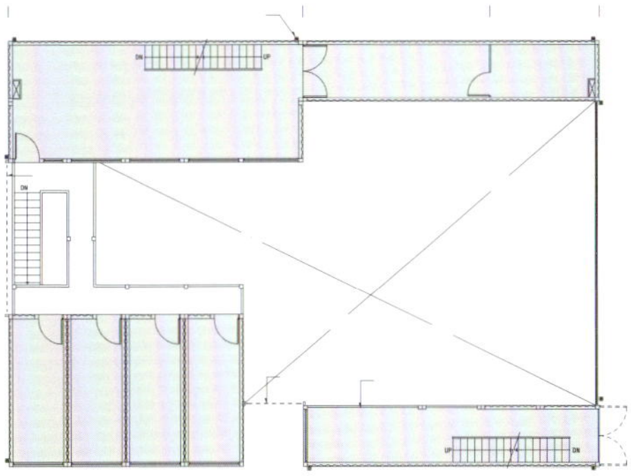

1. Obergeschoss | 1st floor

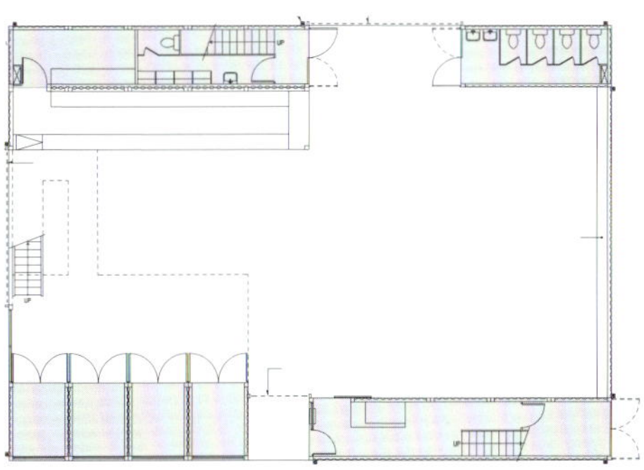

Erdgeschoss | Ground floor

Blick auf den Think Tank, dem Konferenzraum im 2. Obergeschoss
View of the Think Tank, the 2nd-floor conference room

ARCHITEKT | ARCHITECT

TERRAIN: LOENHART&MAYR

GEBÄUDE | BUILDING

MURTURM

GOSDORF, ÖSTERREICH | AUSTRIA

TEXT ANGELIKA FITZ

23

ENTWURF UND PLANUNG AUSSICHTSTURM UND AUSSENANLAGEN | DESIGN AND PLANNING OF OBSERVATION TOWER AND EXTERIOR FACILITIES

terrain: loenhart&mayr BDA architekten und landschaftsarchitekten, München / Graz Kazmairstraße 22 rgb 80339 München | Munich **www.terrain.de**

VERANTWORTLICHE PROJECT MANAGERS

Klaus K. Loenhart und Christoph Mayr

BAUHERR | CLIENT

Gemeinde Gosdorf Orts- und Infrastrukturentwicklungs KG

TRAGWERKSPLANUNG PLANNING OF THE STRUCTURE

osd – office for structural design, Frankfurt am Main

FERTIGSTELLUNG | COMPLETION

März 2010 | March 2010

STANDORT | LOCATION

Gosdorf, Steiermark Österreich | Austria

FOTOS | PHOTOS

Hubertus Hamm, Marc Lins

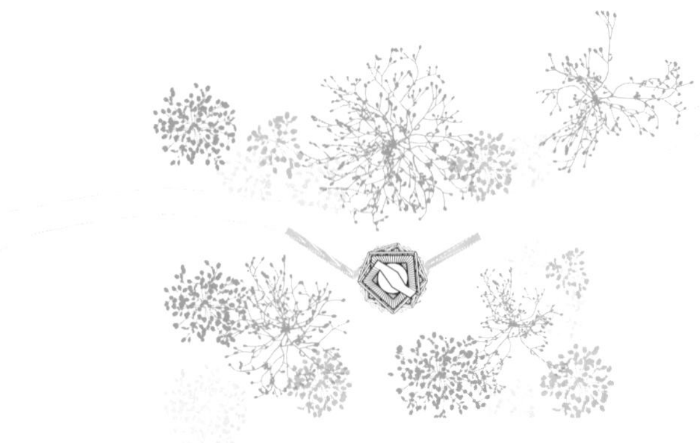

Lage am Weg | Placement on the trail

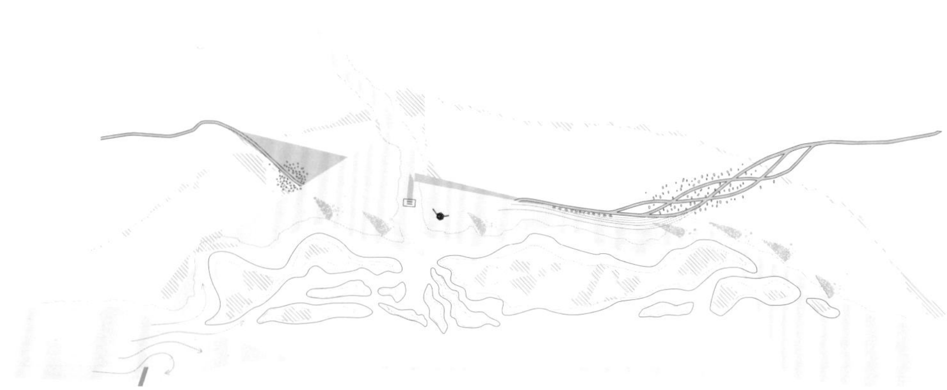

Lageplan und Umgebung | Site plan and environs

In einer Landschaft ohne natürliche Höhepunkte bietet der Murturm Aussicht und Abwechslung.
In a landscape without natural high points, the Murturm offers an observation platform and highlight.

Im Südwesten die malerischen Hügel der steirische Weinstraße, im Osten das steirische Thermenland: die kleine Gemeinde Gosdorf ist umgeben von touristischen Fixsternen und liegt doch etwas abseits. Eine von Mais- und Kürbisfeldern geprägte Ebene entlang des Flusses Mur lässt sich nur schwer als Erlebnislandschaft vermarkten. Die Mur ist hier der Grenzfluss zu Slowenien und die Lage am ehemaligen Eisernen Vorhang mag das ihre dazu beigetragen haben, dass die Zeit an diesem Ort verlangsamt wirkt. Seit Kurzem begreift die Gemeinde diese historische Randsituation jedoch als ‚natürliche' Chance: Die Gosdorfer Auwälder werden Teil des „Grünen Bandes Europa", einem von der europäischen Union geförderten Biotopverbundsystem, das sich entlang der ehemaligen Grenzzone vom Eismeer bis zum Schwarzen Meer erstreckt.
Das Gewässerreferat der steirischen Landesregierung ließ im Rahmen von Renaturierungsmaßnahmen große Schottermassen im Flussraum der Mur bewegen, um deren Fließgeschwindigkeit zu verringern und naturnahe Ausbuchtungen zu gewinnen. Wie der Fluss diese Hilfe zur Selbsthilfe annimmt und wie sich dadurch Flora und Fauna verändern, soll für Wanderer und Radfahrer erlebbar werden. Der Naturschutzbund regte als Projektpartner an, das Büro terrain: loenhart&mayr mit an Bord zu holen, um den Erlebnisfaktor zu intensivieren. Gemäß ihrer

To the south-west the picturesque hills of the Styrian wine route, to the east Styria's thermal landscape: the small town of Gosdorf is surrounded by tourist attractions and yet is somehow still off the beaten track. It is difficult to market this flatland dotted with maize and pumpkin fields along the Mur River as an adventure landscape. The Mur forms the border with Slovenia here, and the Iron Curtain that once ran through the area may have played a role in making time seem to pass so slowly in these parts. In recent years, however, the community has come to view this historical border situation as a "natural" opportunity, and Gosdorf's floodplain woodland is now part of the "European Green Belt", a biotope system subsidised by the European Union that stretches along the former border zone from the Barents Sea to the Black Sea.
In the course of renaturation measures, the Water Department of the Styrian state government has had huge amounts of gravel shifted into the Mur River to slow down its flow and recreate the natural bends in its artificially straightened course. Now, hikers and cyclists are to be given an opportunity to

Direkt am Wegrand gelegen, bietet der Turm gleichsam einen unterhaltsamen Umweg. | Set directly at the edge of the trail, the tower offers an entertaining detour.

Doppelkompetenz als Architekten und Landschaftsarchitekten schlug das Büro zweierlei Maßnahmen vor, einerseits Beobachtungsbauwerke wie Türme oder Stege und andererseits minimale Eingriffe in die Natur wie die abschnittsweise Verdichtung der bestehenden Flora, um die Aufmerksamkeit der Auwaldbesucher zu erhöhen. Bezüglich der Bauwerke votierten die Projektpartner von Land und Gemeinde als Erstes für die Turmvariante, eine mutige Entscheidung, für die der Bürgermeister heftig unter Beschuss genommen wurde. Am Eröffnungswochende, das gleichzeitig Wahlwochenende war, brauchte man sich um die Aufmerksamkeit an der neuen Attraktion keine Sorgen zu machen. Die bunten Dresse der Radfahrer waren schon über den Baumwipfeln zu sehen, bevor die Konstruktion selbst ins Blickfeld rückte.

In einer Landschaft ohne natürliche Höhepunkte bietet die neue Landmarke Aussicht und Abwechslung. Dass die ersten

see how the river has responded to this boost in its natural regeneration process, and how flora and fauna in the area are changing. The Austrian Nature Conservation Society as project partner suggested enlisting the aid of the architects at terrain: loenhart&mayr to find ways of intensifying the discovery factor. Based on their double expertise as architects and landscape architects, the office proposed two kinds of measures: observation platforms consisting of towers or walkways, and also minimal interventions in nature such as consolidating the existing vegetation in certain areas in order to raise visitors' awareness of the lowland forest. With respect to the building plans, the state and municipal project partners voted for the tower variant as a first measure, a bold decision for which the mayor immediately came under fire. On the opening weekend, which also happened to be election weekend, there was hence no need to drum up attention for the new attraction. The colourful garb of the ascending cyclists could already be seen over the treetops even before the structure itself came into view.

In a landscape without natural high points, the new landmark now offers an outlook platform and some variety. As the first steps of the Murturm tower begin directly at the edge of the trail, providing an entertaining detour, the decision to dismount is not difficult for cyclists. The 168 steps that follow will hardly make any visitor gasp for breath, even

Obwohl der Murturm seriell, ...
Although the Murturm was constructed serially, ...

... mit einer Addition von sich wiederholenden Elementen ...
... by adding on repeating elements ...

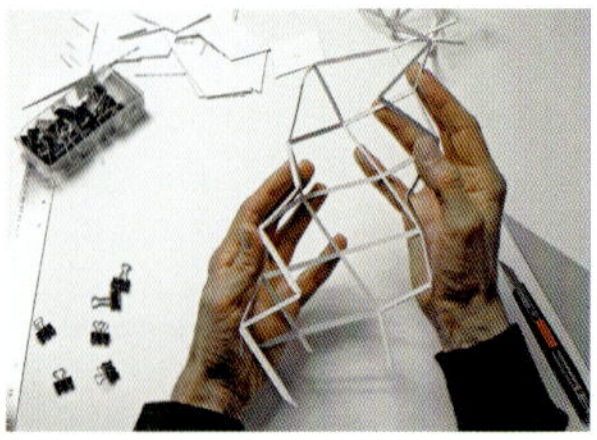

... und Winkelverhältnissen konstruiert ist ...
... at similar angles ...

... erreicht er eine fast organisch wirkende Vielgestaltigkeit. | ... it achieves an almost organic-looking polymorphism.

Wie bei einer DNA-Doppelhelix sind zwei Stiegenverläufe räumlich verschraubt. | Two stairways intertwine, like in a DNA double helix.

Das Bauwerk weitet sich nicht zu einer Aussichtsplattform, sondern führt über eine kleine Brücke zu dem zweiten Wendel. | The stairs do not lead to an observation deck, but rather across a small bridge to a second stairway.

Treppenstufen des Murturms direkt am Wegrand beginnen, den Weg gleichsam über einen unterhaltsamen Umweg weiterführen, erleichtert die Entscheidung, kurz vom Fahrrad zu steigen. Die 168 Stufen, die nun folgen, bringen kaum einen Besucher außer Atem, auch oder vielleicht gerade, weil es keine Zwischenpodeste gibt. Das sorgfältig gewählte Stufenverhältnis von 15,2 x 28,5 Zentimeter erlaubt auch den weniger Sportlichen ein lustvolles Schreiten gen Himmel. Die mit einer Aluminiumverkleidung dreiseitig geschlossenen Stiegenkörper geben Ängstlichen Halt und rahmen zugleich deutlich wechselnde Ausblicke. Weil die Architekten ihre ganze Aufmerksamkeit dem Weg widmeten, kann der Besucher den Weg vergessen und sich dem Durchwandern der unterschiedlichen Etagen des Waldes hingeben.

Nähert sich der Wanderer der Baumwipfelhöhe beginnt ihn eine Brise zu streifen. Dort, wo sich die Brise zum Wind auswächst, erreicht der Weg seinen höchsten Punkt. Mit seinem dynamischen, offenen Tragwerk beginnt der Turm merklich zu schwingen. Das Bauwerk bleibt auch hier ganz Weg, weitet sich nicht zu einer Aussichtsplattform, sondern führt über eine kleine Brücke zu einer zweiten Wegschleife. Es ist also nur das Aufkommen des Windes, das den Ort des Ankommens markiert, ein flüchtiger, aber eindringlicher Ort. Wenn bei Heidegger die Brücke den Ort schafft, dann verkörpert der Murturm die Radikalform einer Brücke, die den Besucher auf einen vertikalen Weg mitnimmt, um ihn dann nur unweit der Einstiegsstelle mit neuen Erfahrungen zu entlassen. Wahrscheinlich nehmen viele Besucher erst beim Hinuntergehen, wenn sich der Blick erstmals vom Schauspiel der Landschaft löst, bewusst wahr, dass sich hier wie bei einer gotischen Zwillingswendeltreppe zwei Stiegenverläufe räumlich verschrauben. Dadurch liefern sich die auf beiden Spuren hinauf und hinab flanierenden Besucher wechselseitig ein Schauspiel. Ungewöhnlich für einen Aussichtsturm, wird nicht nur ganz oben, sondern auf jeder Höhe des Weges eifrig fotografiert, was seine komplexe Attraktivität unterstreicht. Durch die Verwindung erreicht der Murturm eine fast organisch wirkende Vielgestaltigkeit, obwohl er seriell, mit einer Addition von sich wiederholenden Elementen und Winkelverhältnissen konstruiert ist. Die verschiedenen Lichtstimmungen der Fassadenreflexionen verstärken das Vexierspiel. Dass man seine Gestalt auch als DNA-Doppelhelix lesen kann, gefiel dem Naturschutzbund und trägt sicherlich zur Akzeptanz des Turmes bei. Übrigens: der Bürgermeister wurde wiedergewählt.

though, or perhaps precisely because, there are no landings. The carefully selected step height ratio of 15.2 x 28.5 centimetres allows even less athletic climbers to enjoy their ascent towards the sky. Encased in aluminium on three sides, the stairway instils confidence in those afraid of heights, while framing distinct and changing vistas. Because the architects took such care in choreographing this path, visitors can simply forget the climb and instead devote all their attention to taking in the various levels of the forest.

As climbers near the treetops, a breeze begins to play around their ears. And when this breeze becomes a wind, the path has reached its apogee. With its dynamic, open support framework, the tower palpably begins to sway. Here as well, the structure remains all path, not expanding outward to form a viewing platform, but rather leading across a small bridge to a second loop. It is thus only the mounting wind that marks the point of arrival – a transient, but vivid place. If for Heidegger the bridge creates the place, then the Murturm embodies a radical form of bridge, which takes the visitor along a vertical path only to release him again not far from the point of entry with a host of new impressions. Many visitors probably won't notice until they are descending, when their gaze wanders for the first time from the natural spectacle, that two stairways entwine here like a Gothic twin spiral staircase. This means that two groups of visitors, on their way up or down, are also on mutual display. Unusually for an observation tower, people constantly snap pictures not only at the top but also all along the way, underscoring its complex appeal. Its twisting shape lends the Murturm an almost organic-looking polymorphism, although it was in fact constructed serially, by adding on repeating elements and angles. The various moods created by light reflexes off the façade reinforce the mercurial impression made by the tower. The Nature Conservation Society liked the way its shape can be read as a DNA double helix, a feature that surely contributes to the acceptance of the tower. Incidentally: the mayor was re-elected.

DAM JAHRESBERICHT 2010
DAM ANNUAL REPORT 2010

UMBAU
CONVERSION WORK
Das Museum am Schaumainkai blieb wegen notwendiger Umbauarbeiten im Bereich Brandschutz vom 15. 03. 2010 bis 04. 11. 2010 geschlossen.
The Museum on Schaumainkai was closed to be renovated particularly with regard to fire prevention from 15. 03. 2010 until 04. 11. 2010.

Das Deutsche Architekturmuseum zeigte 2010 folgende Ausstellungen:
In 2010 the Deutsches Architekturmuseum hosted the following exhibitions:

Fernsehtürme
TV Towers
8.559 Meter Politik und Architektur
8,559 Meters of Politics and Architecture
03. 10. 2009 – 14. 03. 2010

Martin Elsaesser und das Neue Frankfurt
Martin Elsaesser and the New Frankfurt
10. 10. 2009 – 14. 03. 2010

DAM Preis für Architektur in Deutschland 2009
DAM Award for Architecture in Germany 2009
Die 25 besten Bauwerke in / aus Deutschland
The 25 Best Buildings in / from Germany
14. 11. 2009 – 17. 01. 2010

AGIP – Die Tankstelle des Wirschaftswunders
AGIP – The Gas Station of Postwar Mobility
16. 01. 2010 – 14. 03. 2010

Architekturwelten
Architectural worlds
Sergei Tchoban – Zeichner und Sammler
Sergei Tchoban – Draftsman and Collector
30. 01. 2010 – 14. 03. 2010

Mies van der Rohe Award 2009
Preis der europäischen Union für zeitgenössische Architektur
Prize of the European Union for Contemporary Architecture
In Kooperation mit dem M:AI und der Fundacìo Mies van der Rohe in der Kokerei Zollverein, Essen
In Cooperation with M:AI and Fundacìo Mies van der Rohe at the Kokerei Zollverein, Essen
21. 03. 2010 – 20. 04. 2010

Stadtgrün
Urban green
Europäische Landschaftsarchitektur für das 21. Jahrhundert
European Landscape Architecture for the 21st Century
In Kooperation mit dem und im PalmenGarten
In cooperation with and at PalmenGarten
20. 05. 2010 – 22. 08. 2010

Internationaler Hochaus Preis 2010
The International Highrise Award 2010
06. 11. 2010 – 16. 01. 2011

Von Deutschland nach Argentinien
From Germany to Argentina
Deutsche Einflüsse in der Architektur
German Influences in Architecture
20. 11. 2010 – 20. 02. 2011

Paul Bonatz 1877 – 1956
04. 12. 2010 – 27. 02. 2011

Dauerausstellung im DAM
Permanent exhibition at the DAM

Von der Urhütte zum Wolkenkratzer
From Primordial Hut to Skyscraper

DAM Ausstellungen auf Tour 2010
DAM touring exhibitions in 2010

M8 in China
Zeitgenössische chinesische Architekten
Contemporary Chinese Architects
Berlin, DAZ
05. 12. 2009 – 21. 02. 2010
Dresden, Deutsche Werkstätten Hellerau
25. 03. 2010 – 02. 07. 2010
Oldenburg, bau_werk
02. 09. 2010 – 30. 09. 2010

Gaudí Unseen
Die Vollendung der Sagrada Família
Completing the Sagrada Família
Kolding, Koldinghus
06. 02. 2010 – 02. 05. 2010

Ein Leben für die Architektur
A Lifetime for Architecture
Der Fotograf Julius Shulman
The Photographer Julius Shulman
Herford, MARTa
08. 05. 2010 – 01. 08. 2010

Ausstellung „STADTGRÜN. Europäische Landschaftsarchitektur für das 21. Jahrhundert" im PalmenGarten Frankfurt am Main
"URBAN GREEN. European Landscape Architecture for the 21st Century", exhibition at the PalmenGarten in Frankfurt / Main

Bauhaus Zwanzig-21
Fotografien von Gordon Watkinson
Photographs by Gordon Watkinson
München, Haus der Gegenwart
26. 02. 2010 – 14. 03. 2010
Stockholm, Nordbygg, Nordic Building + Construction Fair
23. 03. 2010 – 26. 03. 2010
Ljubljana, Jakopic Gallery
23. 04. 2010 – 22. 06. 2010

Fernsehtürme
TV Towers
8 559 Meter Politik und Architektur
8,559 Meters of Politics and Architecture
Innsbruck, aut. architektur und tirol
16. 07. 2010 – 18. 09. 2010

Vortragsreihen und Veranstaltungen
Lecture Series and Events

Pecha Kucha Nights
PKN014: 04. 03. 2010, Kunstverein, Frankfurt am Main
PKN015: 10. 04. 2010, Oval am Baseler Platz, Frankfurt am Main
www.pechakuchanight.de

BDB im DAM
Bund Deutscher Baumeister
Sonderführung zu den Ausstellungen des DAM mit Yorck Förster

Die Sanierung der Großmarkthalle
Wolf D. Prix, Horst Peseke, Sven Raecke
DAM + Museum für Kommunikation
28. 04. 2010

Stadt-Grün für Frankfurt
Stephan Heldmann, Michael Landes, Robert Schäfer, Cassian Schmidt, Adelheid Gräfin Schönborn, Mechthild Harting
DAM + PalmenGarten + Frankfurter Allgemeine Zeitung
15. 06. 2010

Das Designethos von Dieter Rams
Dieter Rams's design ethos
Keiko Ueki-Polet, Jürgen W. Braun, Sophie Lovell, Olaf Leu, Michael Schumacher, Peter Eckart
DAM + Museum für Angewandte Kunst
25. 05. 2010
16. 06. 2010

Symposien
Symposia

Martin Elsaesser und seine Zeit(en)
Martin Elsaesser and his times
Christina Gräwe, Jörg Schilling, Thomas Elsaesser, Christian Freigang, Matthias Schirren, Wolfgang Pehnt, Wolfgang Voigt, Floris Paalmann, Ulrike May, Christina Treutlein, Bernd Nicolai, Franziska Wilcken, Romana Schneider, Claudia Wohlfeld-Eckart, Dietrich W. Schmidt, Bettina von Gilsa
DAM + Johann Wolfgang Goethe-Universität + Martin-Elsaesser-Stiftung
11. 02. 2010 – 12. 02. 2010

Stadt-Grün im 21. Jahrhundert
Ulrich Maximilian Schumann, Christophe Girot, Norbert Kühn, Michael Denkel, Jörg Dettmar, Friedrich von Borries, Marc Pouzol und Véronique Faucheur, Melanie Müller, Walter Prigge
DAM + PalmenGarten + GrünGürtel Frankfurt am Main
01. 07. 2010

Vorträge
Lectures

Neue Denkweisen in der Hochhausarchitektur
Ole Scheeren (HighRise Lecture)
DAM + DekaBank
01. 02. 2010

The Oslo Opera House and Ballet
The story behind a spectacular architectural achievement
Tarald Lundevall, Snøhetta Architects, Oslo
Award-winner
„Mies van der Rohe Award 2009. European Union Prize for Contemporary Architecture"
DAM + M:AI
12. 04. 2010

Gymnasium 46° 09'N/16° 50'E
The development of groundbreaking educational settings
STUDIO UP | Lea Pelivan and Toma Plejic
Special Award Emerging Architects
„Mies van der Rohe Award 2009. European Union Prize for Contemporary Architecture"
DAM + M:AI
13. 04. 2010

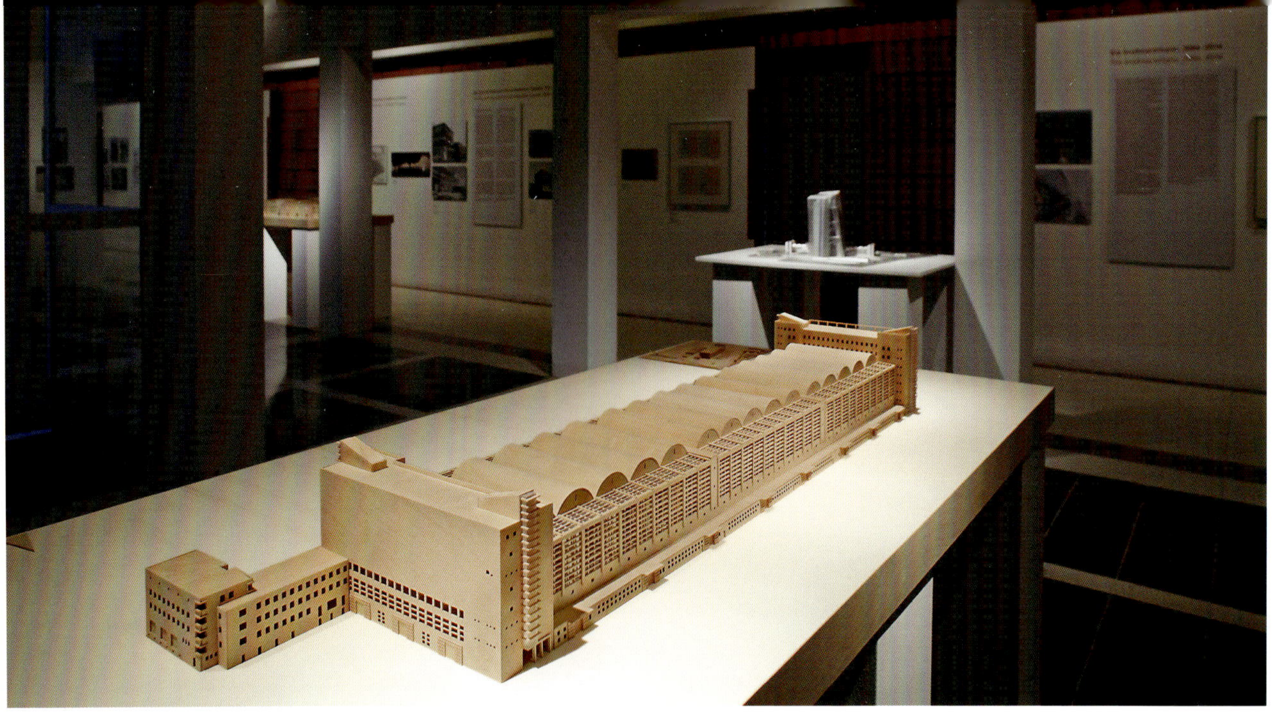

Ausstellung „Martin Elsaesser und das Neue Frankfurt" | "Martin Elsaesser and the New Frankfurt" exhibition

Programm für Kinder und Jugendliche
Programme for children and young people

LegoBaustelle
Lego Construction Site
26. 12. 2009 – 10. 01. 2010
06. 07. 2010 – 15. 08. 2010
DAM + Museum für Kommunikation

Workshops in den Osterferien 2010
DAM + Plus-Energie-Haus
Was ist eigentlich ein Sonnenhaus?
30. 03. 2010

Stadt-Utopie – Kinder bauen ihre Stadt
31. 03. 2010

Architektur – (k)ein Pappenstiel
01. 04. 2010
Module über Module
07. 04. 2010

Handicap – Kinder erleben Räume neu
09. 04. 2010

Workshops in den Sommerferien 2010
DAM + PalmenGarten

Architektur erobert Landschaft – bemalte Flächen werden zu aufrechten Formen
26. + 27. 07. 2010

Baumaterial Natur: Gras
28. – 30. 07. 2010

Höhlen bauen – Architektur für Menschen und Tiere
02. – 04. 08. 2010

Auf Fotosafari im Palmen-Garten – mit der Camera Obscura unterwegs
05. + 06. 08. 2010

Energiequelle Natur: Sonne
09. – 11. 08. 2010

Häuser für tierische Bewohner
30. 01. 2010

Stadtraum mobil
27. 02. 2010

Wandlungsfähig in Grün
29. 05. 2010

Schattenräume
26. 06. 2010

Zurück ins Mittelalter
31. 07. 2010

Fantasiewelten
27. 11. 2010

Projekte
Von Häusern und Menschen – Jugendliche fotografieren Architektur
„Räume in Grün"
DAM + Hostatoschule Frankfurt
14. 6. – 23. 06. 2010

„StadtteilDetektive – Kinder entdecken ihr Frankfurt"
DAM + Ackermannschule Frankfurt
28. 09. – 08. 10. 2010

Lehrerfortbildung
Teacher Training

Historismus
29. 05. 2010

Architektur ganz praktisch – Modellbau im Unterricht
12. 06. 2010

Bau-Bionik
27. 06. 2010

Zukunftsfähiges Bauen (oder: „green-building")
04. 07. 2010

Grüne Stabkonstruktionen
18. 07. 2010

Folgende Kataloge und Veröffentlichungen sind erschienen
The following catalogues and books have been published

AGIP – Die Tankstelle des Wirtschaftswunders
AGIP – The Gas Station of Postwar Mobility
Hrsg. | ed. **Deutsches Architekturmuseum in Kooperation mit** | in cooperation with **ENI Deutschland GmbH**
DAM, Deutsch/Englisch

Architekturwelten
Architectural Worlds
Sergei Tchoban – Zeichner und Sammler
Sergei Tchoban – Draftsman and Collector
Hrsg. | ed. **Eva-Maria Barkhofen**
Jovis Verlag, Deutsch/Englisch

Stadtgrün
Urban Green
Europäische Landschaftsarchitektur für das 21. Jahrhundert
European Landscape Architecture for the 21st Century
Hrsg. | ed. **Annette Becker, Peter Cachola Schmal**
Birkhäuser Verlag, Deutsch/Englisch
mit Beiträgen von
with contributions from

Ausstellung „AGIP – Die Tankstelle des Wirtschaftswunders“ | "AGIP – The Gas Station of Postwar Mobility" exhibition

Marc Treib, Ulrich Maximilian Schumann, Cassian Schmidt, Udo Weilacher, Wolfgang Haber, Inken Formann, Richard Ingersoll, Detlev Ipsen, Christophe Girot, Norbert Kühn

Internationaler Hochaus Preis 2010
The International Highrise Award 2010
Hrsg. | ed. **Michaela Busenkell, Peter Cachola Schmal**
Jovis Verlag,
Deutsch/Englisch
mit einem Essay von
with an essay by
Antony Wood

Von Deutschland nach Argentinien
From Germany to Argentinia
Hrsg. | ed. **CEDODAL,**
Buenos Aires
Ministerio de Relaciones Exteriores,
Comercio Internacional y Culto di Argentina,
Spanisch/Deutsch

Paul Bonatz 1877 – 1956
Hrsg. | ed. **Wolfgang Voigt, Peter Cachola Schmal**
Wasmuth Verlag,
Deutsch/Englisch
mit Beiträgen von
with contributions from
Uwe Bresan, Burcu Dogramaci, Hartmut Frank, Marc Hirschfell, Karl Kiem, Claus Käpplinger, Jooquin Medina-Warmburg, Roland May, Matthias Roser, Wolfgang Voigt

Zu den wichtigsten Neuerwerbungen des DAM zählen
The DAM's most important new acquisitions include

Adolfo Natalini, Florenz
Modell | Model
Haus Saalgasse,
Frankfurt am Main, 1980-84
Übergabe | Handover by
Hochbauamt,
Stadt Frankfurt am Main

Barkow Leibinger, Berlin
Modell | Model
Betriebsrestaurant Trumpf
Schenkung Architekten
Donation by architects

Modelle | Models
16 Studien zum DAM-Pavillon
Schenkung und Dauerleihgabe Architekten | Donation and permanent loan by architects

Ben Willikens, Stuttgart
Serigraphie | Serigraph
Haus der Kunst München, 31/60, 2009
Schenkung Künstler
Donation by artist

Norbert Berghof, Michael A. Landes, Wolfgang Rang
Modelle, Zeichnungen, Dokumente und Möbel
Models, Drawings, Documents and Furniture
Archiv des Büros Berghof Landes Rang, Frankfurt am Main, 1981–96
Schenkung Architekten
Donation by architects

Karl Gruber (1885–1966)
Zeichnungen und Skizzenbücher aus dem Nachlass
Drawings and Sketchbooks from the Estate
Schenkung der Tochter Renate Gruber | Donation by daughter Renate Gruber

Nieto Sobejano, Madrid
Modell | Model
Erweiterung Kunstmuseum Moritzburg, 2008 | Extension of Moritzburg Art Museum, 2008
Schenkung Architekten
Donation by architects

Städelschule Frankfurt am Main
11 Modelle | 11 Models
Pavillonbauten | Pavilion Study Models
Ankauf | Acquisition

Tezuka Architects, Tokio
100 Modelle | 100 Models
Verschiedene Projekte in Japan | Various japanese projects
Schenkung Architekten
Donation by architects

Weitere Schenkungen
Other donations

Fassadenaufrisse | Façade Studies
Kaiserstraße
Frankfurt am Main
Schenkung | Donation by
Dr. Volker Rödel

Werklehre Architekturstudium Karlsruhe 1946–50
Material Studies in Architecture at the University of Karlsruhe 1946–50
Schenkung | Donation by
Martin Giebel

200 Glasdiapositive, ca. 1925/30 | 200 glass slides, c. 1925/30
Nachlass Karl Grabenhorst (1896–1983), Stadtbaudirektor Göttingen, Schenkung der Familie
Estate of Karl Grabenhorst (1896–1983), City Building Director in Göttingen, donation by the family

ARCHITEKTURPREISE
ARCHITECTURE AWARDS

Das DAM ist an der Auslobung wichtiger Architekturpreise beteiligt:
Seit 2007 zeichnet das DAM eines der im Deutschen Architektur Jahrbuch präsentierten Projekte mit dem DAM Preis für Architektur in Deutschland aus. Die Auszeichnung für das beste Projekt 2007 wurde Wandel Hofer Lorch + Hirsch für das Dokumentationszentrum Hinzert verliehen, Peter Zumthor 2008 für das Diözesanmuseum St. Kolumba in Köln, Barkow Leibinger 2009 für das Betriebsrestaurant TRUMPF in Ditzingen und David Chipperfield 2010 für das Neue Museum in Berlin.
Der Internationale Hochhaus Preis (IHP) wird seit 2004 alle zwei Jahre von der Stadt Frankfurt am Main vergeben. Initiiert und organisiert wird er in partnerschaftlicher Kooperation vom DAM und der DekaBank, die außerdem den IHP finanziert. 2004 gewannen den Preis KPF Europe mit De Hooftoren in Den Haag, 2006 Jean Nouvel mit dem Torre Agbar in Barcelona und 2008 Foster and Partners mit dem Hearst Tower in New York. Den IHP 2010 erhält einer der fünf Finalisten am 5. 11. 2010, darunter der Aqua Tower Chicago (Studio Gang), der Burj Khalifa Dubai (SOM), The Met Bangkok (Woha), der Tokyo Mode Gakuen Cocoon Tower (Tange) und das Shanghai World Financial Center (KPF). Der Preis besteht aus einer Statue des Künstlers Thomas Demand und einem Geldpreis von 50 000 Euro.
Der Europäische Architekturfotografie-Preis, alle zwei Jahre ausgelobt, wird bereits zum achten Mal vergeben. Zum ersten Mal fand die Preisverleihung und die Ausstellung der besten Wettbewerbsbeiträge im DAM statt, denn seit 2008 kooperieren der Auslober, die architekturbild e. V. und das DAM. Alle Fotos der bisherigen Preisträger der vergangenen 16 Jahre gehen in die Sammlung des DAM über. Der Preisträger der Edition 2009 unter dem Motto „Neue Heimat – New Homeland" war Stephan Sahm aus München. Die nächste Verleihung findet im Mai 2011 statt.
Der DAM Architekturbuchpreis wurde 2009 zum ersten Mal vergeben. Er wird jährlich gemeinsam mit der Frankfurter Buchmesse ausgelobt und zu diesem Zeitpunkt verliehen. 2009 wurde er an folgende Preisträger vergeben: Marte.Marte, Springer Verlag (Architekturmonografie); Ulrich Müther – Schalenbauten in Mecklenburg-Vorpommern, Niggli Verlag (Historische Monografie); Hans Schwippert – Bonner Bundeshaus, v. Gerda Breuer, Wasmuth Verlag (Dokumentation von Zeitgeschichte mit Architektur); Neues Museum. Friederike von Rauch, Hatje Cantz Verlag (Fotografie/Bildband) und Explorations in Architecture v. Reto Geiser, Birkhäuser Verlag (Lehrbuch). Anerkennungen gingen an Robbrecht en Daem. Pacing through Architecture (Walther König); BDE (Quart); Ponti (Taschen); Rudolf-Bednar-Park, Wien (Niggli) sowie Eduard Neuenschwander – Architekt und Umweltgestalter (gta, Zürich).
Das DAM ist seit 2010 Mitglied des wissenschaftlichen Beirats und der Jury für den alle zwei Jahre ausgelobten European Prize For Urban Public Space, der vom Centre of Contemporary Culture of Barcelona (CCCB) 1999 ins Leben gerufen wurde. Der Preis ging gleichwertig an das „Lesezeichen Salbke" im gleichnamigen Magdeburger Stadtteil (KARO* Architekten, Leipzig) sowie an den Außenraum der neuen Oper in Oslo (Snøhetta Architekten, Oslo). Anerkennungen erhielten: Theater, Podium und Brücke am Grotekerkplein, Rotterdam (Atelier Kempe Thill, Rotterdam); Strandpromenade Benidorm (Office of Architecture, Barcelona); Passage 56 in Paris (atelier d'architecture autogérée, Paris) und Fischerhäuschen im Hafen des galizischen Cangas do Morrazo (Irisarri + Piñera, Vigo, Galizien).
Das DAM ist außerdem Mitglied des Steering Committees für den, alle zwei Jahre alternierend mit dem Public Space Award verliehenen, EU Mies van der Rohe Preis für zeitgenössische Architektur in Europa. Die Preisträger 2009 sind wiederum die Architekten des norwegischen Architekturbüros Snøhetta für ihre Nationaloper in Oslo. Der Nachwuchspreis ging an das kroatische Studio Up für ihr Gymnasium in Koprivnica.

The DAM (German Architecture Museum) is involved in awarding some important architecture prizes:
Since 2007 the DAM has selected one of the projects presented in the German Architecture Annual to receive the DAM Award for Architecture in Germany. The award for best project in 2007 went to Wandel Hofer Lorch + Hirsch for their Dokumentationszentrum Hinzert, in 2008 to Peter Zumthor in 2008 for Kolumba, the art museum of the archdiocese of Cologne, in 2009 to Barkow Leibinger for their Betriebsrestaurant (company restaurant) for TRUMPF in Ditzingen, and in 2010 to David Chipperfield for the Neues Museum in Berlin.
The City of Frankfurt am Main has bestowed its International Highrise Award (IHP) every second year since 2004. The award is initiated and organised in partnership with the DAM and DekaBank, which also funds the IHP. In 2004 the winner was KPF Europe with De Hooftoren in The Hague, in 2006 Jean Nouvel with the Torre Agbar in Barcelona and in 2008 Foster + Partners with the Hearst Tower in New York. The IHP 2010 will be awarded on 5 November 2010 to one of five finalists: the Aqua Tower in Chicago (Studio Gang), the Burj Khalifa in Dubai (SOM), The Met Bangkok (Woha), the Tokyo Mode Gakuen Cocoon Tower (Tange) and the Shanghai World Financial Center (KPF). The prize consists of a statue by the artist Thomas Demand and a cash award of 50,000 euros.
The European Architectural Photography Prize, awarded every two years, was presented in 2009 for the eighth time. The awards ceremony and exhibition of the best competition entries were held that year for the first time at the DAM, which joined architekturbild e. V. in 2008 as co-sponsor of the award. All prize-winning photos from the past 16 years have become part of the DAM collection. The winner of first prize in the 2009 edition, the motto of which was "Neue Heimat – New Homeland", was Stephan Sahm from Munich. The next prizes will be conferred in May 2011.
The DAM Architecture Book Award was presented for the first time in 2009. It will be awarded annually in partnership with the Frankfurt Book Fair and coinciding with that event. The winners in 2009 were: Marte.Marte, Springer Verlag (architecture monograph); "Ulrich Müther – Schalenbauten in Mecklenburg-Vorpommern", Niggli Verlag (historical monograph); "Hans Schwippert – Bonner Bundeshaus", by Gerda Breuer, Wasmuth Verlag (documentation of contemporary history through architecture); "Neues Museum" by Friederike von Rauch, Hatje Cantz Verlag (photography book) and "Explorations in Architecture" by Reto Geiser, Birkhäuser Verlag (textbook). Special mentions went to: "Robbrecht en Daem. Pacing through Architecture" (Walther König); "BDE" (Quart); "Ponti" (Taschen); "Rudolf-Bednar-Park, Wien" (Niggli) and "Eduard Neuenschwander – Architekt und Umweltgestalter" (gta, Zurich).

The DAM has been a member since 2010 of the board of experts and jury of the European Prize for Urban Public Space, which was founded by the Centre of Contemporary Culture of Barcelona (CCCB) in 1999 and is awarded every two years. The joint winners this year are Lesezeichen Salbke, an open-air library in the Magdeburg city district of that name (KARO* Architekten, Leipzig) and the rooftop exterior of the new National Opera in Oslo (Snøhetta Architekten, Oslo). Special mentions went to: the theatre podium and bridge on Grotekerkplein, Rotterdam (Atelier Kempe Thill, Rotterdam); a beach promenade in Benidorm (Office of Architecture, Barcelona); Passage 56 in Paris (atelier d'architecture autogérée, Paris) and the new fishermen's huts in the harbour of the Galician town of Cangas do Morrazo (Irisarri + Piñera, Vigo, Galicia).
DAM is in addition a member of the steering committee for the European Union Prize for Contemporary Architecture – the Mies van der Rohe Award, which is awarded every two years alternating with the European Prize for Urban Public Space. The award-winner in 2009 was the Norwegian architecture office Snøhetta, for its National Opera in Oslo. The "young architect" commendation went to Studio Up in Croatia for their secondary school in Koprivnica.

DAM SPONSOREN
DAM SPONSORS

Alle unsere Aktivitäten im vergangenen Jahr wären ohne die großzügige Unterstützung zahlreicher Sponsoren nicht möglich gewesen. Zu den Sponsoren, die das DAM unterstützt haben, zählen:
The museum's activities in the course of the last year would not have been possible without the generous support of our many sponsors, including:

DekaBank Deutsche Girozentrale, Frankfurt am Main
Gemeinnützige Kulturfonds Frankfurt RheinMain GmbH, Bad Homburg
Kooperationspool der Stadt Frankfurt, Frankfurt am Main
DFMG Deutsche Funkturm GmbH, Münster
Gesellschaft der Freunde des Deutschen Architekturmuseums e. V., Frankfurt am Main
Europäische Zentralbank, Frankfurt am Main
Architekten- und Stadtplanerkammer Hessen, Wiesbaden
HPP Hentrich-Petschnigg & Partner - Architekten, Düsseldorf
Ministerio de Relaciones Exteriores Comercio Internacional y Culto, Buenos Aires
Centro de Documentación de Arquitectura Latinoamericana (CEDODAL), Buenos Aires
Ali Selmi Grundstücksgesellschaft GbR, Frankfurt am Main
Stiftung Polytechnische Gesellschaft, Frankfurt am Main
Hessischer Museumsverband, Kassel
s.boehme & co. KGaA, Frankfurt am Main
ENI Deutschland GmbH, München
S. Tchoban Foundation. Museum für Architekturzeichnung, Berlin

UND FOLGENDE UNTERSTÜTZER
AND THE FOLLOWING SUPPORTERS

Frankfurter Buchmesse, Frankfurt am Main
DESERVE GbR Raum und Medien Design, Wiesbaden
inditec Display & Messegestaltung GmbH, Bad Camberg

GESELLSCHAFT DER FREUNDE DES DAM
THE SOCIETY OF FRIENDS OF THE DAM

Die Gesellschaft der Freunde des Deutschen Architektur Museums wurde im Jahr 1985 als eingetragener Verein ins Leben gerufen. Das Hauptanliegen dieser Gesellschaft ist es, das Deutsche Architekturmuseum, Frankfurt am Main, (DAM) in der Verwirklichung seiner öffentlichen Aufgaben ideell und materiell zu unterstützen und zu fördern.

Zu den Aufgaben und Zielen des Vereins gehören:

- **Vermittlung, Ankauf und Überlassung von Plänen, Zeichnungen und Modellen deutscher und internationaler Architektur-Projekte und Architekten-Nachlässe bzw. -Vorlässe mit dem Ziel der wissenschaftlichen Bearbeitung und öffentlichkeitswirksamen Vermittlung der Arbeitsergebnisse durch das DAM. Vorhaltung eines großen Kontingents von Dauerleihgaben an das Archiv des DAM.**
- **Unterstützung bei der Planung, Vorbereitung und Durchführung von Ausstellungen, Auktionen, Veranstaltungen und anderen anstehenden Aufgaben. Einer der Schwerpunkte ist u. a. die Jugendarbeit bzw. Museumspädagogik.**
- **Herstellung von Kontakten zu Personen, Institutionen und Wirtschaftsunternehmen, die für die partnerschaftliche Unterstützung von Aktivitäten des DAM infrage kommen.**
- **Unterstützung des DAM bei verschiedenen Maßnahmen im Rahmen der Öffentlichkeitsarbeit.**
- **Vorhaltung und Überlassung einer Wohnung für Praktikanten.**

Mitglieder in diesem Verein sind Personen, Institutionen und Firmen, deren Anliegen es ist, einen Beitrag zur Förderung der Qualität der gebauten Umwelt zu leisten. Der Vorstand wird jeweils über einen Zeitraum von fünf Jahren von der Mitgliederversammlung gewählt. Er setzt sich aus Persönlichkeiten aus den Bereichen Wirtschaft, Politik, Bildung, Bankwesen und Kultur zusammen. Dadurch ist gewährleistet, dass Informationen und Kontakte aus den unterschiedlichsten Bereichen zugunsten der Ziele der Gesellschaft der Freunde des DAM genutzt werden können. Um einen intensiven Kontakt zu den Mitgliedern sicherzustellen, wird jährlich mindestens eine Versammlung durchgeführt, anschließend findet eine Sonderführung durch die laufende Ausstellung statt.

Wie Sie sich vorstellen können, erfordern die Aktivitäten der Gesellschaft in hohem Maße Geld, Ideen, ehrenamtliches Engagement und Idealismus. Unterstützen Sie uns bei unserem Vorhaben! Als Mitglieder halten Sie das Jahrbuch des DAM bei Abholung unentgeltlich; auf alle anderen Publikationen des DAM erhalten Sie mit Ihrem Ausweis 20 % Rabatt. Nur als Mitglied können Sie an speziellen Previews und Sonderführungen teilnehmen. Die Jahresgaben der Gesellschaft 1998 bis 2005 erhalten Sie zu einem Vorzugspreis. Es werden Architekturreisen für die Mitglieder angeboten, z. B. Reisen zu Architekturbiennalen (2006 Venedig, 2007 São Paulo, 2008 Venedig). Bitte informieren Sie sich auch speziell unter unserer Website:
http://www.dam-online.de/Gesellschaft der Freunde.

Der Jahresmitgliedsbeitrag beträgt 95,00 EUR für Einzelmitglieder, für Studenten 50,00 EUR und für juristische Personen und Personenvereinigungen 920,00 EUR.

Vorstand: Marietta Andreas (Vorsitz), Prof. Johann Eisele (Stellvertretender Vorsitz), Prof. Helge Bofinger (Schatzmeister), Michael Bahrenberg, Barbara Ettinger-Brinckmann, Prof. Dr. Salomon Korn, Florian Schlüter, Fritz Straub, Francois Valentiny, Prof. Dr. Martin Wentz

The Society of Friends of the Deutsches Architekturmuseum was founded in 1985 as a registered non-profit organisation. The society's main objective is to support and promote the Deutsches Architekturmuseum, Frankfurt/Main (DAM) both intellectually and materially in the execution of its public duties.

The organisation's duties and aims include:

- The mediation, purchase, and sale of plans, drawings and models of German and international architecture projects and architects' estates and bequeathals for the purpose of scientific handling as well as the effective public dissemination of the results of DAM's work. A large contingent of permanent loans is housed in the DAM archive.
- Support in the planning, preparation and realisation of exhibitions, auctions, events and other ongoing tasks. Focuses here include youth outreach and museum education.
- Establishing contact with persons, institutions and companies that come into question as potential partners for the support of DAM's activities.
- Supporting DAM with various PR-related measures.
- Maintaining an apartment for use by interns.

The organisation's members include persons, institutions and firms that are committed to making a contribution to improving the quality of our constructed environment. The Board of Directors is elected for a period of five years by the General Meeting of the members. It is made up of representatives from the worlds of business, politics, education, banking and culture. This ensures that information from and contacts with a wide range of fields can be put to maximum use in furthering the objectives of the Society of Friends of DAM. In order to keep in close contact with members, at least one General Meeting is held every year. It is followed by a special guided tour of the exhibition on show at the time.

As you can imagine, the Society's activities require a large amount of money, ideas, voluntary work and idealism. Why not support us in our objectives! As a member you will receive the DAM Annual free of charge when you pick it up yourself, as well as a 20% discount on all other DAM publications on presentation of your membership card. Only society members are entitled to attend special previews and take part in special tours. You can also obtain the society's annual gifts from 1998 until 2005 at a reduced rate. Architecture-related trips, for example to architecture biennials (2006 Venice, 2007 São Paulo, 2008 Venice) are organised for members. To find out more about these and other benefits of membership, please see our website: http://www.dam-online.de/Gesellschaft der Freunde.

Annual membership costs 95 EUR for private members, 50 EUR for students and 920 EUR for corporate bodies and associations.
The Board: Marietta Andreas (Chairperson), Prof. Johann Eisele (Deputy Chairperson), Prof. Helge Bofinger (Treasurer), Michael Bahrenberg, Barbara Ettinger-Brinckmann, Prof. Salomon Korn, Florian Schlüter, Fritz Straub, Francois Valentiny, Prof. Martin Wentz

Die Gesellschaft dankt folgenden Personen und Institutionen, die sich in besonderem Maße engagiert haben:
We would like to thank our special sponsors:

Architekten- und Stadtplanerkammer Hessen, Wiesbaden
Artemide GmbH, Fröndenberg
aurelis Real Estate GmbH, Eschborn / Taunus
Bauverlag BV GmbH, Gütersloh
Beton Marketing Süd GmbH, Ostfildern
S. Boehme & Co. KGaA; Frankfurt am Main
Bund Deutscher Architekten im Lande Hessen e. V., Frankfurt am Main
Bund Deutscher Baumeister, Architekten und Ingenieure e. V., Berlin-Steglitz
Bund Deutscher Baumeister, Landesverband Hessen, Kassel
Bund Deutscher Baumeister, Bezirksgruppe Frankfurt, Frankfurt am Main
Deutsche Werkstätten Hellerau GmbH, Dresden
F. Dornbracht GmbH & Co. KG, Iserlohn
Frankfurter Allgemeine Zeitung, Frankfurt am Main
Gainestranslations, Frankfurt am Main
HOCHTIEF Projektentwicklung GmbH, Niederlassung Rhein-Main, Frankfurt am Main
Nassauische Heimstätte Wohnungs- und Entwicklungsgesellschaft mbH, Frankfurt am Main
netzwerkarchitekten, Darmstadt
STEFAN FORSTER ARCHITEKTEN, Frankfurt am Main
Treuhandverwaltung IGEMET GmbH, Frankfurt am Main
Xella International GmbH, Duisburg-Ruhrort

Kontakt | Contact:

Gesellschaft der Freunde des Deutschen Architektur Museums e. V.
Geschäftsstelle: Deutsches Architekturmuseum
Schaumainkai 43
60596 Frankfurt am Main
Deutschland | Germany
Telefon | Tel.: **+49 (0) 69 - 97 20 33 66**
Mobil | Mobile: **+49 (0) 178 - 447 53 63**
Telefax | Fax: **+49 (0) 69 - 97 20 33 66**
E-Mail: freundeskreis.dam@stadt-frankfurt.de
http//www.dam-online.de/Gesellschaft der Freunde

Bankverbindung | Bank account:

Commerzbank AG
Frankfurt am Main
KONTO-NR. | Account number: **019 804 1500**
BLZ | Sorting code: **500 800 00**

ABBILDUNGSNACHWEISE
ILLUSTRATION CREDITS

Sämtliche hier nicht aufgeführte Abbildungen wurden uns freundlicherweise von den Architekten für die Publikation ihrer Projekte in diesem Buch zur Verfügung gestellt. Sollten unabsichtlich Referenzen nicht erfolgt sein, bitten wir um Entschuldigung und eine entsprechende Mitteilung an das DAM.
All photographs not listed here were either kindly made available to us by the architects for the publication of their projects in this book. Any omissions are entirely unintentional. We apologise to anyone not acknowledged and would request that details be addressed to DAM.

Umschlag und Umschlaginnenseite | Cover and Inside Front Cover
Hélène Binet

1–16 Hélène Binet
23 Uwe Dettmar
25 links | left
© Institut für Stadtgeschichte Frankfurt am Main;
Foto | Photo: **Jutta Hofmann**
25 rechts | right
© Institut für Stadtgeschichte Frankfurt am Main;
Foto | Photo: **Klaus Meier-Ude**
26 links | left
Sächsischer Landtag;
Foto | Photo: **Unger**
26 rechts | right
© ISOCHROM.com, Vienna
27 Rainer Gollmer
28 links | left **BBR / Stella**
28 rechts | right
© wolfgang tschapeller ztgmbh
29 links | left
© wolfgang tschapeller ztgmbh
29 rechts | right
KölnKongress/Gürzenich, Köln
30 links | left
Foto | Photo: **Bayerische Staatsgemäldesammlungen / Haydar Koyupinar**
30 rechts | right **EPA PHOTO / ANTONIO BAT**
31 links | left **Rose Hajdu**
31 rechts und unten | right and below **© DAM;**
Foto | Photo: **Hélène Binet**
35–39 Jens Masmann, München
41–47 Adam Mørk
49 Michael Reisch, Köln
50 links oben und unten left top and below
Michael Reisch, Köln
50 rechts | right
© nathanwillock.com
51 Michael Reisch, Köln
52 © nathanwillock.com
54–57 Michael Nast, Güstrow, www.lichtkombinat.de
59–61
Michael Heinrich, München
63–67 STEFAN MÜLLER-NAUMANN, MÜNCHEN
69–73 Michael Heinrich, München
75 - 81 © Vitra;
Fotograf | Photographer:
Iwan Baan
83 Michael Heinrich, München
84 links | left **© Louis Hotel;**
Fotograf | Photographer:
Stefan Braun
84 rechts | right
Michael Heinrich, München
85 Michael Heinrich, München
86 © Louis Hotel;
Fotograf | Photographer:
Stefan Braun
87 links | left **© Louis Hotel;**
Fotograf | Photographer:
Stefan Braun
87 rechts | right
Michael Heinrich, München
89–95 ANJA SCHLAMANN, KÖLN / LEIPZIG
97–103 © Zooey Braun
105–113 Stefan Müller, Berlin
115–119 Jörg Schöner, Dresden
120 © 2010 Tishman Speyer;
Fotograf | Photographer:
Klaus Helbig
121 www.klaushelbig.de
123 Thomas Eicken, Eicken und Mack Fotoproduktion
124 / 125 Christian Richters
126 Thomas Eicken, Eicken und Mack Fotoproduktion
127 Christian Richters
129–133 Annette Kisling
134–139 Bernd Hiepe, Berlin
141–145
Frank Grießhammer, 2009
146 oben | top
Frank Grießhammer, 2009
146 Mitte | centre **© Museum Kunst der Westküste**
147 Frank Grießhammer, 2009
149–151 SYRA - SCHOYERER ARCHITEKTEN BDA, Mainz
153 gmp Architekten von Gerkan, Marg und Partner
154 links | left **Public domain**
154 rechts | right **Public domain**
155 links | left **Mario Roberto Durán Ortiz**
155 rechts | right **© FLC / VG BILD-KUNST, Bonn 2010**
156 links | left
gmp Architekten von Gerkan, Marg und Partner
156 rechts | right **Heiner Leiska**
157 links | left
gmp Architekten von Gerkan, Marg und Partner
157 rechts | right
Hans Georg Esch
158 links | left **Jan Siefke**
158 rechts | right **© Atkins**
159 Marcus Bredt
162–164
LIN Finn Geipel + Giulia Andi;
Fotograf | Photographer:
Christian Richters
165–166
LIN Finn Geipel + Giulia Andi;
Fotograf | Photographer:
Jan-Oliver Kunze, LIN
167 links | left
LIN Finn Geipel + Giulia Andi;
Fotograf | Photographer:
François Maisonnasse, LIN
167 rechts | right
LIN Finn Geipel + Giulia Andi;
Fotograf | Photographer:
Jan-Oliver Kunze, LIN
169–171 LIU QIHUA, Shanghai, China
173–177 © PLATOON 2009:
Foto | Photo: **MYOUNG-RAE PARK**
179 terrain_Hamm
180 oben | top **terrain_Hamm**
180 unten links, Mitte links, Mitte rechts | below left, centre left, centre right
terrain: loenhart&mayr
180 unten rechts | below right
terrain_Lins
181 links | left **terrain_Lins**
181 rechts | right
terrain_Hamm
183–185 Uwe Dettmar

AUTOREN KURZBIOGRAFIEN
SHORT BIOGRAPHIES OF THE AUTHORS

WOLFGANG BACHMANN

***1951 in Ludwigshafen / Rhein. Studium der Agrarwissenschaften und Architektur. Diplom 1976 an der RWTH Aachen. Dissertation über die Architektur der Anthroposophen. Drei Jahre Berufspraxis in verschiedenen Architektur- und Ingenieurbüros, begleitend journalistische Tätigkeit. 1982 Redakteur der Zeitschrift „Bauwelt" in Berlin. Seit 1991 Chefredakteur der Zeitschrift „Baumeister" in München; außerdem schreibt er Kritiken, Glossen und Kurzgeschichten über Architektur und darüber hinaus. 2008 „Fachjournalist des Jahres" (2. Preis).**

Born 1951 in Ludwigshafen/Rhein. Studied agriculture and architecture; degree from RWTH Aachen University in 1976. Dissertation on anthroposophically inspired architecture. Three years of professional practice in various architecture and engineering offices while also working as a journalist. From 1982 editor of the magazine "Bauwelt" in Berlin. Since 1991 editor-in-chief of the magazine "Baumeister" in Munich; also writes reviews, glosses and short histories of architecture and other themes. 2008 "Specialist Journalist of the Year" (2nd prize).

FRANK BARKOW

***1957 in Kansas City, USA. 1982 Bachelor of Architecture, Montana State University; 1990 Master of Architecture, Harvard University. 1990–92 Gastprofessor an der Cornell University, Ithaca und in Rom. 1995–98 Unit Master an der Architectural Association London; 2003 The Arthur Gensler Visiting Professor of Architecture, Cornell University, Ithaca; 2004 Cass Gilbert Visiting Professor an der University of Minnesota, Minneapolis; 2005–06 Gastprofessor an der Staatlichen Akademie der Bildenden Künste, Stuttgart; 2000, 2004 und 2008 Gastprofessor an der Harvard Design School, Cambridge; 2008 Gastprofessor an der University of Wisconsin, Milwaukee, School of Architecture & Urban Planning. Seit 1993 gemeinsames Büro Barkow Leibinger in Berlin.**

Born 1957 in Kansas City, USA. 1982 Bachelor of Architecture, Montana State University; 1990 Master of Architecture, Harvard University, Graduate School of Design, Cambridge; 1990–92 Visiting Critic, Cornell University, Ithaca, New York and Rome; 1995–98 Unit Master, Architectural Association, London; 2003 The Arthur Gensler Visiting Professor of Architecture, Cornell University, Ithaca; 2004 Cass Gilbert Visiting Professor, University of Minnesota, Minneapolis; 2005–06 Visiting Professor, State Academy of Art and Design, Stuttgart; 2000, 2004, 2008 Visiting Professor, Harvard University, Graduate School of Design; 2008 Visiting Professor, University of Wisconsin, Milwaukee, School of Architecture & Urban Planning; since 1993 Barkow Leibinger Architects, Berlin, Germany

DIETER BARTETZKO

***1949 in Rodalben. Studium der Kunstgeschichte, Soziologie und Germanistik in Marburg und Berlin; 1984 Promotion über die Theatralik der NS-Architektur. Seit 1994 Redakteur im Feuilleton der „Frankfurter Allgemeinen Zeitung", Ressort Architektur, Denkmalpflege und Archäologie.**

Born 1949 in Rodalben. Studied art history, sociology and German language and literature at Marburg and Berlin; 1984 doctoral thesis on the theatrical aspect of National Socialist architecture.
Since 1994 editor of the architecture, conservation and archaeology section of the review pages of "Frankfurter Allgemeine Zeitung".

CHRISTOF BODENBACH

***1960 in Kestert am Rhein. Schreinerlehre. Studium in Darmstadt, Frankfurt am Main, Kassel und Wiesbaden. 1996 Journalistenpreis. Seit 1997 diverse Lehraufträge an verschiedenen Hochschulen, seit 2004 Pressesprecher der Architekten- und Stadtplanerkammer Hessen. Regelmäßige Veröffentlichungen über Architektur und Städtebau. Lebt in Wiesbaden.**

Born 1960 in Kestert am Rhein. Apprenticed as a carpenter. Studied in Darmstadt, Frankfurt am Main, Kassel and Wiesbaden. Won journalism award in 1996. Since 1997 teaching posts at various universities. Since 2004 press spokesman for the Hessian Chamber of Architects and Urban Planners. Regular publications on architecture and urban planning. Lives in Wiesbaden.

CHRISTIAN BRENSING

***1960 in Bad Ems. 1982–89 Studium der englischen Literatur und Kunstgeschichte in England; Abschluss M. A. Royal College of Art (RCA), London. 1989–90 wissenschaftlicher Assistent am Royal College of Art, London. 1990–92 Zaha Hadid Architects, London. 1993–2004 Ove Arup & Partners Consulting Engineers, London und Berlin.**

2004–05 CBP Consulting Engineers, München. Seit 2006 freischaffender Berater, Autor und Kurator. Lebt in Berlin.
Born 1960 in Bad Ems. 1982–89 studied English literature and history of art in England, final degree M.A. Royal College of Art (RCA), London. 1989–90 assistant lecturer, Royal College of Art, London; 1990–92 Zaha Hadid Architects, London; 1993–2004 Ove Arup & Partners Consulting Engineers, London and Berlin; 2004–05 CBP Consulting Engineers, Munich. Since 2006 freelance consultant, author and curator. Lives in Berlin.

MICHAELA BUSENKELL

***1962 in Schleswig. 1992 Diplom Architektur TU München, Döllgastpreis. Bis 1996 Mitarbeit in Architekturbüros; 1996–99 Volontärin/Redakteurin der Fachzeitschrift „AIT", Stuttgart; 1999–2005 Chefredakteurin von „a-matter, architecture and related". Seit 2005 freie Journalisten- und Kritikertätigkeit, seit 2007 freie wissenschaftliche Mitarbeiterin am DAM.**
Born 1962 in Schleswig. Degree in architecture from the Technical University Munich, Döllgast Award. Worked in architecture offices until 1996; 1996–99 volunteer/editor of the trade journal "AIT", Stuttgart; 1999–2005 editor-in-chief of "a-matter, architecture and related". Since 2005 freelance journalist and reviewer; since 2007 freelance scientific collaborator at the DAM.

OLIVER ELSER

***1972 in Rüsselsheim. Architekturstudium in Berlin. Zahlreiche Architekturkritiken für Zeitungen und Zeitschriften („Frankfurter Allgemeine Zeitung", „Süddeutsche Zeitung", „Texte zur Kunst", „Frankfurter Rundschau", „Bauwelt" etc.) sowie in Katalogen und Büchern. 2006–07 Lehrtätigkeit in Graz und Wien. Seit 2007 Kurator am DAM.**
Born 1972 in Rüsselsheim. Studied architecture in Berlin. Has written numerous architectural reviews for newspapers and magazines ("Frankfurter Allgemeine Zeitung", "Süddeutsche Zeitung", "Texte zur Kunst", "Frankfurter Rundschau", "Bauwelt" etc.) as well as catalogues and books. Taught in Graz and Vienna 2006–07. Since 2007 curator at the DAM .

ANGELIKA FITZ

***1967 in Hohenems (A). Kuratorin und Autorin. Zahlreiche Ausstellungen und Publikationen zu Architektur, Kunst, Urbanismus; aktuell „REALSTADT. Wünsche als Wirklichkeit im Herbst" (gemeinsam mit Martin Heller); zuletzt „Die sanften Wilden. Das Wiener Modell der Stadterneuerung" und „Linz Texas. Eine Stadt mit Beziehungen" für die Europäische Kulturhauptstadt Linz 09; davor u. a. „Wann begann temporär?" und „Ornament & Display" sowie „Reserve der Form". 2005 und 2003 Kommissärin für den österreichischen Beitrag zur Architekturbiennale in São Paulo. Internationale Vortrags- und Lehrtätigkeit.**
Born 1967 in Hohenems (A). Curator and author. Numerous exhibitions and publications on architecture, art, urbanism; currently "REALSTADT. Wünsche als Wirklichkeit im Herbst" (together with Martin Heller) and recently "Die sanften Wilden. Das Wiener Modell der Stadterneuerung" and "Linz Texas. Eine Stadt mit Beziehungen" for Linz 09 European Capital of Culture. Previous publications include "Wann begann temporär?" and "Ornament & Display" as well as "Reserve der Form". In 2005 and 2003 commissioner for the Austrian contribution to the Architecture Biennial in São Paulo. International lectures and teaching posts.

YORCK FÖRSTER

***1964 in Hannover. Studium der Philosophie, Soziologie und Kunstpädagogik an der Universität Frankfurt am Main. Kurator und Publizist. Zahlreiche Vorträge, Publikationen und Ausstellungen. Für das DAM u. a. „Peter Kulka – Minimalismus und Sinnlichkeit" (2005), „Gewahrsam. Räume der Überwachung" (2007), „Heterotopia. Arbeiten von Willem van Genk und anderen" (2008). Partner der kuratorenwerkstatt Förster Gräwe Winkelmann.**
Born 1964 in Hanover. Studied philosophy, sociology und art education at the University of Frankfurt am Main. Curator and journalist. Numerous lectures, publications and exhibitions. Publications for the DAM include "Peter Kulka – Minimalismus und Sinnlichkeit" (2005), "Gewahrsam. Räume der Überwachung" (2007), "Heterotopia. Arbeiten von Willem van Genk und anderen" (2008). Partner in kuratorenwerkstatt Förster Gräwe Winkelmann.

ALMUT GEHEBE-GERNHARDT

Studium der Kunstgeschichte und Germanistik in Frankfurt am Main. Promotion über den Wiederaufbau in Frankfurt am Main mit der erstmaligen Präsentation der Architektengemeinschaft Alois Giefer und Hermann Mäckler. Vortrags- und Publikationstätigkeit mit Schwerpunkt Stadtumbau und Nachkriegsmoderne.
Studied art history and German language & literature in Frankfurt am Main. Doctorate on the rebuilding of Frankfurt am Main, presenting for the first time the work of the architecture cooperative of Alois Giefer and Hermann Mäckler. Lectures and publications on the themes of urban redevelopment and postwar Modernism.

CHRISTINA GRÄWE

***1965 in Idar Oberstein. Krankenschwester, Dipl.-Ing. Architektur. Volontariat am DAM. Freie Kuratorin und Autorin, u. a. Wanderausstellung „A lifetime for architecture – the photographer Julius Shulman", „Stadtvisionen 1910/2010" (Architekturmuseum TU Berlin). Partnerin der kuratorenwerkstatt Förster Gräwe Winkelmann.**
Born 1965 in Idar Oberstein. Nurse, architectural engineer. 2003–05 research volunteer at the DAM. Freelance curator and author, incl. travelling exhibition "A lifetime for architecture – the photographer Julius Shulman", "City Visions 1910/2010" (Architekturmuseum TU Berlin). Partner in kuratorenwerkstatt Förster Gräwe Winkelmann.

OLIVER G. HAMM

***1963 in Limburg / Lahn. Dipl.-Ing. (FH) Architektur. Freier Autor, Herausgeber, Redakteur und Kurator (u. a. „NEU BAU LAND. Architektur und Stadtumbau in den neuen Bundesländern", DAM, 2007). Studium der Architektur an der FH Darmstadt, 1989–92 Redakteur der „db deutsche bauzeitung", Stuttgart, 1992–98 Redakteur der „Bauwelt", Berlin, 2000–07 Chefredakteur „Deutsches Architektenblatt", Berlin, 2008–09 Chefredakteur „greenbuilding", Berlin. 2003 Deutscher Preis für Denkmalschutz (Journalistenpreis). Seit 2003 Mitglied im Fachbeirat der IBA Fürst-Pückler-Land. Lebt in Berlin.**
Born 1963 in Limburg / Lahn. Qualified architectural engineer. Freelance author, publisher, editor, and curator (e.g. "NEU BAU LAND. Architektur und Stadtumbau in den neuen Bundesländern", Deutsches Architekturmuseum, Frankfurt/ Main 2007). Studied architecture at the University of Applied Sciences in Darmstadt. 1989–92 editor of "db deutsche bauzeitung", Stuttgart; 1992–98 editor of "Bauwelt", Berlin; 2000–07 editor-in-chief of "Deutsches Architektenblatt", Berlin; 2008–09 editor-in-chief of "greenbuilding", Berlin. German award for monument preservation 2003 (journalist award).

Member of the IBA Fürst-Pückler-Land advisory council since 2003. Lives in Berlin.

HAORU CHEN

***1972 in Hangzhou/China. Wanderte als Jugendlicher nach New York aus. Studierte Architektur in New York City und arbeitete bei mehreren Firmen in New York. 2001 Rückkehr nach China und Gründung des Citiarc Studio Office, mit Schwerpunkt auf urbane Architekturprojekte in China. Schloss sich 2005 der neuen Architekturabteilung an der China Art Academy (CAA) unter der Leitung von Wang Shu an. Derzeit Gastdozent an der CAA. Mitglied des American Institute of Architecture.**

Born 1972 in Hangzhou/China. Emigrated to New York as a teenager. Haoru Chen studied architecture in New York City and practised in various NYC design firms. In 2001 returned to Hangzhou and created Citiarc Studio Office, which focuses on urban architectural projects in China. In 2005 joined China Art Academy's (CAA) newly established architecture programme headed by Wang Shu. Currently a visiting professor there while practising in his Hangzhou studio. Member of American Institute of Architecture.

CHRISTIAN HOLL

Zunächst Kunststudium in Stuttgart und Münster/Westfalen, dann Architekturstudium an der RWTH Aachen, in Florenz und an der Universität Stuttgart. 1997–2004 Redakteur der „db deutsche bauzeitung". 2004 Gründung von „frei04 publizistik" mit Ursula Baus und Klaus Siegele. Buchveröffentlichungen, freie Redakteurs-, Journalisten- und Kritikertätigkeit sowie Lehraufträge. 2005–2010 akademischer Mitarbeiter am Städtebau-Institut der Uni Stuttgart. Mitglied im Ausstellungsausschuss der „architekturgalerie am weißenhof", Stuttgart.

Studied art in Stuttgart and Münster/Westphalia, then architecture at RWTH Aachen University, in Florence and at the University of Stuttgart. 1997–2004 editor at "db deutsche bauzeitung". Founded "frei04 publizistik" in 2004 with Ursula Baus and Klaus Siegele. Has published books, worked as freelance editor, journalist and reviewer and held posts as lecturer. 2005–2010 academic assistant at the Institute of Urban Planning at the University of Stuttgart. Member of the exhibition committee of "architekturgalerie am weissenhof", Stuttgart.

ULRICH HÖHNS

***1954 in Bothel. Architekturhistoriker und -kritiker, wissenschaftlicher Leiter des Schleswig-Holsteinischen Archivs für Architektur und Ingenieurbaukunst.**

Born 1954 in Bothel. Architectural historian and critic, research director of the Schleswig-Holstein Archive for Architecture and Engineering.

FALK JAEGER

***1950 in Ottweiler/Saar. Studium der Architektur und Kunstgeschichte in Braunschweig, Stuttgart und Tübingen. Promotion an der TU Hannover. Apl. Professor für Architekturtheorie und -kritik an der TU Dresden. Freier Publizist, Kurator und Architekturkritiker bei Tageszeitungen, Fachpresse und Hörfunk. Lebt in Berlin.**

Born 1950 in Ottweiler/Saar. Studied architecture and art history at Brunswick, Stuttgart und Tübingen. Doctorate from Technical University of Hanover. Professorship in architectural theory and criticism at Technical University of Dresden. Freelance writer, curator, architecture critic for newspapers, specialist periodicals and radio. Lives in Berlin.

URSULA KLEEFISCH-JOBST

***1956 in Stuttgart. Studium der Kunstgeschichte, Archäologie und Germanistik in Bonn, München und Rom: Promotion. 1985–88 Forschungsprojekt an der Biblioteca Hertziana in Rom. 1989–90 Mitarbeiterin am Landesdenkmalamt in Berlin. 2001–08 freie Kuratorin am DAM. Seit 2008 leitende Kuratorin am Museum für Architektur und Ingenieurkunst NRW.**

Born 1956 in Stuttgart. Studied art history, archaeology and German language & literature in Bonn, Munich and Rome, culminating in doctorate. 1985–88 research project at the Biblioteca Hertziana in Rome. 1989–90 employee at the Berlin Monument Authority. 2001–08 freelance curator at the DAM. Since 2008 head curator at the Museum of Architecture and the Art of Engineering NRW.

ANNE KOCKELKORN

***1975 in München. Studierte Architektur in Paris und Berlin. Seit 2006 tätig als freie Architekturkritikerin, u. a. für die Zeitschriften „Bauwelt" und „ARCH+". 2008 Ko-Kuratorin des Ausstellungs- und Konferenzprojekts „Tuned City – zwischen Klang- und Raumspekulation" in Berlin. Seit 2009 tätig als wissenschaftliche Mitarbeiterin an der Assistenzprofessur Dr. Laurent Stalder an der ETH Zürich, unter anderem für den Seminarzyklus „Infrastrukturlandschaft Schweiz".**

Born 1975 in Munich. Studied architecture in Paris and Berlin. Since 2006 freelance architecture critic, including for the magazines "Bauwelt" and "ARCH+". Co-curator of the exhibition and conference project "Tuned City – zwischen Klang- und Raumspekulation" in Berlin in 2008. Since 2009 research assistant for assistant professor Dr. Laurent Stalder at the Swiss Federal Institute of Technology Zurich, including for the seminar cycle "Infrastrukturlandschaft Schweiz".

WILHELM KÜCKER

***1933 in Celle. Architekturstudium an der TH München, der TH Wien und der ETH Zürich mit anschließender Promotion. 1963 Gründung eines eigenen Architekturbüros in München. Seit 1975 Honorarprofessor an der TU München, Gastlehrtätigkeiten in den USA, Türkei und Großbritannien. 1983–87 Präsident des BDA. 1981–86 Ratsmitglied der Union Internationale des Architectes UIA, Paris; 1987–90 Vizepräsident. Miembro de Honor del Consejo Superior de los Colegios des Arquitectos de España. Honorary Fellow of the American Institute of Architects AIA. Zahlreiche Veröffentlichungen zur Architekturtheorie und -praxis.**

Born 1933 in Celle. Architecture studies at the Technical University Munich, Vienna University of Technology and the Swiss Federal Institute of Technology Zurich, culminating in doctorate. Founded his own architecture office in Munich in 1963. Since 1975 honorary professor at the Technical University Munich; guest professorships in the USA, Turkey and the United Kingdom. 1983–87 president of the Association of German Architects BDA. 1981–86 member of the council of the Union Internationale des Architectes UIA, Paris; 1987–90 vice president. Miembro de Honor del Consejo Superior de los Colegios des Arquitectos de España. Honorary Fellow of the American Institute of Architects AIA. Numerous publications on architectural theory and practice.

ARNO LEDERER

***1947 in Stuttgart. Architekturstudium in Stuttgart und Wien. Selbstständig seit 1979, ab 1985 in Bürogemeinschaft mit Jórunn Ragnarsdóttir, seit 1992 mit Marc Oei. 1985–90 Professor an der Fachhochschule für Technik in Stuttgart. Ab 1990 Professor an der Universität Karlsruhe. 1997–2005 Leiter**

des Lehrstuhls für Gebäudelehre an der dortigen Architekturfakultät. Seit 2005 Leiter des Instituts für öffentliche Bauten und Entwerfen an der Universität Stuttgart. 2000–05 Beirat im DAM. 2002–06 Wissenschaftlicher Beirat im Bundesamt für Bauwesen und Raumordnung in Berlin. Seit 2007 Mitglied des Beirats der Bundesstiftung Baukultur in Potsdam. Seit 2009 Mitglied im Gestaltungsbeirat für das „Dom-Römer-Areal" der Stadt Frankfurt am Main.
Born 1947 in Stuttgart. Architecture studies in Stuttgart and Vienna. Self-employed since 1979, from 1985 in a shared office with Jórunn Ragnarsdóttir, and since 1992 with Marc Oei. 1985–90 professor at Stuttgart University of Applied Sciences. From 1990 professor at the Karlsruhe Institute of Technology. 1997–2005 chair of building theory and design in the Department of Architecture there. Since 2005 director of the Institute of Public Building and Design at the University of Stuttgart. 2000–05 advisory board of DAM. 2002–06 research council of the German Federal Office for Building and Regional Planning in Berlin. Since 2007 member of the advisory board of the Federal Foundation of Architecture in Potsdam. Since 2009 member of the planning council for the "Dom-Römer-Areal" of the city of Frankfurt am Main.

KARIN LEYDECKER

***1956 in Speyer. Studium der Germanistik, Psychologie, Kunstgeschichte und der evangelischen Theologie in Mainz, Heidelberg und Karlsruhe. 1988 Promotion. Lehrtätigkeit zur Architekturwahrnehmung an der Universität und der Pädagogischen Hochschule Karlsruhe. Schreibt regelmäßig für die „Neue Zürcher Zeitung" sowie für Fach- und Publikumszeitschriften. Zahlreiche Buchveröffentlichungen zur Architektur und Denkmalpflege.**
Born 1956 in Speyer. Studied German language & literature, psychology, art history and Protestant theology in Mainz, Heidelberg and Karlsruhe. Doctorate in 1988. Teacher of architectural perception at Karlsruhe University and School of Education. Regularly writes for the "Neue Zürcher Zeitung" newspaper and for trade and popular journals. Has published numerous books on architecture and historic preservation.

FRANK MAIER-SOLGK

***1959 in München. Studium der Philosophie und Kunstgeschichte, Promotion. Zahlreiche Publikationen zu den Themengebieten Architektur und Städtebau, Gartenkunst sowie Kunst- und Kulturgeschichte. Lebt und arbeitet als freier Journalist, Buchautor und Texter in Düsseldorf und München.**
Born 1959 in Munich. Studied philosophy and art history, culminating in doctorate. Numerous publications on the themes of architecture and urban planning, garden art as well as art and cultural history. Lives and works as freelance journalist, book author and copywriter in Düsseldorf and Munich.

IRENE MEISSNER

***1961 in Kassel. 1980–88 Architekturstudium an der TH Darmstadt; 1988–1995 Mitarbeit bei Kammerer + Belz, Kucher und Partner, Stuttgart; 1995–2001 wissenschaftliche Assistentin am Lehrstuhl für Entwerfen, Baukonstruktion und Baustoffkunde, Prof. Dr.-Ing. Theodor Hugues, TU München. Seit 2001 wissenschaftliche Mitarbeiterin am Architekturmuseum der TU München, Mitarbeit bei zahlreichen Ausstellungen, u. a. „Exemplarisch – Konstruktion und Raum in der Architektur des 20. Jahrhunderts" (2002), „Frei Otto – Leicht bauen, natürlich gestalten" (2005), „Sep Ruf 1908–1981 – Moderne mit Tradition" (2008).**
Born 1961 in Kassel. 1980–88 architecture studies at Darmstadt University of Technology; 1988–1995 employed at Kammerer + Belz, Kucher und Partner, Stuttgart; 1995–2001 research assistant to Prof. Dr.-Ing. Theodor Hugues in the Department of Design, Structural Design and Materials Science at the Technical University Munich. Since 2001 research assistant at the Architecture Museum of the Technical University Munich, assisting with numerous exhibitions including "Exemplarisch – Konstruktion und Raum in der Architektur des 20. Jahrhunderts" (2002), "Frei Otto – Leicht bauen, natürlich gestalten" (2005), "Sep Ruf 1908–1981 – Moderne mit Tradition" (2008).

FRIEDERIKE MEYER

***1972 in Dresden. Architekturstudium in Aachen und Seattle, Design Build Studio in Cuernavaca, Mexiko, Kunstgeschichte in Dresden, Öffentlichkeitsarbeit und Ausstellungen am Festspielhaus Hellerau, Journalistenschule in Berlin. Seit 2000 Redakteurin der „Bauwelt".**
Born 1972 in Dresden. Architecture studies in Aachen and Seattle, Design Build Studio in Cuernavaca, Mexico, history of art in Dresden, public relations and curator at Festspielhaus Hellerau, journalism studies in Berlin. Since 2000 editor at "Bauwelt" magazine.

PETER CACHOLA SCHMAL

***1960 in Altötting. Aufenthalt in Multan/Pakistan, Mülheim/Ruhr, Jakarta/Indonesien, Holzminden und Baden-Baden, Architekturstudium an der TU Darmstadt; 1989 Diplom. Mitarbeit bei Behnisch+Partner in Stuttgart 1989. 1990–93 bei Eisenbach+Partner in Zeppelinheim. 1992–97 wissenschaftlicher Mitarbeiter an der TU Darmstadt. 1997–2000 Lehrauftrag für Entwerfen an der FH Frankfurt. 2000 Kurator, 2006 Direktor des DAM. 2007 Deutscher Generalkommissar VII. Internationale Architekturbiennale São Paulo.**
Born 1960 in Altötting. Has lived in Multan/Pakistan, Mülheim/Ruhr, Jakarta/Indonesia, Holzminden and Baden-Baden. Studied architecture at the Technical University of Darmstadt; diploma in 1989. Worked at Behnisch+Partner in Stuttgart in 1989. 1990–93 at Eisenbach+Partner in Zeppelinheim. 1992–97 Assistant Professor at the TU Darmstadt. 1997–2000 taught architectural design at the University of Applied Sciences in Frankfurt. 2000 curator, 2006 director of the DAM. 2007 German Commissioner for the 7th International Architecture Biennial in São Paulo.

AXEL SIMON

***1966 in Düsseldorf. Studierte Architektur in Düsseldorf und Berlin sowie Geschichte und Theorie der Architektur in Zürich. 1999–2005 Entwurfsassistent an der ETH Zürich, u. a. bei Peter Märkli. Ab 2000 freier Architekturkritiker u. a. beim „Tages-Anzeiger", der „Weltwoche" und internationalen Fachzeitschriften. 2006–09 Begründer und Redakteur des „eMagazins" von swiss-architects.com. Seit 2010 Redakteur Architektur bei der Zeitschrift „Hochparterre".**
Born 1966 in Düsseldorf. Studied architecture in Düsseldorf and Berlin as well as history and theory of architecture in Zurich. 1999–2005 design assistant at the Swiss Federal Institute of Technology Zurich, including for Peter Märkli. From 2000 freelance architecture critic for the "Tages-Anzeiger", "Weltwoche" and other newspapers and for international trade journals. 2006–09 founder and editor of the "eMagazine" of swiss-architects.com.
Since 2010 architecture editor at "Hochparterre" magazine.

IN MEMORIAM

GÜNTER BEHNISCH

(12. 06. 1922 – 11. 07. 2010)

Am 11. Juli verstarb in Stuttgart mit 88 Jahren Günter Behnisch. Eine Würdigung seines Werkes wird im kommenden Deutschen Architektur Jahrbuch 2011/12 erscheinen.

On 11 July, architect Günter Behnisch died in Stuttgart at the age of 88. A tribute to his life's work will be published in the next German Architecture Annual 2011/12.

HANS-BUSSO VON BUSSE

(7. 5. 1930 – 7. 11. 2009)

„Es ist dies das Wagnis des freien Architekten ..., dem Konformismus der Zeit zu widerstehen und ... den Machern aus Staat, Verwaltung und Wirtschaft das abzutrotzen, was ihnen als den Bauherren ... zur Verantwortung aufgetragen ist, nämlich Baukultur zu ermöglichen."

Der dies zu Protokoll gegeben und danach stets gelebt hat, ist Hans-Busso von Busse, der am 7. Mai 1930 im damals oberschlesischen Oppeln geboren wurde.

Nach dem Abitur mit 17 und einer Zimmererlehre folgte das Architekturstudium an der TH in München mit Diplom 1954 und anschließendem Graduate-Studium in den USA am M.I.T. bei Eero Saarinen, Minoru Yamasaki und Paul Rudolph.

Zurück in München wurde für den jungen Architekten das Bauen für die evangelische Kirche zum Schwerpunkt seiner frühen und mittleren Jahre. Gleich die beiden ersten Kirchen in Schaftlach und Erding zeigten Eigenständigkeit im Umgang mit Raum und Material (Holztragwerke) und Einfügung ohne Anpassung in die oberbayerische Ländlichkeit. Es folgten zahlreiche Gemeindezentren, eine Kirche in Stein bei Nürnberg und verschiedene Bauten für die Rummelsberger Anstalten. Auch nach Coburg führten ihn gewonnene Wettbewerbe (Stadtsanierung, Kongresshaus u. a.).

In München gelang ihm mit der Erweiterung des Stadtarchivs das Kunststück, einem öffnungslosen Gebäudetyp eine kraftvoll akzentuierte Gestalt abzuringen und zugleich eine städtebauliche Schwachstelle platzbildend zu bereinigen. Mit dem Terminal 1 des neuen Flughafens in München hatte er sich endgültig in die internationale Architekturgeschichte eingeschrieben. Dass dieses riesige Bauwerk so gar nicht einschüchternd ausgefallen ist, sondern so ganz und gar licht und heiter und filigran konstruiert, verdanken wir ihm.

Von seinen letzten Arbeiten wären der sensible Umbau des historischen Haus Berge zu Witten zu erwähnen und vor allem das Westfälische Museum für Archäologie in Herne: ein architektonischer Glücksfall auch dieses.

Nicht wenige seiner Bauten erhielten Preise. Für sein Gesamtwerk wurde Hans-Busso von Busse mit dem Fritz-Schumacher-Preis und dem Architekturpreis der Landeshauptstadt München ausgezeichnet. Die Akademie der Künste Berlin/Brandenburg und die Bayerische Akademie der Schönen Künste ehrten ihn durch eine Mitgliedschaft.

Als ordentlicher Professor für Entwerfen und Baukonstruktion an der TU Dortmund hatte er von 1976 bis 1995 mit hohem Einsatz am Aufbau der erst kurz zuvor gegründeten Fakultät Bauwesen mitgewirkt.

Hans-Busso von Busse fand bald (1962) zum BDA und nutzte ihn als Plattform. Von 1970 bis 1975 war er dessen Präsident. Sein Wirken an der Spitze des Bundes hat positive Erinnerungen hinterlassen wie kein anderes.

Im Gedächtnis bleibt die Distinktion eines Gentleman, die ihn nie daran gehindert hat, für seine Überzeugung nachdrücklich, ja, wo ihm nötig erscheinend, auch kämpferisch aufzutreten. Gerade dies machte seine Noblesse aus.

"The freelance architect dares ... to resist the conformity of his times and ... manages to wrest from the powers that be in the state, administration and economy that which they have been charged with as building clients, namely to make possible architectural culture."

The architect who went on the record with this statement and who lived by its words was Hans-Busso von Busse, born on 7 May 1930 in the town of Oppeln in Upper Silesia.

After graduating from secondary school at the early age of 17 and apprenticing as a carpenter, he went on to study architecture at the Technical University Munich, earning his Diplom degree in 1954, and then did graduate studies in the USA at M.I.T. with Eero Saarinen, Minoru Yamasaki and Paul Rudolph.

Back in Munich, the young architect was commissioned by the Protestant Church to execute several projects during the early

and middle years of his career. His first two churches, in Schaftlach and Erding, already demonstrated the independent manner in which he handled space and materials (wooden support structures), integrating his structures into the rural landscape of Upper Bavaria but not making any concessions. There followed numerous Protestant community centres, a church in Stein near Nuremberg and various buildings for the Rummelsberger Anstalten. Competition victories also took him to Coburg (urban redevelopment, conference centre, and other projects).
In the extension of the City Archive in Munich, he mastered the challenge of creating a powerfully accentuated form for a windowless building type while at the same time solving a weak spot in the urban fabric with the addition of a public square. With his Terminal 1 for the new airport in Munich he inscribed his name firmly once and for all in the annals of international architecture. It is owing to his skill that this gigantic structure, rather than seeming overpowering, looks light and airy and cheerful.
The sensitive reconstruction of the historical Haus Berge zu Witten and in particular the Westphalian Museum of Archaeology in Herne, likewise an architectural delight, are worthy of note amongst his late works.
Many of his buildings won awards. And for his life's work, Hans-Busso von Busse was distinguished with the Fritz Schumacher Award and the Architecture Award of the State Capital of Munich. The Academy of the Arts Berlin/Brandenburg and the Bavarian Academy of Fine Arts made him an honorary member.
As Professor of Design and Structural Design at TU Dortmund University, he dedicated his energies from 1976 to 1995 to helping to develop the Department of Architecture that had been established there shortly before.
Hans-Busso von Busse joined the Association of German Architects (BDA) early on (1962) and used it as a platform, becoming its president from 1970 to 1975. His work at the head of that organisation left an unparalleled legacy of positive memories.
The man we will remember was a distinguished gentleman who never hesitated to stand up and, if need be, fight for his convictions. This very trait is what accounted for his noblesse.

Wilhelm Kücker

MAX MEID

(18. 7. 1910 – 16. 7. 2009)

Der Bund Deutscher Architekten und die hessische Stadtbauverwaltung begannen 1954 ausgewählte Bauten in Hessen mit dem Prädikat „vorbildliche Leistung" auszuzeichnen. Max Meid schrieb 1956 dazu: „Die Auszeichnung der Leistung – so subjektiv sie wie jede künstlerische Beurteilung auch ist – wird neben ihrer wichtigsten Bestimmung, die Qualität zu heben, Kritik zu wecken, den Ehrgeiz der Bauherren herauszufordern und gutes zeitgemäßes Bauen vor der Öffentlichkeit sichtbar herauszuheben, auch die überaus interessante Folge haben, für spätere Zeiten zu dokumentieren, was in unserer Zeit für gut und einer Auszeichnung für würdig gehalten wurde." Seine Hoffnung, wenn nicht die nachfolgende, dann doch die darauf folgenden Generationen würden diese baulichen Leistungen anerkennen, hat sich nicht erfüllt. Denn gerade die Bauten der Nachkriegsmoderne sind im Rahmen des derzeitigen Frankfurter Stadtumbaus durch Abriss gefährdet.
Der Architekt Max Meid gehörte einer Architektengeneration an, die Ende der 1920er-Jahre zu studieren begann, im Dritten Reich ihre ersten größeren Bauaufträge erhielt und nach 1945 den demokratischen Aufbau der jungen Bundesrepublik entscheidend architektonisch mitgestaltete.
Am 18. Juli 1910 in Berlin geboren, studierte Max Meid von 1929 bis 1934 Architektur bei Hans Poelzig an der TH Charlottenburg in Berlin und schloss dort mit dem Diplom ab. Bis 1937 war Max Meid Baureferendar im Architekturbüro Hans Geber. Hier lernte er den Architekten Helmut Romeick kennen. 1938 beendete er seine Ausbildung mit dem Staatsexamen. Von 1938 bis 1945 war Max Meid Mitarbeiter im legendären Architekturbüro Herbert Rimpl, wo sich viele dem neuen Bauen verpflichtete Architekten versammelt hatten. Er war zuständig für Siedlungs- und Industriebau.
1947 war Max Meid technischer Mitarbeiter im Stadtplanungsamt von Frankfurt am Main. Dort traf er Helmut Romeick wieder. Gemeinsam gründeten sie 1948 als freie Architekten ein Architekturbüro, das eines der bedeutendsten Planungsbüros in Frankfurt am Main werden sollte. Am Wiederaufbau der Frankfurter Altstadt im Jahr 1952 waren sie unter anderem mit den Kammbauten an der Berliner Straße vertreten. Unter vielen herausragenden Gebäuden wie dem AOK-Verwaltungsgebäude von 1956 sollen hier das Parkhaus Hauptwache von 1956, das Hochhaus Schweizer National an der Untermainbrücke von 1964 sowie das Bankgebäude Chase-Manhattan von 1972 besonders hervorgehoben werden.
Max Meid war Vorsitzender und Ehrenmitglied des BDA Hessen und Präsident der hessischen Architektenkammer. 1985 wurde Max Meid mit dem Bundesverdienstkreuz für seine jahrzehntelange Förderung und Pflege der Baukultur im Rahmen der „Auszeichnung vorbildlicher Bauten" geehrt. Am 16. Juli 2009, zwei Tage vor seinem 99. Geburtstag, ist Max Meid in Frankfurt am Main gestorben.
In 1954 the Association of German Architects BDA and the Hessian Urban Planning Office began to award the distinction "exemplary achievement" to selected buildings in Hessen. Max Meid wrote of this in 1956: "The honouring of achievement – as subjective as every artistic judgement – will have in addition to its primary goals of increasing quality, instigating criticism, challenging the ambition of building clients and raising public awareness of good contemporary building the most interesting consequence of documenting for later eras what was considered good and worthy of recognition in our day." His hope that, if not the next generation, then the one succeeding it would acknowledge these architectural accomplishments went unfulfilled, because Frankfurt's post-war Modernist buildings in particular are threatened with destruction in the course of the city's current redevelopment plans.
Max Meid was part of the generation of architects who began their studies in the late 1920s, received their first major commissions during the Third Reich, and after 1945 had a hand in shaping the democratic rebuilding of the young Federal Republic of Germany.
Born on 18 July 1910 in Berlin, Meid studied architecture from 1929 to 1934 with Hans Poelzig at the Technical University of Charlottenburg (today the Berlin Institute of Technology), earning a Diplom degree. Until 1937, Meid was a trainee in the architecture office of Hans Geber, where he made the acquaintance of architect Helmut Romeick. In 1938 he concluded his studies with the state board exams. From 1938 to 1945 Meid was employed in the legendary architecture office of Herbert Rimpl, where many architects dedicated to the

"New Building" movement had gathered. Meid was in charge of housing developments and industrial buildings.
In 1947 he was a technical assistant in the City Planning Office of Frankfurt am Main. There he again met Helmut Romeick. In 1948 the two proceeded to establish their own architecture firm, which would go on to become one of Frankfurt's most important planning offices. Meid and Romeick played a role in rebuilding Frankfurt's Old Town with projects such as the 1952 "Kammbauten" on Berliner Strasse. Among their many outstanding edifices, the AOK administration building from 1956, the Hauptwache car park from 1956, the Schweizer National high-rise at Untermainbrücke bridge from 1964 and the Chase-Manhattan Bank building from 1972 are particularly worthy of mention.
Max Meid was chairman and honorary member of the Hessen branch of the Association of German Architects (BDA) and president of the Hessian Chamber of Architects. In 1985 he was awarded the Federal Cross of Merit for his decades-long promotion and support of building culture in the form of the above-mentioned Award for Exemplary Buildings. On 16 July 2009, two days before his 99th birthday, Max Meid passed away in Frankfurt am Main.

Almut Gehebe-Gernhardt

ELMAR SCHOSSIG

(28. 6. 1950 – 15. 12. 2009)
Die kofferförmigen Aluminiumhallen der Firma Rimowa in Köln standen am viel beachteten Anfang (1985). Zuletzt waren es vor allem Fotografien, die in mehreren Ausstellungen und Publikationen zu sehen waren und den Architekten, Produktdesigner und Fotografen Elmar Schossig als einen Grenzgänger auswiesen, der die Architekturfotografie in Richtung abstrakter Kunst zu bewegen schien – in Richtung kühler, schwarz-weißer, aber auch farbiger Formengebilde, die aus dem rationalen Geist der Objekte geboren waren. Elmar Schossig hatte sich in seinen letzten Lebensjahren der Fotografie zugewandt, nachdem er sich infolge seiner Krankheit vom Büroalltag zurückziehen musste. Davor lag eine lange, produktive und mit vielen Preisen ausgezeichnete architektonische Karriere, die in vielen gemeinsamen Projekten mit Ehefrau Dörte Gatermann oder in Eigenregie eine ungewöhnlich konzentrierte Verbindung von Technik, Funktionalität und Ästhetik demonstrierte. „Die Technik ist nicht der Zweck, sondern ein Mittel unserer Arbeit", hat Schössig einmal gesagt, und sich dabei wohl auch gegen eine skulpturale Architekturmode gewandt, „die die Arbeit der Ingenieure nur ausbeute(t), indem sie sich in Wirklichkeit bloß für die ästhetisch-figurativen Ergebnisse interessierte." Elmar Schossig befand sich hingegen nach seinem Studium an der TU Braunschweig und der RWTH Aachen (Diplom bei Gottfried Böhm) schon in den 1980er-Jahren auf der Suche nach zeitgemäßen Konzepten für ein energiesparendes Bauen, das dabei auf klare ästhetische Linien nicht verzichtete und einen Weg dorthin in einer frühzeitigen Abstimmung mit anderen Fachdisziplinen suchte. Das Kontor 19 im Kölner Rheinauhafen war so ein schnörkelloser, mit seinen eingeprägten grafischen Elementen auf den Fassadenpaneelen aber auch künstlerisch wirkender Bau. Der Turm der Bochumer Stadtwerke (2004) und vor nicht allzu langer Zeit das Capricorn-Haus (2008) im Düsseldorfer Medienhafen sind prominente Beispiele dafür, wie eine ästhetisch überzeugende Umsetzung energetischer Konzepte gelingen kann. Vor allem am Capricorn-Haus wird ein Fokus der Arbeit von Elmar Schossig deutlich: die über die Jahre konsequent entwickelte Auseinandersetzung mit den funktionalen Möglichkeiten von Fassaden, die in der ‚i-modul Fassade' mündete. Es ist die Idee von vorgefertigten multifunktionalen Fassadenmodulen, in denen vom Lüftungssystem bis zu Akustik- und Beleuchtungselementen alles, was sonst an anderer Stelle viel Platz benötigt, integriert ist. Im Fall des Capricorn-Hauses sind die transparenten und geschlossenen signalroten Paneele, zu einem markanten Muster zusammengefügt. In solchen technisch-funktional bedingten Mustern lag eine der Verbindungen zwischen dem künstlerischen und dem technischen Interesse. Viel zu früh, mit 59 Jahren, ist Elmar Schossig im Dezember 2009 in Köln gestorben.
The suitcase-shaped aluminium halls of the Rimowa company in Cologne stood at the much-acclaimed start of his career (1985). But in recent years it was mostly his photographs, on view in several exhibitions and publications, that identified the architect, product designer and photographer Elmar Schossig as a remarkable crossover talent. These pictures seemed to move architectural photography into the realm of abstract art – toward cool black-and-white, but also colour, formal constructions born of the rational spirit of the objects they depict. Schossig turned to photography in the latter years of his life after illness forced him to withdraw from the daily office routine. But before that time he enjoyed a long, productive and award-winning career as an architect, during which many joint projects with his wife Dörte Gatermann, but also on his own, demonstrated an unusually concentrated symbiosis between technology, functionality and aesthetics.
"Technology is not the end, but rather the means of our work," Schossig once said, at the same time turning away from the fashion for sculptural architecture, "which only exploits the work of the engineers by in reality being interested only in the aesthetic and figural results." Elmar Schossig by contrast set out as early as the 1980s, following his studies at Brunswick University of Technology and RWTH Aachen University (Diplom degree with Gottfried Böhm), on a search for modern concepts for energy-efficient building that did not however forego clean, aesthetic lines. He made his way toward this goal by consulting with other disciplines early on in each project. Kontor 19, in Cologne's waterfront Rheinauhafen, exhibits a pared-down structure but exudes an artistic air with its façade panels featuring embossed graphic elements. The tower of the Bochum Municipal Utilities Building (2004) and, more recently, the Capricorn-Haus (2008) in Düsseldorf's Medienhafen are prominent examples of how energy concepts can be implemented in an aesthetically convincing manner. Particularly in the Capricorn-Haus, a focus of the Schossig's work becomes evident: an engagement that evolved consistently over the years with the functional possibilities of façades, culminating in the "i-modul façade". This idea involves prefabricated, multifunctional façade modules integrating everything from ventilation system to acoustic and lighting elements – in other words, all those services that would otherwise take up a great deal of space in the building.
In the case of the Capricorn-Haus, the transparent and self-contained signal-red panels are arranged to create a striking pattern. This kind of technical -functional pattern was just one of the ways Schossig found to link artistic with tech-

nical interests. Elmar Schossig died much too young, at 59, in December 2009 in Cologne.

Frank Maier-Solgk

JULIUS SHULMAN

(10. 10. 1910 – 15. 7. 2009)

„All began just by chance"– so hat Julius Shulman (*1910 Brooklyn, New York – † 2009 Los Angeles) gern die Frage nach dem Beginn seiner Karriere als Architekturfotograf beantwortet. Die zufällige Begegnung mit Richard Neutra im Jahr 1936 legte den Grundstein zu einer über Jahrzehnte währenden Karriere. Und noch viel mehr: Shulman war Geburtshelfer eines eigenen Genres, der Architekturfotografie. Auch wenn er sich nicht als Häuserfotograf festlegen ließ, hat er darin – überwiegend autodidaktisch – seine Kunst am weitesten entfaltet und ist international berühmt geworden. Shulman inszenierte ein Haus und seine Umgebung. Seine Fotos sind Ergebnisse stunden- oder sogar tagelanger akribischer Vorbereitung. Oft entstand nur ein Foto, DAS Foto, das ihn zufriedenstellte, mit dem er die Häuser der Wirklichkeit entrückte und eine neue, erwünschte Realität entstehen ließ.

Versuche sich zurückzuziehen scheiterten. Wer Shulman noch mit weit über 90 Jahren zwar mit Stock, aber hochkonzentriert (seit 1999 an der Seite seines Partnerfotografen Jürgen Nogai) Einstellungen diskutieren sah, erkannte schnell, dass der Ruhestand nicht seine Lebensform war.

Das Deutsche Architekturmuseum hatte 2005 das große Glück, noch vor der Übergabe des Archivs mit geschätzten 100 000 Negativen an das Getty Research Institute direkt in Shulmans Studio eine Ausstellung zu seinem 95. Geburtstag vorzubereiten. Zur Eröffnung reiste der alte Herr vergnügt an und bannte das Publikum über Stunden mit einem überaus charmanten Vortrag.

Sein Haus in den Hollywood Hills stand Besuchern stets offen. Dort ist Julius Shulman im Juli 2009 gestorben, nachdem er über 70 Jahre lang die Architektur dokumentiert hat wie kaum ein anderer.

"All began just by chance." This is what Julius Shulman (*1910 Brooklyn, New York – † 2009 Los Angeles) liked to reply when asked how he got his start as an architectural photographer. His chance encounter with Richard Neutra in 1936 laid the foundation for a decades-long career. But more than that: Shulman ended up playing the role of midwife to what would become a genre in its own right. Even though he did not let himself be pinned down as merely a photographer of buildings, this is the field where he was able to unfold his art to the fullest – primarily as an autodidact – and the metier in which he rose to international fame. Shulman carefully staged his photographs of a building and its environment. His pictures are thus the result of hours or even days of painstaking preparation. Often his efforts produced only a single photo that met his exacting demands, THE photo with which he succeeded in transporting the building beyond the quotidian world and creating a new, more desirable reality.

Attempts to retire failed. Anyone who witnessed Shulman discussing angles and settings at well over 90 years of age, supporting himself on a cane and yet with full concentration (from 1999 at the side of his partner photographer, Jürgen Nogai), soon realised that retirement was not for him.

In 2005, the German Architecture Museum had the great good fortune, even before the archive of an estimated 100,000 negatives was handed over to the Getty Research Institute, of preparing an exhibition right in Shulman's studio on the occasion of his 95th birthday. The old gentleman made a special trip to attend the opening, captivating the audience for hours with a charming talk.

Julius Shulman always welcomed visitors to his home in the Hollywood Hills with open arms. This is where he passed away in July 2009, after documenting architecture like no other for over 70 years.

Christina Gräwe

Architekten-Register der Jahrbücher
Index of architects in the annuals 1980–2010/11

Die fett gesetzten Jahresangaben verweisen auf Essays und Textbeiträge

The dates in bold refer to essays and other texts

IMPRESSUM | IMPRINT

Herausgegeben von | Edited by **Peter Cachola Schmal und** | and **Yorck Förster**
im Auftrag des | on behalf of **Dezernats für Kultur und Wissenschaft, Kulturamt der Stadt Frankfurt am Main**

Die Deutsche Nationalbibliothek verzeichnet diese Publikation in der deutschen Nationalbibliografie; detaillierte Bibliografische Daten sind im Internet über http://dnb.ddb.de abrufbar | Deutsche Nationalbibliothek holds a record of this publication in the Deutsche Nationalbibliografie; detailed bibliographical data can be found under: http://dnb.ddb.de

Library of Congress Control Number is available; British Library Cataloguing-in-Publication-Data: a catalogue record for this book is available from the British Library

Prestel Verlag, München
in der Verlagsgruppe Random House GmbH
Königinstraße 9
80539 München
Tel. +49 (0) 89 24 29 08-300
Fax +49 (0) 89 24 29 08-335
www.prestel.de

Prestel Publishing Ltd.
4 Bloomsbury Place
London WC1A 2QA
Tel. +44 (0) 20 73 23-50 04
Fax +44 (0) 20 76 36-80 04

Prestel Publishing
900 Broadway, Suite 603
New York, N.Y. 10003
Tel. +1 (212) 995-27 20
Fax +1 (212) 995-27 33
www.prestel.com

Prestel books are available worldwide. Please contact your nearest bookseller or one of the above addresses for information concerning your local distributor.

Deutsches Architekturmuseum
Schaumainkai 43
60596 Frankfurt am Main
Tel. +49 (69) 212-38 844
Fax +49 (69) 212-36 31-86
E-Mail: info.DAM@stadt-frankfurt.de
www.dam-online.de

Koordination und Redaktion DAM | Editorial direction and coordination DAM: **Yorck Förster**
Projektleitung Prestel | Project Management Prestel: **Anja Besserer**
Übersetzung aus dem Deutschen | Translaxtion from the German: **Jennifer Taylor**
Übersetzung aus dem Englischen | Translation from the English: **Elizabeth Schwaiger**
Lektorat | Copyediting: **Dr. Willfried Baatz (deutsch** | German**), John Sykes (englisch** | English**)**
für | for **alpha & bet VERLAGSSERVICE, München**
Gestaltung | Design: **LIQUID | Agentur für Gestaltung, Augsburg**
Herstellung | Production: **Christine Groß**
Art Direction | Art Direction: **Cilly Klotz**
Satz | Typesetting: **LIQUID | Agentur für Gestaltung, Augsburg**
Lithografie | Lithography: **Reproline Mediateam, München**
Druck und Bindung | Printing and Binding: **APPL aprinta druck GmbH & Co. KG, Wemding**

Anzeigenverkauf | Advertising sales**:**
medienpunkt.e.K., Raimund T. Arntzen
Am Aichberg 3
86573 Obergriesbach
Tel. +49 (0) 8251-88 80 852
E-mail: zentrale@medienpuntonline.de

FSC
Mix
Produktgruppe aus vorbildlich bewirtschafteten Wäldern, kontrollierten Herkünften und Recyclingholz oder -fasern
Product group from well-managed forests, controlled sources and recycled wood or fibre
Zert.-Nr. SGS-COC-004238
www.fsc.org
© 1996 Forest Stewardship Council

Verlagsgruppe Random House FSC-DEU-0100
Die FSC-zertifizierten Papiere für dieses Buch BVS und PlanoPlus liefert Papyrus.
The FSC-certified paper BVS and PlanoPlus has been supplied by Papyrus.

ISSN 1865-3545
ISBN 978-3-7913-5063-9 (Buchhandelsausgabe | Trade edition**)**
ISBN 978-3-7913-6307-3 (Museumsausgabe | Museum edition**)**

Linoleum Global 3
Designing the future

PORSCHE MUSEUM

Schiebetürantrieb CS 80 MAGNEO

Türdrücker Premium 8800

Türassistent PORTEO

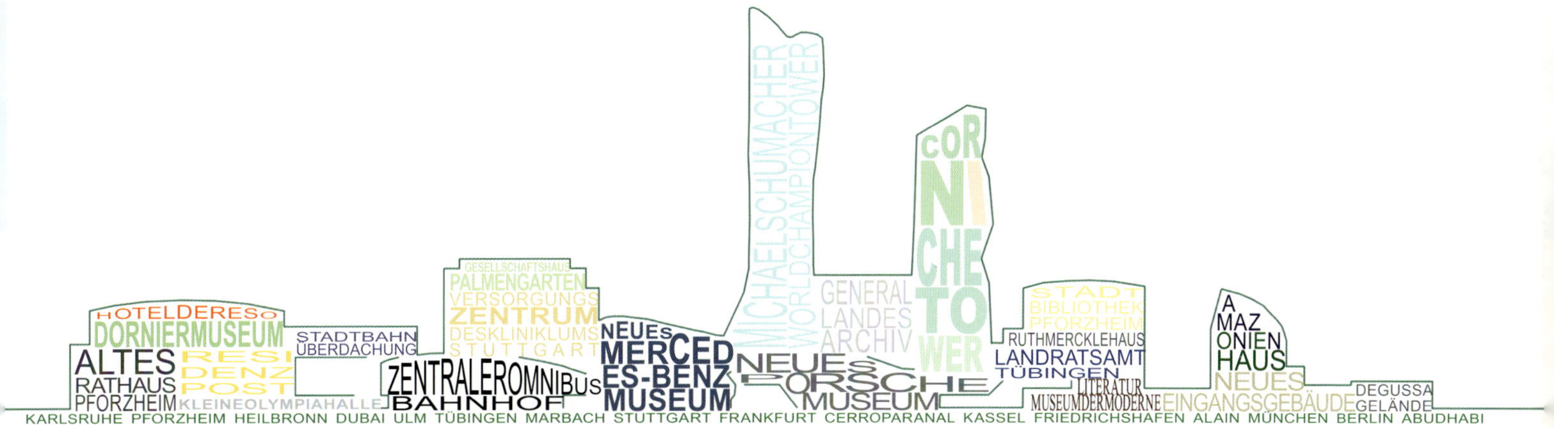

WENZEL + WENZEL

FREIE ARCHITEKTEN | DIPL.-ING. | PARTNERSCHAFT

Komplizen für Visionäre

Wenzel + Wenzel Freie Architekten | 76199 Karlsruhe | Donaustraße 24 | +49 721 / 59840-0 | karlsruhe@w-w.de | www.w-w.de

VMZINC®–
Die Haute Couture
der Architektur.
VMZINC® – Am Anfang ist es nur ein chemisches Element. Am Ende mehrfach prämierte Baukunst. Neben unseren bereits bekannten Qualitäten QUARTZ-ZINC® und ANTHRA-ZINC® begeistert vorbewittertes Zink jetzt mit drei weiteren Oberflächen: PIGMENTO® rot, blau und grün. Drei Farbnuancen, die zu Neuem inspirieren, die sich harmonisch in die Landschaft integrieren oder sich bewusst von ihr absetzen. In jedem Fall werden Sie Zink von nun an mit anderen Augen sehen.
Umicore Bausysteme GmbH
Gladbecker Str. 413 | 45326 Essen
Tel.: 0201 836 06 0 | Fax: 0201 836 06 60
vmzinc.germany@umicore.com
www.vmzinc.de
Museum, Bilbao, Spanien
VMZINC